PICKETT

LEADER OF THE CHARGE

A Biography of General George E. Pickett, C.S.A.

EDWARD G. LONGACRE

 White Mane Publishing Company, Inc.

This White Mane Publishing Company, Inc. publication
was printed by
Beidel Printing House, Inc.
63 West Burd Street
Shippensburg, PA 17257-0152 USA

In respect for the scholarship contained herein, the acid-free paper used in this book meets the guidelines for permanence and durability of the Committee on Production Guidelines for Book Longevity of the Council on Library Resources.

For a complete list of available publications
please write
White Mane Publishing Company, Inc.
P.O. Box 152
Shippensburg, PA 17257-0152 USA

Library of Congress Cataloging-in-Publication Data

Longacre, Edward G., 1946–
        Leader of the charge : a biography of General George E. Pickett,
    C.S.A. / Edward G. Longacre.
            p.   cm.
        Includes bibliographical references and index.
        ISBN 1-57249-006-3. -- ISBN 1-57249-126-4 (pbk.)
        1. Pickett, George E. (George Edward), 1825–1875. 2. Generals-
    -Confederate States of America--Biography.   3. Confederate States of
    America.   Army--Biography.   I. Title.
    E467.1.P57L66   1995
    973.7'13'092--dc20
    [B]   95-40941
                                                                  CIP

PRINTED IN THE UNITED STATES OF AMERICA

For Wendy, Gregg, and Taylor

CONTENTS

LIST OF ILLUSTRATIONS AND MAPS

PREFACE

Thanks to that climactic, catastrophic charge on the third day at Gettysburg, his name is known to almost everyone who knows anything at all about the American Civil War. That name ranks in familiarity with those of Robert E. Lee, Stonewall Jackson, J.E.B. Stuart, Ulysses S. Grant, and William T. Sherman. The man behind the name, however, is less well known; consider, for instance, that this is the first full-length biography of George Edward Pickett to be published in nearly a century.

Pickett is probably best known to present-day readers through Michael Shaara's Pulitzer Prize-winning novel about Gettysburg, *The Killer Angels* (New York, 1974). In this fact-based work of fiction, Pickett is portrayed as fun-loving and jovial, a hopeless romantic, and brave to the point of recklessness—as well as foppish, eccentric, shallow, and simple-minded. Pickett's colleagues joke about his perfumed hair and teenaged sweetheart, and they are endlessly amused by what he says and does. Even his friend and superior, Lieutenant General James Longstreet, finds him clownish and immature; Shaara has Longstreet call Pickett "my permanent boy."[1]

Engaging in campfire conversation, Shaara's Pickett manages to trivialize complex subjects such as the constitutional basis of secession. At other times he views the war as a gala festival. In one scene, Longstreet informs him that the Army of Northern Virginia is concentrating in southern Pennsylvania, to which Pickett replies: "Oh, very good." Shaara adds that "Pickett was delighted. He was looking forward to parties and music."[2]

In some passages from the novel, Pickett is made to look pathetic. He cannot understand why he makes such a poor impression on people, a lack of self-awareness that troubles him no end. Shaara writes: "Pickett was always saying something to irritate somebody, and he rarely knew why, so his method was simply to apologize in general from time to time and to let people know he meant well and then shove off and hope for the best."[3]

Although Shaara was a gifted novelist, his portrait of Pickett seems overdrawn. Still, *The Killer Angels* does not stray far from the manner in which both contemporary observers and historians have characterized the Virginia gentleman who commanded one of the premier divisions in Robert E. Lee's army. Unable or unwilling to come to terms with him, some historians have tended to portray Pickett simplistically, skimming the surface of his character and personality. Others have lost touch with the man beneath the image in their quest to make him one of the more poignant symbols of the Lost Cause. Still others fail to look beyond that tragic attack of July 3, 1863, characterizing its nominal leader as an absurd anachronism, the epitome of a discredited mode of warfare.

Like the vast majority of human beings, there was more to George Pickett than met the eye. He was a complex individual composed of conflicting elements of personality. He could exude romantic charm one moment and cold, unremitting hostility the next. Outwardly the proper gentleman, he could also be a rakehell who fondly indulged weaknesses for drinking and gambling. Under fire he was sometimes reckless in his disregard of danger; at other times, he was conspicuously protective of his physical safety. At Gettysburg, one of the pivotal epochs of the war, he elected not to accompany his troops in their suicidal charge, but at Five Forks—long after the Confederate cause had been effectively lost—he risked his life in a futile effort to rally his broken division. Seemingly the embodiment of Southern chivalry, he showed no compunction about waging guerrilla warfare, and he perpetrated atrocities that forced him to flee the country in 1865 to escape prosecution as a war criminal.

That a man capable of so many contradictory impulses can be portrayed as shallow and simplistic owes much to the characterizations of contemporaries. A number of military associates appear to have been alienated by Pickett's flamboyant personality, scandalized by his penchant for high living, antagonized by the rank and authority he attained through the patronage of influential superiors such as Longstreet, and made envious by the enduring fame he won at Gettysburg. Among those who disliked or disapproved of Pickett were several who left influential memoirs, notably Brigadier Generals G. Moxley Sorrel and Eppa Hunton and Colonel John Cheves Haskell. Such men stated or strongly implied that Pickett was childish, incompetent, even cowardly. Each of these accusations is false. They also erred in trying to brand as a dimwit a man who could converse intelligently, even astutely, on political, social, and economic topics; who could translate works of literature into a Native American tongue; and who could insert French and Latin passages into his personal correspondence.

Another writer of influence who tended to portray the general as stereotypical and one-dimensional—albeit for a different reason—was his widow, La Salle Corbell Pickett. In numerous books and articles written after the war, Pickett's third wife (whom he married two months after Gettysburg when he was thirty-eight, she barely fifteen) attempted to convince the reading public that her late husband was the incarnation of Southern values and Confederate valor. To La Salle, George Pickett could do no wrong: he was fearless, dashing, a charming romantic, an instinctive leader and master strategist beloved by his troops and respected and admired by every leading light in his army from Lee on down.

La Salle Corbell Pickett's penchant for hero-worship led her to exceed the literary license granted a memorialist and to violate the rules that guide the historian. In her quest to sanctify George Pickett as Southerner, general, husband, and father, she fabricated many of the wartime and postwar letters he supposedly wrote to her. Along with some genuine letters, she published many of the bogus missives, under claim of authenticity, in two collections fifteen years apart.[4] Much of the material contained in the fraudulent letters she lifted from the writings of her husband's contemporaries, virtually all of whom had passed from the scene by the time she published. Two examples among many are *Pickett's Men*, a book published in 1870 by his inspector-general, Major Walter Harrison, and the wartime letters of his artillery commander, Major James Dearing.[5]

To a certain extent Mrs. Pickett's behavior is understandable if inexcusable. Even the most reputable editors of her time occasionally played fast and loose with first-person accounts; for instance, Robert Underwood Johnson and Clarence Clough Buel quietly rewrote the memoirs of Union and Confederate contributors to *Battles and Leaders of the Civil War* (4 vols. New York, 1887-88).[6] Furthermore, her husband's death at fifty in 1875 left Mrs. Pickett on the brink of poverty, forcing her to live by her natural talent as a writer, using the only saleable material at her disposal. Then, too, one can appreciate how the sensitive and clever widow of a high-ranking officer steeped in controversy as was Pickett after Gettysburg and Five Forks might strive to polish his image. Through her abilities as a dramatist she could make her husband appear even more romantic, more colorful, and more integral to the Confederate effort than he was.

Of course, by putting fanciful words into her husband's mouth and high-toned thoughts in his head, Mrs. Pickett has greatly complicated the efforts of would-be biographers to sift fact from fiction and produce something more than a portrait in primary colors and broad brushstrokes. It can be done—collections of authentic Pickett correspondence are available to let the man speak for himself, as are the wartime letters and postwar writings of many of his contemporaries disposed to characterize him as objectively as possible. Still, obstacles of unusal size and number strew the path of the writer wishing to locate the man beneath the glibness and the glitter—which may help explain why so few have undertaken the journey.

ACKNOWLEDGMENTS

Many individuals and institutions assisted in the preparation of this book. Above all else I wish to thank Patrick A. Bowmaster, a doctoral candidate in history at Virginia Tech and my research assistant, whose diligent, thorough, and imaginative handling of numerous manuscript sources proved extremely valuable to me. I am also indebted to Lieutenant Colonel Bob Spore, United States Air Force Reserve, who suggested this project, and to Martin Gordon of White Mane Publishing Company, Inc., who was instrumental in bringing it to fruition. Mark Brown of the John Hay Library, Brown University Library, made available to me the largest known body of authentic Pickett correspondence. Lisa Malden and Judith Sibley of the United States Military Academy Library and Archives were unfailingly helpful in answering what must have seemed an unending series of inquiries about Cadet Pickett. Mike Vouri of the Whatcom (Wash.) Museum of History and Art permitted me to make use of his original research into Pickett's prewar service in the Washington Territory. My wife, Ann, provided clerical (and moral) support throughout the project.

Others who assisted me, to one degree or another, include Fred Bauman of the Division of Manuscripts, Library of Congress; De Ann Blanton, Michael Musick, and Mike Pilgrim of the Military Reference Branch, National Archives; Christina M. Deane, Special Collections Department, Alderman Library, University of Virginia; Joan Grattan, Special Collections, Milton S. Eisenhower Library, The Johns Hopkins University; Christiana Green, William R. Perkins Library, Duke University; William C. Luebke, Virginia State Library and Archives; Ellen Nemhauser, Robert W. Woodruff Library, Emory University; Donald Pfanz of the Fredericksburg-Spotsylvania National Military Park; Lee Shepherd and Eileen Parris of the Virginia Historical Society; Dr. Richard J. Sommers, U.S. Army Military History Institute; Guy Swanson of the Museum of the Confederacy; and Don Welsh and his staff of reference librarians at the Earl Gregg Swem Library, College of William and Mary.

ONE — An Officer, A Gentleman, A Virginian

For two hours or more Confederate cannon atop the ridgeline had pounded away at the blue lines a mile to the east, shattering parts of a stone wall along a parallel ridge, detonating caissons and limbers, creating havoc in the enemy's rear. Now the guns were quieting and the climactic hour of battle was drawing near.

From among the trees that fringed the ridge came foot soldiers in gray and butternut-brown, thrashing through foliage until they reached open ground where they began to form columns of attack. The soldiers' faces were grim and grimy; their eyes were cold and hooded, the eyes of men who had seen too much killing and were about to see more of it. Minutes before, as their army's cannonade reached crescendo, they had spoken animatedly of its effects. Now they were silent; only the shouts of officers, shuttling them into line, were audible above the continuing din. Within their ranks flags ablaze with stars and bars hung limp in the breezeless heat. After several minutes the shuffling ceased. Their lines dressed, the men poised to move forward across the sun-baked valley where untold numbers of riflemen in blue, surrounded by double-shotted cannon, awaited them.

The officer who would lead them sat his coal-black charger under a sheltering tree. He was a dapper man of compact build, sporting a well-manicured moustache and imperial and long hair that curled from beneath a gilt-spangled kepi. Minutes before, this man had spurred along the ridge, reining in and dismounting beside a long-bearded officer who stood silently amid a knot of aides. Major General George Edward Pickett snapped off a salute, handed his superior a dispatch he had just received, and quietly inquired, "General, shall I advance?" Lieutenant General James Longstreet, commander of the First Corps, Army of Northern Virginia, scanned the communique, which called for a decision he desperately wished to avoid. He looked up, then turned away. He tried to speak, could not, bowed his head as if in despair—and nodded.

His subordinate required no further reply: "I shall lead my division forward, sir." Pickett saluted again, remounted, and galloped back to the line of trees.[1]

Once back with his troops, he cried out the order they had been awaiting and added a personal appeal: "Up, men, and to your posts! Don't forget today that you are from old Virginia!" Officers on foot and horseback repeated the order, carrying it the length of the line. Pickett's voice rose above all others: "Forward! Guide center! March!" Slowly, warily, but without hesitation, the column started forward.[2]

The general rode with the leading rank for a short distance, cantering among the files, shouting encouragement to everyone within earshot. Some observers thought George Pickett animated to the point of euphoria. Survivors of the attack would describe him as anxious, even eager, to cross the mile-long valley and close with the enemy.

They were wrong. In their eagerness to move forward in close alignment with their comrades, including those in supporting columns off Pickett's left flank, these men lost sight of their commander. Few if any saw him pass to the rear, where he sat his black horse as the lines moved forward without him. Once the last rank had advanced into the distance, he and his staff trailed after it at a cautious gait, then stopped and waited.[3]

Pickett would not take part in the charge that would earn him a form of immortality he neither sought nor desired. He would watch from a safe distance the carnage that enveloped his truncated division of Virginians as it made its valiant but futile attempt to break the midpoint of the Union line below Gettysburg. In less than an hour his command would be reduced to a bloody remnant, formless and leaderless, its men walking, limping, crawling back to the starting-point of their assault.

On this hideous day in July George Pickett would observe not only the death of his division; he would view the demise of a military career once considered among the most promising in the officer corps of the Army of Northern Virginia. He would also witness a brutal end to the romance, the pageantry, the grandeur of war—qualities that had lent meaning to his life for the past three decades.

* * *

In his lifetime George Edward Pickett came to represent different things to different people but in his own mind he was, first and always, a Virginia gentleman. He was born in Richmond on January 25, 1825, into a family celebrated for producing "people of culture and education . . . [who] have ever taken an active part in the affairs of their day, though few of them sought or held political office."[4]

The Pickett pedigree—among the finest in the Old Dominion—was of ancient French origin. One branch of the family, which originally spelled its name Picquett, came to England under William the Conqueror in 1066, while another line crossed the English Channel five centuries later to escape the Huguenot persecutions. Apparently the branch that sought religious freedom was the first to emigrate to the New World. Family tradition has it that three Huguenot brothers came to the Colonies in the mid-seventeenth century, one settling in Virginia, another in Massachusetts Bay, the third in what would become North Carolina.

The Virginia Picquetts resided initially in Middlesex County along the Rappahannock River and in Westmoreland County along the state's Northern Neck, but by the latter 1600s they had migrated northwestward. The earliest recorded reference to an ancestor of George E. Pickett lies in a will drawn up by his great-grandfather, William Pickett, and probated in Fauquier County shortly after William's death in 1766.

Via that document William divided his earthly possessions among his wife and seven children. His youngest son, George, parlayed his inheritance into a successful career as a businessman, senior partner in the Richmond mercantile firm of Pickett, Pollard & Johnston. George's second son, Robert, inherited enough money to purchase a comfortable home at Sixth and Leigh Streets in Richmond where he lived with his wife, Mary Johnston Pickett, child of another prominent Richmond family, and to share in the ownership of a colonial-era plantation on Turkey Island, along a loop of the James River about a dozen miles southeast of the Virginia capital.[5]

On this spacious estate that his grandfather and namesake had purchased from another First Family of Virginia, the Randolphs, young George Pickett spent hours that provided him with pleasant memories. One latter-day acquaintance wrote that George grew to adolescence "in hunting and fishing and the fresh air life of the Virginia country boy." Often he would tramp the trails and woodlands of Turkey Island in company with his parents, his several cousins, aunts and uncles, and one or more of his family's slaves. When he reached young manhood he shared the hike with his brother, Charles, fifteen years his junior, and their younger sister, Virginia. Rarely did he enjoy the serenity of a solitary tramp through the woods. On his deathbed four decades later, facing a last, lonely journey, he told a visiting priest: "You know, father, I never was a solitary bird. I was never alone except sometimes in the twilight or in the woods. . . ."[6]

Despite living the "fresh air life," George did not grow tall or robust. Always somewhat below average height, he developed a slight physique and delicate, almost feminine features including unusually small hands and feet, soft gray eyes, and dark brown hair that he frequently wore long. One biographer claims that the boy inherited from his mother a tendency toward frail health; malaria and intestinal ailments, contracted in childhood, caused him discomfort at intervals throughout his life. The heart disease that contributed to his early death may have begun to stalk him in his youth.[7]

Born to wealth and privilege in a neo-feudal society, George could hardly have escaped growing up pampered, sheltered, and spoiled. In his early years he exhibited a sometimes-healthy, sometimes-harmful tendency to disobey orders and defy authority, if only to establish his independence and individuality. This quality persisted after his parents sent him off, at age twelve, to the Richmond Academy, a preparatory school for the sons of the gentry. There, despite his slight build, George got into more than his share of schoolground fights. It is said, however, that his willingness to challenge older, bigger schoolmates won their respect as did his penchant for staging all manner of pranks in and outside the classroom.

From his earliest days at the Richmond Academy George demonstrated that he was not a brilliant student. He felt inhibited by the school's strict code of conduct and he did not incline toward many of the subjects the academy stressed, such as English grammar and mathematics. Apparently, however, he developed something of an aptitude for at least one foreign language, French, for he would rank fairly high in this subject during his later schooling.

Outside the classroom, young Pickett was exposed to influences more conducive to his innate interests. While not a military institution in the formal sense, the Richmond Academy occasionally organized its students into a corps of cadets and exposed them to military drill and a smattering of tactics.[8]

Despite his youthful aversion to taking orders, the military appealed to young Pickett. In many ways he had been primed for a soldier's life even before his formal education began. From his earliest years he had been inculcated into the military tradition of "the Fighting Picketts of Fauquier County." According to one chronicler of George's forebears, "at the time of their country's need, they responded to a man." Fifteen family members served in the Revolution, including his grandfather and great-uncle, the latter rising to become lieutenant colonel of the Third Virginia Regiment of Infantry. Numerous other Picketts attained high rank during the War of 1812, two of them as colonels. Among the present generation, several Pickett cousins were serving, or had served in, the military, the highest-ranking being his uncle, Captain John Symington, a career officer in the ordnance department. That the son of a gentleman should consider a military career was not an oddity; in the mid-nineteenth century the profession of arms was not considered beneath the station of those born to wealth and status.[9]

Supposedly George's parents suffered so greatly from the effects of the financial panic of 1837 that by the time he reached sixteen they could no longer afford to send him to the Richmond Academy. He was as yet too young to secure an army commission and so his parents suggested he read law. George was none too keen about the idea but he enjoyed few options. His mother enlisted the aid of her older brother, Andrew, an established barrister, in helping the boy gain entrance to the profession. The Picketts arranged for George to study under his uncle's tutelage, but to do so the teenager had to travel several hundred miles from home. Seeking a more promising professional venue than Virginia could provide, Andrew Johnston had emigrated to western Illinois, hanging out his shingle in the bustling but as yet uncrowded prairie town of Quincy.

By the time George Pickett went to live with him, Andrew Johnston had not only made a name in jurisprudence but had become prominent in the Illinois chapter of the newly formed Whig Party. In 1839 Johnston had served as secretary at the party's first state convention, before taking a legislative seat at the new Illinois capital of Springfield. Either at the convention or in the legislature, where he served as assistant clerk of the lower house, Johnston became acquainted with a tall, unpolished but arresting colleague from Springfield named Abraham Lincoln. The fellow-Whigs would become friends. Sharing Lincoln's interest in things literary as well as political, Johnston would be responsible for placing in a Quincy newspaper the only poetry and prose the future President would ever publish.[10]

When his nephew arrived in Quincy, Johnston did his utmost to introduce him to, and interest him in, the law. In this effort he failed miserably; his parents' desires notwithstanding, young George had neither the mind nor the heart the profession demanded. Returning home to a family whose financial situation remained uncertain appeared out of the question. Long-distance consultation with his sister and her husband prompted Johnston to focus, instead, on the boy's natural inclination to the military life. The uncle's professional connections raised the possibility that George might partake of the free and highly valuable education offered by the United States Military Academy at West Point, New York, which produced not only army officers but some of the most successful civil engineers in the country. Despite his less-than-brilliant record in formal education, the young man appeared receptive to this idea and Johnston, in the summer of 1841, set about obtaining an Academy appointment for his nephew.

As befit an up-and-coming politician, his quest was short and successful. His Springfield acquaintances included a United States Congressman who happened to be a fellow Southerner and a brother Whig. Kentucky native John T. Stuart agreed to consider George Pickett for the next Academy appointment to come his way. Apparently Johnston sought the support of other local Congressmen in the event that Stuart failed to deliver; at the same time, he persuaded his brother-in-law, Captain Symington, to write Stuart in George's behalf. In a matter of weeks, the youngster's name stood atop the list of Academy applicants in Stuart's district.

In the late summer of 1841 Stuart apparently confided to Captain Symington that were he reelected to Congress the following February he would make the nomination in George's favor. Late in August Andrew Johnston wrote Stuart asking whether George's family might "look for his appointment in February next." Presumably he was assured that such was the case. In the end Stuart decided not to stand for reelection but came through anyway. On April 19, 1842, Secretary of War John Canfield Spencer sent George his conditional appointment to the Military Academy. The young man promptly returned his acceptance along with his father's consent to George's serving in the U.S. Army "eight years unless sooner discharged."[11]

Because Stuart had once been a law partner of Abraham Lincoln, tales later surfaced that the latter had helped obtain George Pickett's appointment. An equally enduring myth is that Lincoln himself secured Pickett's place in the West Point Class of 1846—a neat trick since Lincoln was not a national Congressman at the time George applied and thus lacked the power to nominate applicants.

In the writings she published after her husband's death, La Salle Corbell Pickett created the enduring fiction that Lincoln not only secured her late husband's appointment but that the future President took an avid interest in his Academy career as well as in his service as a Confederate officer. To support her claims, Mrs. Pickett fabricated at least two letters from the Illinois legislator to his young protege, one supposedly written before and one shortly after George's matriculation at the Academy. The general's widow was also responsible for the fiction that her husband was so grateful to Lincoln for his interest and assistance that he never permitted anyone, in his presence, to criticize his benefactor.

Mrs. Pickett went to elaborate lengths to persuade her readers that her husband and the President remained close even in the throes of civil war. She concocted and several times repeated the tale that Lincoln, visiting dying Richmond at the close of the conflict, stopped by the house at Sixth and Leigh, introduced himself to the general's widow, assured her that he bore no ill will toward her husband, and exchanged kisses with one-year-old George Pickett, Jr. By evoking the image of the martyred President, a supposed friend of the South whose lenient plan of Reconstruction had been thwarted by radicals in his own party, Mrs. Pickett invested her story with mythic properties while exploiting a reunion theme popular with her postwar audience.[12]

By the time Mrs. Pickett wrote, on the threshold of the twentieth century and after, close acquaintances of "her soldier" and of Lincoln, who might have exposed her accounts as fabrications, were few. One who doubted the credibility of her stories was Union Major George A. Bruce, who had been in Richmond during Lincoln's April 1865 visit and who in after years contributed to the history of the war. Like other critics North and South, Bruce chose not to go public with his contention that Mrs. Pickett was perpetrating a literary fraud. He never doubted, however, that the Lincoln-Pickett relationship was a carefully crafted piece of fiction.[13]

* * *

From the outset of his West Point career, Cadet Pickett demonstrated by word and deed that he would neither cowtow to authority nor submit to what he considered the Academy's narrow, arbitrary, unrealistic, harshly punitive, and inconsistently applied code of conduct. Such behavior, coupled with his determined indifference to the scholastic demands of the institution, ensured that his stay on the upper Hudson would be a memorable one in the most perverse sense of the term.

In the early 1840s the U.S. Military Academy was beset by a public relations crisis, one it believed had been decisively overcome

U.S.M.A. Archives

Antebellum West Point

years before. During the presidential administrations of Democrats Andrew Jackson and Martin Van Buren, critics in Congress and the public at large had repeatedly accused the Academy of being insufficiently equalitarian. Their most frequent accusation was that by seeking to institutionalize and professionalize military life West Point hoped to create an elitist officer corps. Academy officials did not expect to encounter a new round of criticism under the Whig administrations of William Henry Harrison and John Tyler, but by 1841 opponents were again launching what one Academy apologist termed "absurd allegations that the cadets were drawn from the wealthy classes in the country, or were principally sons of high functionaries under the government."[14]

During George Pickett's first year at West Point, such accusations prompted Major Richard Delafield, Superintendent of the Academy, to have incoming students fill out a form that recorded "the circumstances of life of the parents of the cadets." No one was required to sign the form, so that "the information might not affect the social relations among the cadets themselves." Thus it cannot be determined if Cadet Pickett identified himself as springing from moderate or reduced circumstances—either answer would have been appropriate.

During the first year the survey was in use, Academy officials failed to break down the results in a meaningful manner, but during the remainder of Pickett's West Point career the totals indicate that only three to five percent of the cadet corps came from families classified as wealthy or "independent in life" and that less than ten percent were the sons of state or federal employees. In reporting the results of the first few years' survey, Colonel Joseph G. Totten, the army's chief engineer, opined that the Academy's appointment system "has been exercised in a praiseworthy and impartial manner. In truth, it is one of the noblest features of this institution, that it gives a helping hand to so many of the poorer youths of our country. . . ."[15]

Perhaps Academy officials did too good a job of proving that indigent students were as welcome as the sons of upper- and middle-class families. Before Cadet Pickett's schooling was done, the pendulum of criticism would swing in the opposite direction. By 1844, with government retrenchment in full sway, congressional critics began to complain that the institution was such a drain on the economy that it should start paying its own way by charging tuition of at least a portion of its student body. Academy officials fought long, hard, and successfully to prevent this policy from being instituted. Had they lost the fight, it is doubtful whether George Pickett, given his family's depleted finances, could have completed his education. Much of the debate over West Point's admission policies generated heat rather than light, but the clamor did highlight the school's perilous status as a bastion of militarism in a nation that had inherited an anti-military bias from its British forebears.[16]

One admirable result of the admissions controversy was that Academy officials had to redefine, carefully and thoughtfully, the mission of the institution. Heretofore basically known as a school for engineer officers, West Point now viewed its primary objective as to "provide well-instructed officers for the *several arms* composing our army, in sufficient numbers for a peace[time] establishment, based upon the principle of skeleton regiments and corps, susceptible of sudden enlargement" in time of war.

A secondary intent of the Academy was to "introduce into the country military science and tactics, and to diffuse them through the militia." This mission would placate the Jeffersonians and Jacksonians in high places, who saw the nonprofessional soldier as the true bulwark of the American military establishment. Finally, the Academy sought to foster "some means of preserving and diffusing the *improvements* in the science and art of war," thereby affording army officers "of all arms of service, an opportunity of gaining from such a nursery of their profession every thing new in the lines of their respective arms. . . ."[17]

Pointing up this new emphasis on all arms of the service, in recent years the Academy had broadened its scholastic base to place general military science on a par with engineering. Still, the curriculum relied heavily on higher mathematics, natural philosophy, and the other physical science courses that underlay the engineering profession. An incoming student like George Pickett, who lacked a basic grasp on these core subjects, could be expected to fare poorly. This proved to be the case early on; at the start of his "plebe" year he experienced major difficulties in trying to assimilate algebra, geometry, and trigonometry, which constituted the greater part of the fourth-class year course of study. Even so, at the end of his first year he ranked in mathematics forty-ninth out of his class of seventy-two students, a higher standing than achieved by classmates destined for prominence as field commanders, including Cadmus Wilcox and John Gibbon of North Carolina.

Contrary to the myth that Pickett did poorly in every phase of his coursework, he proved strong enough in French—digesting complex passages from *Leviznc's Grammar, Berard's Lecon's Francaises,* and the *Voyage du Jeune Anacharsis*—to attain a ranking of twelfth, only a few forms below Pennsylvanian George B. McClellan, one of the acknowledged brains of the Class of 1846. Despite his respectable performance in such a notoriously difficult course, however, Pickett finished his first year ranking no higher in "general merit" (overall achievement) than fifty-fifth out of seventy-two cadets.[18]

One reason why Pickett closed out his plebe year in the bottom quarter of his class was that scholastic achievement was not the only factor governing class standing. The Academy's time-honored practice of awarding demerits and punishments to cadets who violated its stringent code of conduct proved to be George Pickett's downfall. That code served to complicate the lives of students such as he, convivial to a fault and with a fondness for stunts and pranks of the sort rarely appreciated by schoolmasters.[19]

Pickett's sociability led him to flout Academy rules designed to promote mature behavior, self-control, and decorum. He would visit the quarters of close friends such as fellow-Virginians Dabney H. Maury, Ambrose Powell Hill, and Birkett D. Fry, and New Yorker Alfred Gibbs after lights' out or during imposed study hours. His illicit fraternizing often included the use of pipe and cigar tobacco, a popular amusement forbidden under the code of discipline. At intervals he would accompany equally venturesome companions to off-limits haunts such as Benny Havens's Tavern, that den of iniquity so celebrated in story and song. A classmate walking guard duty one wintry night found a drunken Cadet Pickett lying unconscious in a snowbank after a visit to Benny Havens's. Only the guard's solicitude saved Pickett from discovery by the authorities, from disgrace and expulsion—and perhaps from a slow death by freezing.[20]

In addition to being fond of unlawful amusements, Cadet Pickett was troubled by a defective body-clock. During his first year at West Point he was gigged for being late for roll call, late for drill, late for breakfast and dinner, late at reveille, late at retreat, late at guard-posting, late for chapel services—in fact, late for just about every function and ceremony at which attendance was compulsory. Then there was the Academy's dress code, which demanded that cadets wear such uncomfortable attire as stiff linen collars and scarf-like stocks—elements of uniform that Cadet Pickett could not tolerate. From his earliest weeks on the Hudson he wore under his gray uniform the soft collar he favored, sometimes a cravat as well—and he continued to do so despite racking up demerit after demerit.[21]

His aptitude as a class clown proved another barrier to high standing. In a blatant bid for attention, he repeatedly appeared at drill in nonmilitary clothing. While marching he would swing his arms exaggeratedly as though to poke fun at the rigid bearing of his peers. Once he tried to start a food fight in the mess hall; on another occasion he was caught urinating on Academy property. Perhaps his most notable prank was an attempt, while marching in formation, to trip a file of fellow cadets, presumably to watch them collide and fall like so many tenpins.[22]

At first glance, Pickett's self-destructive bent appears difficult to reconcile with his evident intention to graduate and become a career officer. In her postwar writings, Pickett's widow offers a clue to his bizarre behavior. She claims that her husband's defiance of the Academy's dress code was a studied, calculated effort. He would wear soft collar and tie so long as he felt he could afford the black marks and punishments they entailed. He curbed his harmful behavior, however, whenever he found himself approaching the magic number of 200 demerits per year that constituted grounds for immediate dismissal. He appears to have followed this same course with regard to other infractions as well.[23]

If La Salle Corbell Pickett's analysis of her husband's behavior is correct—and in this instance, at least, her words have the ring of credibility—his was a carefully crafted pattern of defiance, designed to show his contempt for a petty, capricious, and unmanly system of control that robbed cadets of initiative and self-expression—a system that also condoned the distasteful and mean-spirited hazing practices of upperclassmen. Pickett knew the rules and was prepared to play by them; he readily accepted the consequences of his actions in order to make what he considered a valid statement of disapprobation.

This pattern of conduct, however, does not appear to have outlived his Academy career. Some historians have cited his record of disobedience at West Point as proof of a life-long disdain for higher authority. A careful look at his active-duty record discloses no incidents of insubordination, or refusal to obey given orders. George Pickett may have been a rebellious youth, but as an army officer he unfailingly subordinated himself to proper authority—sometimes with disastrous results for himself and the troops he led.[24]

Pickett's campaign to flout the established order at West Point produced predictable effects. He did no worse than mediocre in a few courses such as English grammar and military drawing, and he showed some aptitude—as he surely should have—for tactics. His conduct, however, ensured that he would never attain a lofty class standing. In his plebe year, when he gained the highest ranking he would enjoy at the Academy, he amassed 167 demerits. His deportment improved only slightly during his third-class year, when he accumulated 140 demerits for infractions such as failing to police his tent during summer encampment, permitting his musket to rust, and wearing his hair too long (a precursor of his Civil War service, when his curly hair grew almost to shoulder-length).

In his junior year—when he was charged with, among other things, "highly unsoldierlike conduct" for being out of uniform, smoking on the parade ground—his demerits climbed to 155. During his senior year, he surpassed himself, committing almost every sin of omission and commission possible at the Academy. As he stood on the verge of graduation he also teetered on the brink of expulsion, having attained the nearly fatal total of 195 black marks. His delinquency record ran to four legal-size pages of double-column entries, a record to that time.[25]

Pickett's natural inclination to rebelliousness was strengthened by the company he kept. Only occasionally would he befriend studious, well-behaved students such as George McClellan. For the most part he avoided the straightlaced "grinds" in his class such as the dour, ascetic Virginian Thomas Jonathan Jackson—who fifteen years hence would win the appellation "Stonewall" on the first major battlefield of the Civil War. Rather, Pickett appeared to adopt as his compatriot every hell-raiser who matriculated at the Academy.

One of the most innovative and energetic of these kindred spirits was Henry Heth, Class of 1847, eldest son of George's aunt, Margaret Pickett Heth and Lieutenant John Heth of the United States Navy. "Cousin Hal" had been a favorite companion since early youth, visiting frequently at the Pickett home in Richmond and hiking, hunting, and picnicking with the family on Turkey Island. The youngsters' reunion at West Point developed into a three-year effort to see how much illicit merriment they could initiate without getting booted out. In his memoirs Heth admitted that his scholastic record at the Point was "abominable. My thoughts ran in the channel of fun. How to get to Benny Havens occupied more of my time than Legendre on Calculus. The time given to study was measured by the amount of time necessary to be given to prevent failure at the annual examinations."

In keeping his pledge to enjoy himself and live dangerously, Heth appears to have outstripped his relation. With impunity he broke regulations that Cadet Pickett feared even to bend such as by making clandestine excursions to neighboring Newburgh and far-off New York City when supposedly confined to barracks or to the post hospital. In so behaving Heth realized he was "running a great risk, but I was so in the habit of taking risks, that I presume I became callous."[26]

If he found it hard to keep pace with his cousin, George devoted much time and attention to the effort, leaving him with little of either to apply to his studies. During his last two years at West Point, his already-low class standing took a nose dive. At the close of his second class year he ranked last in two of the three courses for which his class was graded, natural philosophy and chemistry. In his senior year he finished last or next-to-last in three of five courses: engineering, ethics, and artillery tactics. Even in the basic instructional course offered by the Academy—infantry tactics—he ranked no higher than fifty-second out of fifty-nine cadets.[27]

Such a dismal performance has spawned the popular misconception that Pickett was not very bright, a value judgment that colors some historians' evaluations of his later career. In fact, he was neither slow-witted nor stupid; rather, he failed to take his studies seriously. As one of his classmates, William M. Gardner, remarked, Pickett was "a jolly good fellow with fine natural gifts sadly neglected." There appears to be much truth in that evaluation.

His terrible grades, added to his ever-growing demerit count, ensured that he would finish at the foot of his class two years running. At graduation, July 1, 1846, he won the unenviable title of class "immortal." His scholastic record was bad enough; one of its consequences was that it denied him an active-duty assignment to his service branch of preference, the cavalry, and ensured him a berth in the less glamorous infantry. Even worse, in some respects, was his record in conduct during his first class year, which enabled him to overtake Cousin Hal in their race for notoriety. By ranking two hundred and tenth out of 213 students, Academy-wide, George finished eight places lower than Henry Heth (who was himself destined for immortality, graduating at the bottom of the Class of '47).[28]

Still, George Pickett managed to graduate; thirteen of those who had entered the Academy with him in the summer of 1842 failed to complete their education for one reason or another including academic deficiencies greater than his. Although neither an accomplished student nor a paragon of discipline, on that bright, sultry first day in July George Pickett became a brevet second lieutenant in the United States Army. In so doing he joined a list of promising young officers, many of whom would distinguish themselves in combat. The class roll included future Confederate Generals Jackson, Maury, Wilcox, Gardner, John Adams, David R. Jones, and Samuel Bell Maxey, as well as Union generals-to-be McClellan, Gibbs, Jesse Reno, Darius Couch, Truman Seymour, Samuel D. Sturgis, George Stoneman, Innis N. Palmer, and George H. Gordon.[29]

George Pickett had completed his studies at an advantageous time. His nation would readily overlook his dubious record of academic achievement in its search for young officers to lead its ground forces in war—a war that had broken out during his last year at the Academy. He welcomed the conflict for it promised an opportunity to prove that his grades, his class standing, and his crimes against institutional rectitude did not accurately reflect his potential as a soldier.

TWO — Baptism of Fire

In the spring of 1846, years of smoldering resentment between the United States and Mexico, most recently raked into life by President James Knox Polk's annexation of Texas, ignited with a resounding crash. That March the Mexican government declared war on its North American neighbor and two months later, following the commencement of hostilities on the north side of the Rio Grande, the United States Congress reciprocated. The result was America's first foreign war—a war of invasion, occupation, conquest, and acquisition.

It was also the first war to be directed, to a great extent, by West Point graduates. The impact of hostilities on the institution was immediate and powerful. War news animated cadet discussions, enlivened the proceedings of the Academy's debating society, and made many a cadet, plebe and upperclassman alike, dream of how he might contribute to his country's initial attempt at empire-building.

As the conflict progressed—twenty-two months would pass between Polk's war message and the Treaty of Guadalupe Hidalgo, by which America won enough foreign soil to create half a dozen states— it also fomented discord and divisiveness among the Academy's population. Cadets from the North and Northwest began to view the war, as Polk's political opponents proclaimed it, a war to extend the reach of slavery and to expand the political influence of those who profited from the Peculiar Institution. The debate over the war's political, social, and economic influences did not heat up until after George Pickett graduated, but he knew where he stood on the issue and he would not have hesitated to speak his mind. His Southern birthright and his

15

unquestioning acceptance of slavery would have ensured his support of the war effort even if the conflict had not promised him an opportunity to advance in his chosen profession.[1]

Although he viewed the war as a means of firming up the rather shaky foundation of his nascent career, he put off entering it until the close of the two-months' leave to which he was entitled upon graduation. Having enjoyed only one extended furlough during his four years at West Point—in June and July 1844, at the end of his third class year—he looked forward to resting at home with his family, to clearing his memory of the institutional restraints that had so long oppressed him. Immediately following commencement exercises he bade farewell to his classmates, to his cousin and other lowerclassmen with whom he was acquainted, then took a canal boat down the Hudson and the overland stage to Richmond.

He enjoyed his first few weeks of relaxation in Richmond and on Turkey Island but long before the leave was up he had grown restive. He was, after all, an army officer—or he would be as soon as his commission came through—and the languid pace at which his family lived, especially in the bucolic James River country, had an unsettling effect. He no longer had a sense of belonging in such a quiet, unchallenging corner of the world, especially when colleagues and superiors were fighting fifteen hundred miles away. Not even the increasingly pleasant hours he passed in the company of pretty, seventeen-year-old Sally Harrison Steward Minge—whose family, originally of Charles City County, were long-time neighbors of the Picketts in Richmond—could erase the impression that he was idling far from the place where duty demanded he be.[2]

By the end of July he was downright anxious to move on. He had read in a Washington newspaper of his posting, at his brevet rank, to the army's newest regiment, the Eighth Infantry, but he lacked official confirmation of the appointment. He began to fear that the War Department, in its haste to mobilize men and supplies to Mexico, had passed him by, stranding him in a bureaucratic limbo. On the last day of the month he wrote directly to Secretary of War William L. Marcy to ask if there had been some mistake: he wondered if "my orders might have been forwarded to Illinois from which State I received my appointment as cadet. I shall be much obliged to learn from you it is so, in order that I may write on for them immediately and hand in my acceptance as quickly as possible."

He was correct to blame a geographical misunderstanding. The same day he wrote, his notice of appointment reached Andrew Johnston in Quincy. His uncle immediately informed Washington of the error; within a week the misdirected form was in Pickett's hands.

The day he received it he scrawled his acceptance and testified that he had taken the accompanying oath of allegiance to serve "honestly and faithfully" in the service of the United States in accordance with all applicable statutes and articles of war.[3]

Valentine Museum
Lieutenant George E. Pickett

Along with his appointment Pickett received an order under date of July 17. The communique directed him to report, before his furlough ended in late September, at the headquarters of his regiment, currently located near the recent battlefield of Monterey, in northeastern Mexico. His attempt to comply proved to be an ordeal. Dutifully, he left his family and Sally behind on the morning of September 3 and travelled southwestward to New Orleans via the Ohio and Mississippi Rivers. Due to low water on the Ohio, he failed to reach the Crescent City until the last week of the month.

Hoping to recoup lost time, he sailed for Brazos Island aboard the first vessel on which he could book passage, a supply steamer. To his chagrin, long after leaving New Orleans the ship experienced engine trouble that forced her to return to port. The return trip took ten days, by which time Pickett was already overdue at Monterey.

Not until mid-October could he find a berth on another steamboat passing down the Gulf of Mexico. He made it to the mouth of the Rio Grande without further difficulty but once there he marked time for three days seeking additional transportation. Finally he was carried up the Rio Grande to Camargo, Mexico, from which point he trekked overland to Monterey.

Pickett's frustrating journey came to a close on November 9, when he reported to the headquarters of the Eighth Infantry, an element of Major General Zachary Taylor's army of occupation in and around Monterey. One of the first faces to meet his gaze was an unsmiling one; it belonged to the regimental adjutant, First Lieutenant

John D. Clark, a martinetish North Carolinian. Having heard nothing of the newcomer's travail on the way south, the adjutant had listed him as absent without leave to date from September 30. Pickett's belated appearance was all the more disagreeable because the Eighth Infantry was critically short of commissioned officers. Thus Lieutenant Clark sharply ordered him to provide a written account of his journey, explaining every delay and detention.

Although probably disgusted at being treated like a truant, and almost certainly distressed that his active-duty career should get off to such a ragged start, the new subaltern did as ordered. He described his itinerary in great detail and made a credible defense of his conduct. The litany of difficulties so obviously beyond his control must have satisfied his inquisitor, for no sanction was taken against the newest addition to the Eighth United States Infantry.[4]

* * *

As if the rigors of travel were not enough of an ordeal, four days after reaching Monterey Pickett took to a sickbed, probably the result of a malarial ailment contracted during his enforced stay in the unhealthy lowlands along the Gulf. He required a month in the military hospitals around Monterey before he could join his regiment. On December 13 he reported for duty, pale and weary, at the camp of Company I of the Eighth at Saltillo, fifty-five miles southwest of Monterey in the southern Sierra Madre Mountains.

Despite the salubrious climate that had made Saltillo a health resort, he quickly found that he had company among the ranks of the unwell: three of the four officers in his unit—Captain Collinson P. Gates, First Lieutenant Joseph Selden, and Second Lieutenant Alfred Crozet—were on sick leave or were lying, feverish and weak, in camp. For some time before Pickett's coming, the company had been in charge of its senior noncommissioned officer. Thus, George Pickett found himself in command of the first active-duty unit to which he was assigned.

Donning the mantle of command, he must have wondered whether he could shoulder his new responsibilities with confidence, or whether inexperience would give rise to self-doubt and cause him to falter. For instruction and advice he looked to his new colleagues but found few enough on hand to help him; the dearth of leadership was of regimental proportions. Although the Eighth had lost only a few officers in battle, several others including Colonel (and Brevet

Brigadier General) William Jenkins Worth and Lieutenant Colonel Thomas Staniford had been detached from the outfit to head occupation commands.

Pickett quickly acquainted himself with those few officers who remained in the ranks, forming especially close relationships with two assigned to Company A, Brevet Major George Wright and Second Lieutenant James ("Pete") Longstreet, graduates, respectively, of the West Point Classes of 1822 and 1842. Each was destined to become Pickett's commanding officer at different points in the latter's career. While the Pickett-Wright association would be mainly of a professional nature, the bonds of friendship that linked Pickett and Longstreet would be among the strongest to grace the mid-nineteenth-century army.[5]

National Archives
James Longstreet

Along with Lieutenant Selden, who soon came off sick leave to relieve Pickett in company command, these officers proved instrumental in helping the new arrival settle into the pace of regimental affairs and in general to become familiar with the duties of an infantry subaltern. Another source of counsel and advice was Brevet Major William R. Montgomery, who two months after Pickett's arrival at Saltillo succeeded to the command of Company I and thus became the Virginian's immediate superior. Under the tutelage of these officers, Pickett put in countless hours on the drill-field, familiarizing the many recruits in his company with the intricate evolutions that had so taxed his patience at West Point.

While assuming his new duties, Pickett took the occasion to visit the camps of other regiments outside Monterey. There he was befriended by older West Pointers, including two members of the Class of 1843 whom he had known briefly at the Academy, Second Lieutenants Ulysses S. Grant of the Fourth Infantry and Rufus Ingalls of the First Dragoons. Ingalls was an amiable, outgoing sort whose friendship was Pickett's for the taking. Grant, however, was quiet, stolid, seemingly dour—a contrast to Pickett's courtliness and sociability. Despite their dissimilar backgrounds—the aristocratic Virginian and the rough-hewn Northwesterner had few experiences in common beyond scholastic difficulties at the Academy—Pickett came to respect and admire the older officer. Their friendship would span decades and would survive the fire of a war that placed them at sword's point.[6]

Lieutenant Pickett had less than a month to acquaint himself with his new comrades and responsibilities before the Eighth Infantry quit its station at Saltillo. In common with other units in Taylor's command, early in January 1847 the regiment marched to the coast and at Tampico boarded transports for Lobos Island in the Gulf of Mexico. Taylor's victory at Monterey appeared to have put the *quietus* on active campaigning in northern Mexico. Meanwhile, Brevet Lieutenant General Winfield Scott, commanding general of the army, was mapping a 270-mile advance from the Gulf to Mexico City by which he hoped to capture the enemy's capital and conquer a peace. To bolster his expeditionary force he had been assigned roughly half of Taylor's army, the divisions of Worth and Brigadier General David E. Twiggs. Scott would leave the able but prickly Taylor, with his reduced force, to sew up the last pockets of resistance in northern Mexico.[7]

From Lobos Island, where "Old Fuss and Feathers" was assembling his host, the forward contingent of the Eighth Infantry—six companies including Pickett's, under the overall command of Major Wright—sailed on February 6 for the anchorage of Anton Lizardo, twelve miles south of Scott's initial objective, the fortified port of Vera Cruz. The journey down the coast was slow and much-interrupted; Pickett and his comrades did not leap ashore until sunset on March 9. The Virginian was among the first troops to set foot on Collado Beach, where for the first time he came under enemy fire. Thanks to the distance between his position and the guns of the Castle of San Juan de Ulua on Gallega Reef, he weathered the barrage without injury. At once he supervised his company in erecting a line of investment westward toward Malibran, then northwestward to the coastal village of Vergana.[8]

For the next three weeks Wright's detachment took part in the siege of Vera Cruz, which the regiment's historian termed "almost wholly a bombardment . . . the duty of the infantry mainly that of guarding the trenches." Initially hopeful of a quick and heroic baptism of battle, Pickett found trench warfare a frustrating experience. For him the only satisfying aspect of the siege (beyond its successful denouement) was the communique he received in early March announcing that he had been promoted to the full grade of second lieutenant. The news that he was now a full-fledged commissioned officer was overshadowed, however, by an accompanying notice that he had been transferred to the Second United States Infantry. Having only recently begun to feel at home in the ranks of the Eighth, he must have been pained by the prospect of starting over elsewhere. Apparently, however, the reassignment was countermanded, for Pickett's name never appeared on the rolls of the Second Infantry.[9]

Following the fall of Vera Cruz, Scott took up his movement toward the Mexican interior via Puebla. His path led through the pass of Cerro Gordo where he encountered forces under General Antonio Lopez de Santa Anna, the newly restored commander of the Mexican forces. If Lieutenant Pickett expected that Santa Anna would provide him with his first battle experience, however, he was disappointed. The Eighth Infantry saw no direct involvement in the fighting near Cerro Gordo on April 17-18, which closed with the enemy in headlong flight and the road to Puebla wide open. For two days after the battle the regiment guarded some of the several hundred Mexicans who had been slow to flee the scene of Santa Anna's defeat.[10]

Once the prisoners had been paroled, Pickett and his comrades spent warm, lazy weeks on occupation duty at Puebla while General Scott awaited reinforcements and tried to achieve peace through negotiation. At Puebla the regiment attended to administrative duties, assimilating three understrength companies that had been reorganizing in the rear of the army and welcoming the return from detached duty of Major Carlos A. Waite, who assumed command by virtue of seniority.

Other regiments were also reorganizing; one result was an announcement that Lieutenant Pickett had been transferred to the Seventh Infantry. He may have fought the transfer; in any case, he managed to postpone its effective date. Finally, on July 1, Pickett bade an unhappy farewell to Majors Waite and Wright, Lieutenant Longstreet, and his other comrades, and left the regiment—only to return nine days later. Concurrent with his transfer, General Scott's headquarters had directed Second Lieutenant Samuel Bell Maxey of the Seventh Infantry—a boisterous Kentuckian who had finished one notch above Pickett in the Class of 1846—to join the Eighth. As Maxey later explained, "both desiring to remain with the regiments with which we had served, and this being the desire of our superior officers, an exchange was effected," permitting both officers to rejoin their original units. To Maxey, the outcome suggested that Lieutenant Pickett had already won the "entire confidence" of his commanders.[11]

Upon his return, Pickett assumed company command for the second time in his brief career. As result of officer reassignments announced by Major Waite, he temporarily took over Company A, which had been leaderless for some time while Major Wright served as second-in-command of the regiment and Pete Longstreet, recently promoted to first lieutenant, replaced Lieutenant Clark as adjutant.[12]

Not until early August, when the Mexican government rejected Scott's offer of an armistice, did the army resume its northwestward movement along the bank of Lake Xochimilco. Approaching Mexico City from below, Scott dispatched two divisions toward the fortified camp Santa Anna had built outside the village of Contreras; meanwhile, the American commander continued north with Worth's command toward the post of San Antonio. On August 19 his detached force overwhelmed the camp near Contreras. The defeat compelled the garrison at San Antonio to flee to the Churubusco River and that stream's namesake village. The following day Worth supervised a four-pronged assault on Churubusco and its environs along the direct approach to Mexico City. It was at Churubusco that Lieutenant Pickett tasted combat for the first time.[13]

The Fifth United States Infantry, leading regiment in Colonel Newman S. Clarke's brigade of Worth's division, spearheaded the attack at Churubusco. That regiment, however, bogged down against enemy resistance short of the town, whereupon Clarke sent in the Sixth and Eighth Regiments. As the brigade leader reported, under Major Waite the Eighth rushed up the Churubusco road "almost breathless with exertions to keep closed up." When scouts reported the advance of a body of lancers from the direction of Mexico City, Colonel Clarke faced Waite's people to the right, then sent them through a cornfield onto the road the horsemen occupied. By the time it got into position to repel a thrust, the lancers were in retreat along with other elements of Santa Anna's force. Minutes later, the Eighth was hastening north in pursuit.

Giving way to caution, General Worth halted and recalled the outfit before it could reach the riverline defenses above Churubusco, which included a *tete de pont*, or fortified bridgehead. The attackers required possession of the bridge but to reach it they must surmount a high-banked, cannon-studded earthwork protected by a ditch twenty feet wide.

As Worth and Clarke sized up the position, the Eighth Infantry guarded the rear of Captain James Duncan's celebrated Battery A, Second United States Artillery, then shelling the retreating enemy. When word came to resume the advance, Major Waite left two companies with Duncan and led the balance of the regiment, including Pickett and Company A, toward the bridge. On the flank and to the rear, most of the Fifth Infantry moved up in support, while the Sixth Infantry prepared to strike the *tete de pont* from another direction.[14]

About 150 yards from the earthwork, the regiments ground to a halt under a torrent of shell and musketry. As though oblivious to it all, Captain James V. Bomford and Lieutenant Longstreet rushed forward, leading Company H to the edge of the ditch, Pickett's company close behind. From that point Bomford and Longstreet crawled to the southern base of the bastion, hauling the regimental colors with them. Climbing upon the shoulders of their men, both officers were boosted up and over the wall of the ditch. Then they splashed through the moat and, with musket balls whipping around them, scrambled up the fort's parapet. Impressed by their daring, Pickett followed their lead; behind him the rest of the regiment surged up and over the ditch. Once inside the fort, they began to press the defenders rearward at bayonet-point.

Soon after entering the earthwork Pickett was slightly wounded, probably by a fragment of shell or a spent ball—the first of only two wounds he would receive in the course of a long military career. Shrugging off the stinging blow, he remained with his troops, fighting his way across the parapet with pistol and sword until enemy resistance abated. Once the fort was securely in American hands, he helped turn its guns on nearby works that had yet to surrender.

By sundown, the victory at Churubusco was complete. The key to success appears to have been the impetuous offensive of Bomford and Longstreet, which Pickett had helped sustain. Although other regiments including the Fifth and Sixth Infantry had penetrated the *tete de pont* within minutes of the Eighth's entry, the colors of Major Waitè's outfit had been the first to fly from the crest of the work.

Library of Congress
Attack on *tete de pont* at Churubusco

The victory had great personal meaning for Lieutenant Pickett. Not only had he displayed daring and fortitude in his first battle, he had sufficiently distinguished himself to win plaudits in Major Waite's after-action report and a recommendation for promotion. Since no vacancies existed in the commissioned ranks he received the brevet of first lieutenant for the "gallant and meritorious conduct" he had exhibited on August 20.[15]

* * *

With the southern approaches to Mexico City secure, Scott's reunited army poised for the kill on the road to the capital. Santa Anna's call for an armistice postponed the invaders' final offensive for more than two weeks, but once it became clear that the Mexican leader was playing for time in which to concentrate and strengthen his forces General Scott renewed his advance during the first week in September.[16]

By this time Lieutenant Pickett, who was recuperating from his recent wound, had been transferred from line to staff service, sharing with another officer the post of adjutant recently relinquished by James Longstreet; for a time he also took on the responsibilities of regimental quartermaster. These behind-the-lines assignments, however, did not keep him out of combat once active campaigning resumed. He had partaken of battle and he decided that he liked the keen tang of it—the exhilaration of shared danger, the pride that came from keeping one's head and doing one's duty even as the hot breath of mortality seared the flesh.[17]

Scott's carefully chosen route led toward the western defenses of Mexico City including the hilltop castle known as Chapultepec. Before moving up to strike that critical objective, the commanding general felt compelled to deal with a pair of obstacles about half a mile to the west: a granary suspected of harboring ordnance supplies, the Molino del Rey, which was defended by two infantry brigades with a third in close support; and an adjacent building of stone, the Casa Mata, held by 1,500 foot troops and artillerymen. On September 8, Worth's division assaulted both objectives, gaining lodgements that eventually forced the enemy to evacuate but in the process suffering numerous casualties including the wounding of Major Waite and Brevet Majors Wright and Montgomery of the Eighth Infantry.

Adjutant Pickett, anxious to prove that his performance at Churubusco had not been a fluke, took part in the assault on the Casa Mata but found no opportunity to distinguish himself. After huddling under a heavy fire in advance of the enemy position, watching as men around him toppled one after another, he readily heeded orders to withdraw. After disengaging, the survivors of his outfit re-formed in the rear, supporting Duncan's battery as it laid a deadly barrage upon both positions. Eventually the cannonade enabled Worth to launch a new offensive that carried Molino del Rey. Once the mill fell into Yankee hands the defenders of the Casa Mata withdrew, permitting some regiments in Clarke's brigade to occupy the works. Meanwhile the Eighth, under the ailing Captain Montgomery, undertook "to collect and remove our killed and wounded, thickly scattered over the field." Noting the scope of his regiment's losses, Pickett must have marvelled that he had escaped without harm from such a precarious position.[18]

Once the fighting of the eighth died down, Scott's main army pushed eastward, thrusting the troops dislodged from Molino del Rey and the Casa Mata inside the walled citadel of Chapultepec, key to the defense of the enemy capital. By the morning of the thirteenth, Scott was ready for the climactic offensive of his campaign. That morning he launched a multi-column assault on the hilltop fortress, Regulars and volunteer troops attacking simultaneously from the west, southwest, and south.

At the outset Colonel Clarke's brigade was held in reserve, but when the assault slowed, the command was hastened forward to bolster the line and recoup momentum. As part of this movement, the Eighth Infantry took up a position in a woods at the western base of Chapultepec Hill, where, as Major Montgomery reported, his men "received a galling fire from small arms." Unable to remain in such a place, the major waved his sword and ordered the regiment at the double-quick across a field sewn with land mines and up the slope beyond to the crest. The regiment responded with a burst of pent-up emotion, Lieutenant Pickett and his comrades charging toward the top "over ditches, rocks, and breast-works" against a blizzard of musketry, shell, and roundshot.[19]

At the crest, facing the walls of the fortress, officers and men sought shelter while steeling themselves for a final push. For twenty minutes they huddled under a constant fire from the ramparts as scaling ladders came forward. In the meantime, other regiments secured unsteady footholds around the castle. Pickett watched with admiration as Lieutenant Lewis A. Armistead led a storming party of the Sixth Infantry into the ditch that surrounded the citadel. Fifteen years hence, then-General Pickett would have the good fortune to make then-General Armistead one of his ranking subordinates.[20]

Preparations at last complete, the soldiers of the Eighth Regiment surged forward, placing the ladders against the walls of the fort and ascending them as fast as they could go. Numerous attackers lost their footing, many toppling, wounded, into open air. When his turn came, Pickett led Company A up the ladders in rear of Lieutenant Longstreet and H Company. On the first parapet, Longstreet grabbed the regimental colors as they fell from the hands of their wounded bearer, himself falling minutes later with a musket round in his thigh. As he lay on the stone walk he handed the colors to his friend Pickett and urged him to place them where they belonged. The adjutant needed no prodding; with adrenaline coursing through his system he clambered up the steps to the uppermost parapet, missiles flitting all around him. Reaching the top in a breathless rush, he shot down at least one defender who sought to bar his path, hauled down the Mexican flag, and ran up the banner of the Eighth Infantry. Moments later other Americans clustered about him; one planted the national standard beside the regimental colors.

From his lofty perch the lieutenant watched with a curious sense of detachment as the fighting swirled beneath him. Eventually, the sounds of battle tapered off as attackers flooded the parapets, putting the last defenders to flight. The abrupt diminution of resistance made it appear that Pickett's dramatic feat—like Bomford's and Longstreet's at Churubusco—had torn the life from the enemy garrison. Observing from a distance the American flags waving upon the crest, Santa Anna is supposed to have cried out: "I believe if we were to plant our batteries in hell the damned Yankees would take them from us!"[21]

Whatever its effect on the Mexican commander, Pickett's flag-raising had a major impact on some enemy soldiers not engaged in the day's combat. During the fighting at Churubusco the Americans had captured eighty-five deserters—many of them of Irish ancestry—whom the Mexicans had organized into a special all-foreign unit known as the San Patricio Battalion. General Scott had sentenced to death the majority of the turncoats; at his order, twenty had been hanged a few days before the fighting at Chapultepec. Early on September 13, one of Scott's subordinates placed thirty other San Patricios on a makeshift gallows within view of the fortified castle and announced that they would die as soon as the American flag went up over the ramparts. The hangings came off as scheduled; thus, by his heroics Pickett indirectly played the role of an executioner.[22]

* * *

Pickett's role in the capture of Chapultepec, whose fall precipitated the surrender of Mexico City, would number among the storied achievements of Scott's campaign in Mexico—indeed, in the annals of American military history. His exploit brought him numerous benefits. It gained him prominent mention in Scott's after-action report, which received nationwide circulation. It brought him a second brevet, that of captain, for gallant and meritorious conduct. It won him the adulation of his men, the respect of fellow-officers—even the admiration of the enemy. Shortly after the battle, a local priest (possibly a member of the Franciscan convent adjacent to Chapultepec) presented him with a crucifix as a token of his esteem. Staunch Anglican Pickett revered the cross as a talisman; he attached it to a chain that he wore about his neck for the rest of his life.[23]

The young hero saw no direct action during the mopping-up operation that cleared Scott's path into Mexico City. As the American commander entered the capital to accept the surrender of its military and political officials, much of his army settled into occupation duty on the city's outskirts. Initially the Eighth Infantry camped at Tacubaya, southwest of Mexico City, then outside the village of Jalapa. At Jalapa Brevet Captain Pickett tried to adjust to a much reduced pace, returning to his adjutant's paperwork while exchanging the additional duties of quartermaster for those of regimental commissary officer.[24]

The mundane routine of filling out returns, filing requisitions, and stockpiling beef and crackers was unsettling to one recently immersed in the hectic violence of combat. He remained at this duty, however, for several months as negotiations toward a formal surrender of Santa Anna's army dragged on. He broke the monotony of camp life as best he could, playing cards with James Longstreet once his friend recovered from his wound, and joining his cousin Henry Heth, a subaltern in the Sixth Infantry, on visits to the cantinas of Jalapa, where the pair "painted that town red."[25]

The winter that followed the victory at Chapultepec slowly turned into spring; when spring became summer it found the Eighth Infantry still on occupation duty. It was the regiment's fate to be a part of the last division to be withdrawn from Mexico City and its outlying districts. Not until July 1848, with the ink barely dry on the Treaty of Guadalupe Hidalgo, did the outfit depart the scene of stasis and routine to return to the States. With mixed emotions, Lieutenant Pickett marched to the coast and boarded the steamer *Missouri* en route to his next duty station, Jefferson Barracks, outside Saint Louis. While he disliked the thought of leaving the scene of his recent triumphs, perhaps never to return, he could hope that more challenging assignments and equally rewarding service awaited him above the Rio Grande.[26]

THREE — Service on Two Frontiers

Back in the States, Pickett found that he had traded one form of military occupation for another. This was bad enough; but the new venue suffered by comparison to the old.

The Eighth Infantry remained at Jefferson Barracks for only a few months; by the autumn of 1848 the regiment, which had been reorganized, refitted, and recruited back to strength, was deemed fit for the task of subduing the Native Americans who inhabited Texas, flashpoint of the war just ended. By December the outfit had been placed in garrison at Camp Worth, outside San Antonio, headquarters of the several units of infantry, cavalry, and artillery that kept the peace in Texas. There the regiment began to acquaint itself with the frontier constabulatory duties it would shoulder for the next decade and longer.[1]

After Chapultepec, Pickett had found service in Mexico nearly as slow-paced and tedious as his weeks at home before joining his regiment. Yet, in Mexico he could while away occupation duty by partaking of the wares and amusements of local civilization: hearty food, abundant drink, and the company of sultry-eyed *senoritas*. He enjoyed none of those diversions during his early days in southeast Texas. Life on the rim of the Great American Desert was bleak and foreboding like the landscape itself, complete with its own brand of dangers. If barren vistas and roving bands of Comanches and Kiowas were insufficient to unsettle a soldier's mind, he could always fix his attention on the tarantulas, the poisonous centipedes, the rattlesnakes, the scorpions, and the other varmints that crossed his path with exasperating regularity.

Fortunately for the acting adjutant of the Eighth Infantry, short weeks after reaching Texas he was able to escape, at least temporarily, from the desert primeval. At year's end he started off on what turned into a six-month leave, during which he reimmersed himself in the genteel life of his youth. In Richmond and on Turkey Island he played the returning hero, accepting the adulation of relatives and friends who clamored endlessly for retellings of his exploits at Churubusco and Chapultepec. On this extended visit he paid greater attention than ever before to Miss Sally Minge, whose bright eyes and lustrous hair lingered in his mind's eye long after he returned to the rude surroundings of San Antonio in April 1849.[2]

* * *

The presence of the Eighth Infantry in East Texas was supposed to place a check on Comanche depredations. Indian raids on homesteads continued unabated, however, for the hostiles did not fear reprisal: before it could punish them the army had to catch them. Each time the army was ordered out in pursuit, the marauders quickly moved beyond the range of the slow-footed infantry. A little over a year after the regiment's arrival at San Antonio, the *Texas State Gazette* noted that "the idea of repelling mounted Indians, the most expert horsemen in the world, with a force of foot soldiers is here looked upon as exceedingly ridiculous."[3]

More uniformly successful than its record of preventing and punishing Indian attacks was the regiment's continuous effort to establish strategic outposts that would gradually reduce the sphere of Comanche operations. By August 1849 the Eighth Infantry had concentrated around Austin, where Pickett received word of his promotion to first lieutenant. Later that year he was reassigned to Company I, the unit that established Fort Gates on the left bank of the Leon River. At this post Pickett spent three and a half years learning the business of small-unit command under conditions that only occasionally approached those of wartime.[4]

As if the very act of fortifying was a powerful deterrent, the regiment observed few hostiles in the vicinity of Fort Gates through the early months of 1850. For Lieutenant Pickett release from inactivity came infrequently, such as in early January when he led a mounted detachment of seven men in chasing down a band of "Tonkaways" who had stolen army horses. The company commander pushed on determinedly, eventually overtaking the horse-thieves and returning the stolen property. Upon returning to the post, however, he settled back into a life of monotony in a desolate, torrid corner of the world that appeared to lack even the rudiments of civilization.[5]

At times the unchanging routine, the aridness of existence, approached the unbearable. Whenever possible he took leave, if only to visit friends at other equally isolated posts. He came to welcome detached service, even if it promised only court-martial duty or supply-train escort service, so long as it took him to population centers where the surroundings were new and he could feel less isolated.

Eventually, he could no longer go it alone. Fortunately, he did not have to: by December 1850, through frequent correspondence and infrequent visits to Virginia, he had been courting Sally Minge for several months. Just before Christmas he took an extended leave for the first time in almost two years. By train and stagecoach he joined his betrothed at the Franklin, Louisiana, home of Sally's sister, Mrs. Margaret Wilkins. There the happy couple were wed on the afternoon of January 28, 1851.[6]

The lieutenant and his bride enjoyed a long honeymoon; not till July did they make their way to the Leon River country, towing a wagon crammed with trunks of clothing and wedding presents. By then Sally was six months pregnant.

One can only imagine the life Mrs. Lieutenant Pickett experienced at Fort Gates over the next four months. A child of the landed gentry, a stranger to want and privation, she could not have been prepared for the primitive conditions that characterized her new home. Doubtless she made friends among the officers' wives, most of whom, by sheer necessity, had come to terms with the harshness of frontier life. From these women she may have learned enough survival skills to withstand the barren vistas, the extreme weather, the natural perils that faced one at every turn.

But acquired stoicism could not have enabled Sally Minge Pickett to surmount the limitations of the medical and surgical care available to the frontier army. When complications arose during pregnancy, her health suffered irreparable damage. In November she died, along with her infant son, during delivery. Her grieving husband sent their bodies to Richmond for burial in the Pickett family plot at Shockoe Hill Cemetery.[7]

Prior to this time, Pickett had been a happy-go-lucky sort impervious to misfortune, let alone tragedy. Sally's death changed all that. For months he seemed unable to throw off the pain and gloom that her memory brought him. In fact, at intervals throughout the rest of his life he was susceptible to moodiness and depression. He seemed unwilling to strive for happiness, for fear that once he attained it, it would be taken from him.

Given the bleakness of Pickett's life before Sally joined him, after her passing he must have seriously considered leaving the army. Perhaps the camaraderie of sympathetic colleagues, the solicitude of commanding officers who felt some measure of his grief, persuaded him to remain in the service.

The sympathy expressed by family members also helped him deal with the pain. In a letter written more than a year after Sally's death he revealed to his cousin, Elizabeth Heth Vaden, the continuing severity of his grief as well as his gratitude for her efforts to comfort him. Although he had torn up several previous replies, fearing each to be "too gloomy and melancholy," he persevered because he felt himself to be in her debt. Then, too, a return letter would have a therapeutic effect: "*She* is always connected in some way with you, and when I write to you I wish constantly to speak of that dear being who is now an angel in heaven."

The more he wrote of his wife, the more he descended into the sort of gloom he had hoped to avoid. He thanked his cousin for her unwillingness to leave him to "my desolation," although "I sometimes think Lizzie that I am not worthy of consolation, that I do not deserve the commiseration and kindness which has been bestowed upon me. I know it and feel it—I am no longer the same person, the buoyancy of youth is past. I look forward to nothing with pleasure. It is sinful to cherish such feelings, still there are many times when I cannot stifle them."

One means of blocking such thoughts was to submerge himself in professional activity: "I have just returned from a tour of Court Martial duty—which thank God has served in some measure to occupy and divert my thoughts from their usual melancholy train." He then assured Lizzie that he was trying to conquer his tendency to isolate himself from companions. As a first step toward rehabilitation he had acquired "one of the prettiest little setter dogs you ever saw." He considered the animal (named "Hal," after Lizzie's brother) not only a pet but the finest friend he had in the army.[8]

In point of fact, by the time he wrote, Lieutenant Pickett had made the acquaintance of someone who would fill the void in his life in a way no dumb animal could. A month after his wife's death, shortly before Christmas 1852, he had taken leave, returning to Virginia to continue his emotional recuperation in the bosom of his family. He remained at home until late the following April, visiting not only his relatives but also friends at nearby army installations. When not in a sociable mood, he would take solitary walks along the seawall at Fort Monroe, that venerable installation at the tip of the Virginia Peninsula. One day in early spring he was lying under an umbrella on the beach of Old Point Comfort, reading a book, feeling thoroughly alone, when La Salle Corbell of Chuckatuck, Virginia, not yet four years old, found him and, as she always claimed, fell in love with him.

The little girl, visiting with her grandmother at the post, had been drawn away from her guardian by the forlorn picture presented by a young man in uniform, "always apart from the others, and very sad." La Salle herself was sad and lonely, having been forced into isolation from most of her family because of a contagious respiratory ailment. "I could imagine," she wrote six decades later, "but one reason for his desolation and in pity for him, I crept under his umbrella to ask him if he, too, had the whooping-cough."

The officer hesitated before giving her a warm smile, raising his cap in salutation, and replying in the negative. The answer only heightened his inquisitor's curiosity, for there was a palpable air of tragedy about him that even a child could discern. She knew this soldier must be suffering from an inner pain so great that he must also go off by himself to avoid afflicting others.

The poignant pose he struck would have captivated La Salle Corbell's interest even had she not been struck by his delicate good looks and sartorial splendor. To the end of her days she would cherish her first glimpse of him "as he lay stretched in the shade of the umbrella, not tall, and rather slender, but very graceful, and perfect in manly beauty. With childish appreciation, I particularly noticed his very small hands and feet. He had beautiful gray eyes that looked at me through sunny lights—eyes that smiled with his lips. His mustache was gallantly curled. His hair was exactly the color of mine, dark brown, and long and wavy, in the fashion of the time. The neatness of his dress attracted even a child's admiration. His shirt-front of the finest white linen, was in soft puffs and ruffles, and the sleeves were edged with hemstitched thread. . . ."[9]

Her wonderment at high pitch, she continued to question him, probing toward the source of his melancholy. Slowly, hesitantly, feeling the need to open himself to this young stranger, he confessed that his heart had been broken by a sorrow almost too great to bear. When the child asked how one's heart could break, "he replied that 'God broke it when He took from him his loved ones and left him so lonely'." The details of his bereavement so moved his listener that "in return for his confidence I promised to comfort him for his losses and to be his little girl now and his wife just as soon as I was grown up to be a lady."

Her earnest sympathy must have touched him, for he responded with a gesture that created an immediate bond between them. Taking from his guard-chain a ring that he obviously treasured, he slipped it onto her finger while placing in her hand a golden heart inscribed with his wife's name. Sixty years later the recipient of these gifts (which she still owned) recalled that when her grandmother came up to reclaim her at last, "I crept out from under the umbrella pledged to Lieutenant George E. Pickett of the United States Army. Then and to the end he was my soldier. . . ."[10]

Although he invited her to return for further conversation, it is doubtful that Pickett expected to see this precocious child again. If so, he was mistaken, for both remained at the fort for several days, during which their acquaintance turned into friendship. As La Salle told it, he taught her to write her first words ("Sallie," and "Soldier") and he sang to her in a "clear, rich voice . . . frequently accompanying himself on the guitar."

When Sallie's visit was over and the curious couple parted, Lieutenant Pickett probably expected that their meeting would produce nothing more than a touching memory. His confidante, however, had other ideas. La Salle Corbell was a mere child but a willful and determined one. She knew her own mind and heart, and both told her that one day she would marry George Pickett.[11]

* * *

He heard from Sallie soon after returning to his regiment in Texas. Her first letters, which she dictated to her mother or grandmother, amused him, then gradually, imperceptibly, warmed his heart. He replied to her childish missives, and so began a correspondence that frequently rescued him from melancholy. It would take years before the realization set in but when it did he would look back upon their first meeting with a deep sense of gratitude for the healing properties of fate. Denied her love, he would tell Sallie in 1863, life "would be but a blank to me . . . as it was when you found me wandering and lost, without a hope or guiding star."[12]

Another happy distraction in Pickett's life was the frequency with which he changed duty stations during the next three years in contrast to his static existence since arriving at Fort Gates in late 1849. While he was visiting in Virginia, the headquarters of the Eighth Infantry had been moved to a new installation on the San Saba River later known as Fort McKavett. Five months after his return to Texas, the regiment shifted northwestward to the confluence of the Colorado River and Oak Creek, where fatigue parties built Fort Chadbourne. Pickett remained at this outpost, established to protect the emigrant route from Fort Smith, Arkansas, to Santa Fe, New Mexico Territory, for only a couple of months before relocating to San Antonio, where he served a stint of quartermaster service. A month later, January 1853, he led Company C of the regiment back to Fort McKavett on scouting duty. The following month he was reassigned to Company I, which he commanded at Fort Chadbourne until relieved in May 1853 by Lieutenant Longstreet, then rejoining the regiment after a long period of detached duty. That August, after helping Longstreet complete work on Chadbourne, Pickett joined him at the head of a four-company battalion posted to San Antonio. In October the Eighth was reunited at Fort Clark, a semi-permanent post guarding the road between San Antonio and El Paso, but it quickly moved to Ringgold Barracks on the lower Rio Grande. During the first weeks of 1854, with Indian troubles heating up in West Texas, the regiment shifted cross-state to Fort Bliss, along the boundary with the New Mexico Territory. The long list of station changes finally ended in November with the outfit's return to Fort Davis, by which point Pickett was for a second time commanding Company E.[13]

For much of Pickett's seven-year tour of duty in Texas, he served in hostile territory, where his regiment was, in the words one of his superiors, "actually engaged in war" with various Indian tribes. With rare exceptions, however, Pickett did not come into sustained contact with the enemy, which carefully chose when and where it would engage the United States Army. On a few occasions he helped repulse hit-and-run attacks, usually at night, when raiding parties of Comanches and Kiowas struck cantonments and corrals. Not once did he take part in anything approaching a pitched battle. It was a strange, sometimes baffling, existence for a young soldier whose brief experience in combat had been limited to conventional warfare and European-model tactics.[14]

Thus he was extremely pleased when granted the opportunity to leave Texas for a locale physically and militarily more fertile. Late in 1854, when it became apparent that the nation's expanding internal-security responsibilities would bring about a larger army, Pickett tried to position himself for a berth in a new regiment. His efforts bore fruit, probably as the result of his close relationship with George Wright, his old company commander, who early in '55 was appointed colonel of one of four new regiments of horse and foot, the Ninth United States Infantry. That March Pickett received notice of his promotion to the full grade of captain and his assignment to command Company D of the Ninth. The new regiment was scheduled to recruit, mass, and organize at his old port-of-call, Fort Monroe.

Although he was saddened by the necessity of leaving friends such as Longstreet, the lure of a new and more challenging duty station and an increase in rank and pay kept him from looking back. In early June he took ship up the Gulf Coast to New Orleans. Ahead lay Virginia, home and friends, and the girl whose heart he had won during a spring day at the beach.[15]

* * *

Reaching Richmond at the commencement of summer, he remained with his family during a several-weeks' leave, not reporting to Fort Monroe until August. There he conferred with Colonel Wright; made the acquaintance of superiors previously unknown to him including Wright's second-in-command, Lieutenant Colonel Silas Casey; was introduced to his subordinates in Company D, First Lieutenant John E. Howard and Second Lieutenant James W. Forsyth; and met with his noncommissioned staff. In succeeding weeks, as troops reached Hampton Roads from the recruiting depots of the Northeast, he organized the would-be soldiers into squads and platoons and began to drill them. In off-hours he paid heed to the rumors swirling about Old Point Comfort, attempting to glean from them the location of the regiment's first tour of duty.[16]

As he marched proudly at the head of his company on the drill-plain, Pickett became the object of attention of many civilian visitors. None was more attentive than La Salle Corbell. Now all of seven years old, the precocious lass from Chuckatuck had importuned her family to come up to Fort Monroe that she might gaze wistfully upon "Her Soldier" for the first time in three years. She remained quite convinced that one day she would wed this handsome and dashing officer twenty-three years her senior.

Given the plethora of responsibilities incumbent upon Captain Pickett as he formed his company, he could not have shared a great deal of time with his young admirer. Sallie and he spent some time on the beach where they had met, building sand castles and watching ships put out into Hampton Roads. After a few days she had to go home, but she returned to Fort Monroe when she learned he had received orders to sail to a duty location three thousand miles away, where an Indian war was raging.

On a raw day in early November, as she recalled decades later, "the first real sorrow came to me when I watched the *St. Louis*, the United States transport, go out to sea with my soldier on board . . . bound for Puget Sound where was the new station, Fort Bellingham, which I thought must be farther than the end of the world."[17]

Here her memory failed her on two counts. Fort Bellingham was a year away from being built, and while Captain Pickett's regiment was indeed heading for the Washington Territory—specifically, Fort Vancouver, on the Columbia River—he was not accompanying it aboard the *St. Louis*. Her Soldier had embarked on another transport bound for Florida, where four months of court-martial duty awaited him.[18]

* * *

Fighting between white settlers of the Washington Territory and their Native American neighbors had broken out in the summer of 1855. Its roots lay in tribal leaders' dissatisfaction over the Treaty of Walla Walla, which Governor Isaac Ingalls Stevens had persuaded the Yakima, the Palouse, the Pisquouse, the Kilikatat, and ten other "confederated tribes" of the Yakima Nation to sign in June of that year. Under the imperfectly understood terms of this treaty, the signatories found themselves forced onto Yakima Valley land too circumscribed to support their expansive lifestyle. There the tribes had to contend against the increasing encroachment of homesteaders, trappers, and gold miners. Local tribes that had not acceded to the treaty including the Spokanes and the Coeur d'Alenes, felt even less constrained in blocking the path of white exploration and settlement. They and their Yakima neighbors rose up with increasing frequency, falling upon miners and Indian agents, killing the whites and confiscating or destroying their property.[19]

In the fall of 1855 United States troops already in the Washington Territory under Major Granville O. Haller of the Fourth Infantry invaded the Yakima Valley to determine the causes of the unrest. To the soldiers' consternation, they were driven out with severe loss. Over the next several months clashes between the Yakimas and enemy soldiers and civilians spread to both sides of the Cascade Mountains including westward into the Puget Sound country. It was in response to these expanding hostilities that the Ninth Infantry was sent to Fort Vancouver.

When Captain Pickett, fresh from his detached service in Florida, reached the Columbia River territory in March of '56, he found that his company, along with Company H of the Ninth under Lieutenant Colonel Casey and Major Robert S. Garnett, had been transferred to Fort Steilacoom, situated a mile east of Puget Sound near the frontier village of Olympia. While this detachment pacified Puget Sound, Colonel

Wright and the balance of the regiment would join territorial forces in freeing the Yakima and Walla Walla Valleys of unrest.[20]

Pickett's early weeks in northwestern Washington passed pleasurably. He was able to renew his association with comrades posted to the area including Rufus Ingalls and George B. McClellan. In company with these and other friends he lounged in the officer's club at Steilacoom, playing billiards and poker and rehashing old times over cigars and whiskey.

When weather permitted him to take the field, Pickett's active service was limited to a single engagement. On March 1 his unit, along with Company H of the Ninth and detachments of the Fourth Infantry and Third Artillery, tangled with hostiles on White River near Muckleshute Prairie. After inflicting some casualties and chasing the survivors into the hills, the expeditionary force returned to the snug confines of Fort Steilacoom. Pickett's unit remained in garrison until late summer, when Brigadier General William S. Harney, Commander of the Department of Oregon, directed Lieutenant Colonel Casey to send Company D to Whatcom County in the northwest corner of the territory to protect the settlements and coal mines on Bellingham Bay against Indian attack.[21]

When he reached his new post on August 26, the captain had as his primary objective replacing a small blockhouse built by the settlers with a major fortification of the most advanced design. On a strip of relatively flat land that a siting commission had selected a year earlier—eighteen miles from the border with British North America (Canada) at the mouth of the Nooksack River—he laid out the pattern for what would become Fort Bellingham.

The site was a logical choice, the only extensive tract of cleared ground along that heavily timbered shoreline. Pickett's only concern was that it straddled the claim of Charles E. Roberts, a former Hudson's Bay Company employee who had erected a cabin in which he lived with his German-born wife. Mr. Roberts was off serving in the territorial forces then battling the northern tribes; Maria Roberts, however, was at home to meet Captain Pickett—but not to greet him. When her visitor politely informed her that he must evict her from her home, which he would then raze to make way for the fort, she angrily ordered him off her property. Not even his well-meaning efforts to explain military necessity and eminent domain could calm her Teutonic fury.

Pickett's Virginia courtliness had its limits. Unable to work his logic upon his hostess, he resorted to physical measures: at his order, a labor detail from Company D removed the roof of her cabin. Amid imprecations half in English and half in German, Mrs. Roberts retreated to the end of her property line, whereupon Pickett formally

Whatcom Museum of History and Art

Captain Pickett's sketch of Sehome, Washington Territory, 1859.

claimed all 640 acres of the Roberts homestead for the federal government. (Later he saw to it that the government paid what it considered a fair price for the property while permitting the former owners to rebuild on the adjacent beach.)[22]

Preliminaries attended to, the captain set to work to build an outpost that would stand as a monument to his hitherto-unknown talents as an engineer. Over the next two months he designed and his soldiers constructed corner blockhouses, their walls twelve feet high and eight to eighteen inches thick, lashed together at the top to form palisades. The two-story blockhouses, equipped to mount 6- and 12-pounder howitzers, gradually enclosed a cantonment area 240 feet square, containing barracks, officers' quarters, and storehouses. Beyond the perimeter of the stockade Pickett placed outbuildings including a barn, a carpentry shop, a laundry, an officers' mess, a blacksmith's shop, and a dispensary. On the east side of the fort he cleared land for a drillground. Later he supervised the building of a road between the fort and the sleepy village that would become the city of Bellingham. He also built the first bridge ever to span Whatcom Creek.

By any indication, Fort Bellingham was an impressive facility. Examining the outpost in December 1858, the army's inspector-general, Colonel Joseph K. F. Mansfield, pronounced the fort "beautifully situated" and the various interior dwellings "ample" in space and accommodations: "The troops are well-quartered and there seems to be nothing wanted of consequence." In sum, the fort was "a cheap and good post, creditable to the parties that performed the duty." Such praise was not the expected lot of one who had fared so poorly in his engineering courses at West Point. The quality of the fort's design suggested that Pickett was possessed of gifts not amenable to mathematical measurement.[23]

Perhaps to its creator's chagrin, the military capabilities of Fort Bellingham were never tested. Not long after its erecting, Colonel Wright put an end to the Indian conflict of 1855-56 through the almost unprecedented practice of negotiating fairly with the leading chiefs. On Puget Sound, Captain Pickett settled down to a peacetime regimen that permitted him to interact with the Native American population. Years later his wife would claim that "he made friends even of his enemies, learning the dialects of the different tribes that he might be able to teach them better principles of life than any they had known." The tongue in which he became most fluent, however, was Chinook, not a true Native American dialect but a commercial language that whites—principally representatives of the Hudson's Bay Company—had devised to facilitate trade with the northern tribes.[24]

Pickett did befriend one former enemy. When peace descended upon Puget Sound he sought escape from dull routine by joining a survey team bound for the Canadian border. He accompanied the surveyors to the Indian villages of the peninsula along Semiahmoo Bay, where he met a Haida woman who hailed from "Russian America"—a land later known as Alaska. Pickett was struck by her dark-eyed beauty, she by his courtly ways and exotic mannerisms. In time she came to fill a place in his heart empty since the death of his wife, one not yet occupied by La Salle Corbell.

This Indian maiden (a "princess," by legend) returned with Pickett to Fort Bellingham, where they decided to live as man and wife. Ample precedent existed for a soldier to take an Indian wife, or *klootchman*, in a marriage of convenience: one of Pickett's sometime subordinates, First Lieutenant Robert H. Davis, nephew of former Secretary of War Jefferson Davis, wed a Native American woman at about this time. Reportedly, Pickett's friend Sam Grant had done the same years before when posted to the wilds of Oregon.[25]

Whatcom Museum of History and Art
James Tilton Pickett, ca. 1860

Their wedding took place in mid-1856 at the home of one of Puget Sound's more prominent landowners. According to a local historian, the rite "was solemnized both according to tribal ceremonials of the bride's people, and according to the 'Boston Way'"—the norms of white society. At the height of the ceremony "the gloved right hand of the bride was clasped in the gloved right hand of the bridegroom," a simple gesture of romantic union.

The couple moved into a partially completed two-story frame house that Captain Pickett was having built atop Peabody Hill, three and a half miles from his fort. The house symbolized Pickett's intent to sink roots in this gleaming sliver of God's country, as did his purchase of property along Bellingham Bay.

He and his princess lived together—by all accounts, happily—for the next year and a half while Pickett continued in command of Fort Bellingham. The marriage produced a son, James Tilton Pickett, born on December 31, 1857, and named for his father's friend, the adjutant general of the Washington Territory. The arrival of his first-born was a joyous occasion for Pickett but one all too reminiscent of an earlier birth. Despite the diligent ministrations of Pickett's friend and chief surgeon, Lieutenant George Suckley, his wife did not long survive delivery. When she died early in 1858, Pickett for the second time in six years was beset by an oppressive loneliness and a sense of abandonment.[26]

FOUR – Fighting Redcoats and Bluecoats

Pickett was still in command of Fort Bellingham in the summer of 1859 when an improbable series of events ignited an international dispute over territorial expansion and commercial rights. Permitted to escalate, the dispute eventually brought the United States and Her Britannic Majesty's government to the brink of all-out war. It was Pickett's fate to be drawn into the center of this notorious *cause celebre*, a circumstance that made his name famous throughout the U.S. Army and anathema to British officials in the Pacific Northwest.

The controversy sprang from conflicting claims to San Juan Island, a trading enclave in Puget Sound roughly midway between the coasts of Washington and Vancouver's Island, British Columbia. The Oregon Treaty of 1846 settled decades of territorial rivalry between the two nations by giving the United States undisputed possession of all land south of the Forty-ninth Parallel. According to the terms of the treaty, the dividing line between American soil and British North America extended "to the middle of the channel which separates the continent from Vancouver's Island; and thence southerly through the middle of the said channel . . . to the Pacific Ocean."

While the treaty settled the thorniest aspects of the boundary dispute, it did not make clear who owned San Juan Island. The treaty's reference to "the middle of the channel" was inadequate, for two channels surrounded the island: Haro Strait, near Vancouver's Island, and Rosario Strait, which ran close to the U.S. mainland. Each country claimed the island as its own, America arguing that the boundary ran through the former defile, Britain insisting that the latter channel marked the boundary.[1]

In terms of population, San Juan was an English possession. Most of its few inhabitants were employees of the Hudson's Bay Company, whose presence on the island dated to 1845. The powerful trading concern had built a salmon-curing station on the island in 1850 and three years later a sheep ranch. In contrast, by mid-1859 only two dozen Americans had settled on the island. Even so, six years before, the territorial legislature of Washington had incorporated San Juan into what became Whatcom County.

The island's British and American settlers had long lived in unpeaceful coexistence. By 1859 the Americans had accumulated a long list of complaints against their more numerous neighbors, whom they accused of gross indignities, violations of civil rights, and efforts to provoke the northern Indians to attack homesteads. Many of the Americans' grievances stemmed from the policies of Sir James Douglas, the bluff and imperious governor of British Columbia and a former officer of Hudson's Bay. The extent of British involvement in tribal unrest cannot be determined, but it was true that many of her majesty's subjects regarded American squatters as trespassers on property guaranteed to England by treaties, explorations, and trading rights of long standing. Governor Douglas was especially desirous of ridding San Juan of foreign influences and as commander-in-chief of British military and naval forces in the Northwest, he believed he had the power to make his wish a reality.

If the American government could have controlled the local situation, there would have been no confrontation over San Juan. Back in 1855, when unrest on the island had first attracted attention in the nation's capital, Secretary of War Marcy had urged Governor Stevens to avoid antagonizing the British until a binational commission could reexamine the boundary question. No such commission had been formed, however, and by 1859 relations between the American settlers and British political and commercial representatives in the region abruptly degenerated as the result of a pig run amok.[2]

On or about the first of July a breeding boar owned by the Hudson's Bay Company broke free of its pen and began rooting in the vegetable patch of one Lyman Cutlar. The enraged Yankee grabbed his rifle and shot the errant swine, whereupon the animal's owners threatened legal recourse. Some hours after the killing a delegation of officials from British Columbia including the chief factor of Hudson's Bay (who happened to be Governor Douglas' son-in-law) swept down on Mr. Cutlar's cabin, ordered him outside, heatedly interrogated him, berated him for his lawless effrontery, and threatened to carry him off to Vancouver's Island to face trial under British law. When the unrepentant homesteader reacted by threatening to treat his unwanted guests as he had the pig, they beat a hasty retreat—only to return the following day accompanied by a squad of constables.[3]

Having anticipated their return, Cutlar hid from his accusers in the home of another American, who also felt threatened by the British officials. On July 11, as unrest spread across the island, a band of homesteaders flagged down a passing ship carrying General Harney, the departmental commander, then returning from an inspection tour of the upper reaches of his domain. When apprised of the situation, the hot-tempered Missourian, a dedicated anglophobe, immediately pledged that U.S. troops would be dispatched to the island to prevent further harassment of American citizens.[4]

The handiest troops were those at Fort Bellingham. At Harney's behest, on July 18 Lieutenant Colonel Casey ordered Pickett and Company D to protect lives and property on San Juan. It took a few days for the captain to round up his men, procure the necessary transportation and supplies, take on the firepower necessary to hold any position he took up, await the arrival of a relief garrison at Fort Bellingham—and provide, in his absence, for the care of his nineteen-month-old son. Finally, on the twenty-seventh, a warship landed at Griffin Bay, depositing Pickett, Lieutenants Howard and Forsyth, fifty-four enlisted men, one six-pounder gun, and two mountain howitzers on the southeastern shore of the island.[5]

As per his orders from Harney, Pickett immediately set out to secure a perimeter. For the better part of that day his men labored on earthworks and revetments and trained their cannon on the most likely route of British advance. Late that day Pickett permitted a small delegation of civil authorities, whom Governor Douglas had dispatched aboard the man-of-war H.M.S. *Satellite*, to meet with him. The leader of the party, Major John F. De Courcy, whom Douglas had recently appointed justice of the peace for San Juan, demanded to know what the American troops were up to. Pickett bluntly informed his visitor of his intentions, whereupon De Courcy told the captain "that it was his duty to warn him off the premises and island." Pickett informed De Courcy that he had appointed his own justice of the peace, who alone had jurisdiction over the island. Unable to make headway with the stubborn Virginian, Governor Douglas's representative retreated, spluttering with rage. Within a few days his report of the standoff caused a second British man-of-war, *Tribune*, Captain G. Phipps Hornby, to heave to in Griffin Bay, her thirty-one guns trained on "Camp Pickett."

Soon after Major De Courcy departed, the camp's namesake issued a proclamation declaring that, by General Harney's authority, he was establishing a military post on the island, one to whom settlers might flock when in need of protection. Ostensibly the soldiers were there to prevent Indian raids but Pickett's true intent was implicit in his announcement that "this being United States territory, no laws other than those of the United States, nor courts except such as are held by virtue of said laws, will be recognized or allowed on this island."[6]

His words had predictable effects. In Vancouver, Sir James issued a formal protest against the U.S. "invasion" and reasserted British claims to San Juan. His message strongly implied military retaliation. Pickett must have suspected as much, but he appears to have advanced toward the inevitable confrontation with a clear conscience and a sense of anticipation. The crisis could not be blamed on him; he was merely following the orders of his superior—a kindred spirit to Pickett in his overriding desire to do what he felt needed doing regardless of the consequences. Moreover, after years of inactivity and personal upheaval on Bellingham Bay, the captain was looking forward to some action.

* * *

By August 30, the increasingly short-tempered Governor Douglas ordered the Hudson's Bay representative on San Juan to declare Pickett and his men trespassers on British property, a charge they were to answer in a British Columbia court. Not surprisingly, Pickett ignored the court order, although he could not be said to be bargaining from a position of strength. By this point Camp Pickett was as strong as heavy earthworks, a small garrison, and a few cannon could make it, but its commander admitted that "it is not comfortable to be lying within range of a couple of war steamers." The situation grew even stickier the next day, when a third warship, the ten-gun *Plumper*, arrived off the island to bring Pickett's opposition to just shy of 1,000 sailors, soldiers, and marines. Still, Pickett maintained his determined, belligerent stance.[7]

Such a standoff was not easily ended. On August 3, Pickett received a communication from Captain Hornby, the senior naval officer off San Juan, to come aboard his ship and discuss the situation with a view to a mutually acceptable resolution. Pickett blandly replied that "my wish corresponds with yours to preserve harmony between our respective governments," but he demanded that the meeting be held in his camp. Hornby agreed, and he met with Pickett and his subordinates early that afternoon. Throughout the ensuing conference, the naval officer acted with unfailing politeness, calling Pickett's attention to Secretary Marcy's 1855 dispatch cautioning Governor

Stevens against stirring up trouble with his neighbors. Hornby reiterated Governor Douglas's protest against Pickett's presence, warned that continued recalcitrance could precipitate a clash, and "to prevent the chance of such collision" proposed a joint military occupation of the island.

Pickett sternly replied that he could not accede to joint occupation, but he would refer the matter to his superior. This course was not acceptable to his guest—no one on the British side wished to entrust the dispute to a man of Harney's temperament—and the seaman implied that an armed response was imminent. In a post-conference communique to Pickett, Hornby noted that, having offered concessions toward an amicable settlement, his was no longer the responsibility for any violence that occurred.

His host did not see it that way. Replying to Hornby's faintly condescending letter, Pickett tried to thrust any blame back to the British, arguing that should Hornby impose a joint occupation before Pickett could clear the suggestion with Fort Vancouver "you will then be the person who will bring on a most unfortunate and disastrous difficulty, and not the United States officials."[8]

By this point Pickett was probably hoping for a way out of the crisis without seeming to disobey his orders. Unfortunately, when he passed Hornby's suggestion on to General Harney, the bellicose commander would have none of it. Seeing in Pickett's response to Hornby's threats a note of defiance that he considered admirable, Harney advised his subordinate to remain firm. In reporting the confrontation to General-in-Chief Scott on August 18, Harney embellished the Hornby-Pickett conference with a militant flamboyance: "The senior officer of three British ships-of-war threatened to land an overpowering force upon Captain Pickett, who nobly replied that whether they landed fifty or five thousand men, his conduct would not be affected by it; that he would open his fire, and, if compelled, take to the woods fighting." He later recommended Pickett for a brevet promotion on the basis of the "cool judgment, ability, and gallantry" the captain had displayed in facing down an enemy.[9]

Rather than calm aroused passions, Harney escalated the crisis by sending army reinforcements to, and seeking naval support for, the island. Already he had ordered Colonel Casey to dispatch Brevet Major Haller's company of the Fourth Infantry from Fort Steilacoom to San Juan. Arriving off Griffin Bay on August 1 aboard the *Massachusetts*, the same ship that had conveyed Pickett and his unit to the post of danger, Haller at first hesitated to land for fear of precipitating a fight. To avoid that possibility, he communicated with both Pickett and his opponents while still aboard the *Massachusetts*.

Haller's most significant contribution to the standoff was a piece of news, just received from abroad, that he brought Captain Hornby—news that dampened any enthusiasm Her Majesty's government might have entertained for an armed clash in the Pacific Northwest. The European war that had been raging for some months among Sardinia, France, and Austria appeared to have reached a climax during the recent battle of Solferino, a tactical defeat for England's ally, Austria. Now that the Austrians were reported retreating from the Italian peninsula, placing England on military alert, Captain Hornby realized that the last thing his government needed was a war in North America. When Hornby relayed Haller's news, even the blustery Governor Douglas decided that his naval forces—to whom he had granted authority to land and take San Juan by force—should proceed cautiously.[10]

Eventually Major Haller disembarked his unit, and nine days later Lieutenant Colonel Casey slipped past the porous British coastal blockade to place another five companies of foot soldiers and artillerymen at Pickett's disposal. As per his orders from Harney, Pickett refused to relinquish command to Haller, but upon Casey's arrival he resumed the role of dutiful subordinate. At once he carried out Casey's order to strengthen the island's defenses. By the close of August no fewer than 461 soldiers occupied Camp Pickett and its environs, bolstered by eight 32-pounder cannon and three howitzers.[11]

Around the time of this influx of defenders, the crisis in Griffin Bay began to ease at last. A few days before Casey's landing, Rear Admiral Robert L. Baynes, commander of British naval forces in the Pacific, had arrived off Victoria to confer with Governor Douglas. Aware of the recent events in Europe and unimpressed by Sir James's claim that national honor was at stake over San Juan, the admiral decided upon a conciliatory course. Appalled at the thought that two mighty nations might go to war over the death of a pig, he resolved to do nothing provocative until the entire situation could be referred to London for a conclusive judgment. The most he would do in the meantime was to keep "a Ship of War in Griffin Bay to watch over British interests."[12]

* * *

At about this same time, reason finally began to emanate from the American side, if not from Harney's headquarters. Once details of the "Pig War" made the slow, circuitous journey to Washington, D.C.,

President James Buchanan and his military and diplomatic advisors were at least as shocked and upset by Harney's actions as the British had been. Buchanan's acting secretary of war notified the departmental leader that "the President was not prepared to learn that you had ordered military possession to be taken of the island of San Juan" without a direct order from the War Department. The general was to refrain from further action until a less precipitate policy could be formulated at the highest levels.[13]

So disturbed was the President by Harney's rashness that he took the unusual step of sending the seventy-three-year-old General Scott on the long sea and land voyage to Puget Sound. The opposing sides rested uneasily on their arms until the General-in-Chief reached Fort Vancouver in late October.

Over Harney's protests, Scott quickly resolved to implement the proposition Captain Hornby had advanced on August 3. Proceeding to Victoria, he proposed to Governor Douglas a joint military occupation of San Juan, no more than 100 American and British troops "to be posted in separate camps or quarters, for the equal protection of their respective countrymen in the island." When Douglas suggested instead a joint occupation by civil officials that Scott lacked the power to approve, the latter slyly maneuvered his host into accepting his plan. Under terms of the agreement reached at Victoria, the imposition of a joint force would be accompanied by the withdrawal of the original American contingent as well as of the ships in Griffin Bay. For his inspired mediation of the crisis, Scott received the praise and gratitude of the Buchanan administration.[14]

Since George Pickett had come to symbolize U.S. intransigence in the face of British reason and fair-dealing, Governor Douglas stipulated that he would be among the first troops to withdraw. In early December the captain headed back to Fort Bellingham, which had been allowed to fall into disrepair in his absence. He was in an unhappy mood, and not because of the renovations that lay ahead. The circumstances of his leaving suggested that he was beating a shameful retreat. Even worse, by publicly repudiating the basis for the U.S. presence on the island General Scott had made his spirited defense of American interests look silly. Pickett was also miffed that Scott had waited until he was absent from San Juan—on court-martial duty at Fort Vancouver—before notifying him of his relief.

His displeasure at the conciliatory attitude of the General-in-Chief increased when Scott, in his well-publicized official report of the episode, accused Harney and Pickett of injudicious and precipitate action that risked a disastrous outcome. Two months after his removal, Pickett complained that "Genl. Scott has . . . cast an implicit censure upon me for *Obeying Orders*." By then he was likewise upset by a rumor that he had been removed for behavior "obnoxious to the British Officials." Thus he sought and won Captain Hornby's assurance that "our intercourse had been of the most courteous nature, and aside from official matters of the most pleasant and agreeable kind." Pickett could also take comfort from a unanimous resolution by the territorial legislature of Washington, thanking him "for the gallant and firm discharge of his duties under the most trying circumstances on the Island of San Juan."[15]

Pickett got a measure of revenge for his unceremonious relief, thanks to the continuing impulsiveness of his department commander. Before General Scott left the Northwest to return home, he attempted to persuade Harney to relinquish command at Fort Vancouver and accept transfer to the Department of the West, headquartered at St. Louis. The embittered brigadier refused to leave short of a direct order. To discomfit his superior further, in April 1860, less than four months after Pickett had resumed command of the fort he had built on Bellingham Bay, Harney ordered Company D back to San Juan, relieving the American occupation force, a company of the Fourth Infantry, and sending it to Fort Steilacoom. Officially Pickett's new mission, like his old, was to protect American settlers from British-induced Indian depredations. Harney, however, had never accepted the idea of joint occupation, and coming as it did only a few weeks after 87 British marines set up a campsite on the northwestern side of the island, the order appeared another manifestation of Harney's anti-English bias.[16]

When news of Harney's most recent act of insubordination reached the East—along with a new flurry of British protests— President Buchanan and General Scott acted swiftly to settle the controversy once and for all. On June 8 Harney was relieved of his command and recalled to Washington, where he was reprimanded by the secretary of war. He would never again hold an active-duty command.

This time, Captain Pickett was permitted to remain on San Juan, where, once Harney's departure mollified the British, the "most amiable relations" existed between the occupation forces. Displaying a spirit of conviviality long suppressed, Pickett strove to outdo the foreigners by extending the most lavish hospitality to them. He later reported himself as grateful for the many courtesies they paid him in return. Meanwhile, he pursued a "mild but fair" policy in regard to the northern tribes who had settled on the island.[17]

★ ★ ★

He retained command of Camp Pickett until the early summer of 1861. In the interim, he found his attention increasingly drawn not to redcoated marines or Native Americans in warpaint but to the escalating sectional tensions that had been pulling his country apart for some years. Born and reared a Virginian, Pickett could not have escaped being affected by the American South's struggle against the perceived despotism of Northern politicians, especially those agitating for an end to slavery.

As best he could from the forest primeval, he followed with growing alarm the course of the national schism. The crisis appeared to reach flashpoint in November 1860 upon the election of his uncle's old friend, Abraham Lincoln, to succeed Buchanan in the White House. By Christmas of that year, following the secession of South Carolina, the Union seemed on the brink of collapse. Not only the Deep South was threatening to follow the Palmetto State into rebellion, but numerous Virginians were also counseling disunion.

The implications of secession and the prospect of civil strife placed Captain Pickett in a profound dilemma. He owed allegiance to the United States Army, which had provided him with a career, a home, and an identity; he shuddered at the thought of firing on the same flag he had raised above Chapultepec. On the other hand, he would never take part in a war to coerce or subjugate Virginia should she leave the union. Such a course—which would violate every precept of family honor and regional loyalty—was unthinkable for a man of Pickett's background.

Appreciating the depth of his quandary, some contemporary observers, looking back upon the controversy over San Juan Island, would invest it with conspiratorial trappings. According to Pickett's widow, his West Point friend George McClellan would come to believe that Pickett, in league with General Harney, Governor Stevens, "and other Democratic Federal officers on that coast," had precipitated the Pig War as a way to unite the country against Great Britain "and so avert the civil strife which they feared they saw approaching." For his part, Major Haller contended that Pickett had indeed tried to foment war, not to unite his country but to bring on a disastrous defeat at the hands of the British that would have prevented the federal government from putting down secession. Given the total absence of evidence to support either theory, neither appears worthy of serious consideration. By all indications, when he fortified San Juan Island in that summer of 1859 Pickett acted from no other motive than to fulfill General Harney's wish that the tail of the British lion be given a twist or two.[18]

Not to say that Pickett would have shied from an opportunity to postpone, if not prevent, civil war. He hoped to the last that he would have to take up arms against neither state nor country. He assured Sallie that he had "always strenuously opposed disunion, not as doubting the right of secession . . . but as gravely questioning its expediency." On the other hand, the adage "charity begins at home" had special meaning for him: "While I love my neighbor, i.e., my country, I love my household, i.e., my state, *more*, and I could not be an infidel and lift my sword against my own kith and kin, even though I do believe . . . that the measure of American greatness can be achieved only under one flag."[19]

* * *

He could stave off his decision only so long. It was mid-June before news of Virginia's secession, ratified by public referendum late the previous month, made its circuitous way to the Pacific Coast— lagging not far behind word of other momentous, conscience-wracking events. On April 12-14 South Carolina troops had shelled into surrender the U.S. garrison at Fort Sumter, Charleston harbor. Immediately afterward President Lincoln called on those states still a part of the federal union to furnish 100,000 recruits to confront "combinations too powerful to be suppressed." Lincoln's move, inevitable as it was, drove Virginia and the upper South to secede. By the time Pickett received the news of his state's reaction, a government was being organized in Richmond, capital of the new nation. Already many Southern-born colleagues such as Longstreet had resigned their commissions in preparation for offering their services to the army of the Confederate States of America. On June 25, Pickett sadly but resolutely followed suit.[20]

What appears to have forced his hand was an order to close down the fortified camp that bore his name and embark with his troops for San Francisco. Issued on the eleventh by Pickett's regimental commander, Colonel Wright, now head of the District of Oregon, the directive probably anticipated that all available forces would soon be dispatched to the scene of activity in the East. Previous to receiving the evacuation notice, Pickett had warned his superior that the local tribes were stirring. On the twenty-first Wright countermanded his order, announcing that because of "the threatening attitude of the Indians on the waters of Puget Sound," Camp Pickett would remain open indefinitely. By then, however, the prospect of leaving Washington had jarred Pickett into a realization that it was time to go, and time to stand by his home state. He would return to Virginia in the hope that war might be averted but ready to serve the Confederacy if eleventh-hour negotiations failed.[21]

He did not depart immediately. For three weeks after handing in his resignation—apparently while awaiting its acceptance—he remained in command of Camp Pickett, while making occasional trips to the mainland to put his affairs in order. Not until late July did he extend existing arrangements for the care of his four-year-old son and the property he would leave behind. He gave his friend Major Tilton one hundred dollars to provide for "the welfare of my little boy . . . during my absence." The note indicated that he expected to see Jimmie at some future date—he told Tilton he "hoped to come out here again"—but this appears to have been wishful thinking. Whether or not he admitted it, he must have known that their coming separation would be final.

For the past two years while Pickett served on San Juan Island, his son had lived with a couple homesteading along Bellingham Bay, William and Catherine Collins; through Major Tilton Pickett had provided the couple with money to support James's upbringing. Now the Collins' care of Jimmie would continue indefinitely, although Pickett apparently assured Tilton that should he be killed in the coming war "his aunt in Virginia will look out" for the boy. It is doubtful, however, that the captain expected his old-stock Southern family to take a half-breed youngster from the frontier into their home, caring for him as one of their own. In all probability, he regarded young James as the legacy of a part of his life on which, regrettably, he must turn his back.[22]

Pickett's departure from the Washington Territory began on July 24, the date of his relief by Captain T. C. English, whose company of the Ninth Infantry would now garrison San Juan. Two days later Pickett accompanied Company D to Fort Steilacoom aboard the *Massachusetts*. Upon his arrival he penned his final communication as an officer in the United States Army, informing district officials that, in compliance with orders, he had turned over his unit's property to the post commander.[23]

After a round of farewells among Steilacoom's garrison, he began the long journey south and east, moving overland through Portland, Oregon, to San Francisco, where he boarded a ship bound for the Pacific Coast of Panama. From there he would have travelled by steam train through the Panamanian jungle until able to take ship up the coast to home.[24]

The trip was a gloomy one, not only because of the war clouds gathering overhead but because he had been forced to leave a place where, despite some bad times, he had known personal and professional satisfaction. The only rewarding aspect of the journey was the company he kept: he travelled with a family friend, twenty-five-year-old Samuel Barron, Jr., of Richmond, until recently a naval officer assigned to Pacific waters. Sam hailed from a distinguished seagoing family; his father, one of the senior officers in the United States Navy, had recently resigned his commission to offer his services to Virginia and the fledgling Confederacy.[25]

Originally Pickett and his friend intended to strike Washington, D.C., before heading home to Richmond, but circumstances forced them to alter their destination as well as to travel under assumed names. In the final days of August they landed in New York City, which they found a hotbed of anti-secessionist sentiment. Soon after they had left the Northwest, the first major land battle of the war had been fought near Manassas Junction, Virginia, a couple dozen miles south of the national capital. The resulting Confederate triumph still had New Yorkers in a truculent mood. The atmosphere was difficult enough for the travelers to tolerate, but on the day they docked, news-boys were trumpeting reports that Sam Barron's father had been taken captive by his former service. "Poor Sam," La Salle Pickett quoted her husband as writing, "had a hard fight to hide his feelings and to avoid arrest."

Once in the city, the companions appeared to go their separate ways but met by prearrangement at the home of a physician named Paxton, a Southern-born friend of both men. They spent the night as guests of the Confederate sympathizer and the next morning left the city by train, heading north rather than south. Reluctant to travel directly to Virginia for fear of being unmasked as traitors to the United States flag, Pickett and Barron went home via a wide detour through Canada.[26]

Precisely why Pickett chose such a roundabout route is unknown, although other future Confederates returned home that way. While his itinerary is also a mystery, one student of Pickett's career suggests that when he crossed back into America he passed through Kentucky and Tennessee. All that is certain is that he had returned to his home state ("barely escaping arrest several times") by the second week in September, reaching Richmond on the thirteenth. There, Sam and he shook hands and parted, Pickett's friend en route to embark on a career in the Confederate Navy that would include a tour aboard one of the most celebrated commerce raiders of the war, the C.S.S. *Florida*.[27]

★ ★ ★

Pickett's homecoming was something less than he expected. By now his parents were deceased, but he had supposed that cousins, aunts, and uncles would greet him warmly as they had on past occasions. Instead, upon reaching the old house at Sixth and Leigh, he found that many relations and neighbors had given him up for lost. A few openly expressed disapproval that he had arrived so late to join in the effort to defend hearth and home. Other family members had gone into Confederate service immediately upon Virginia's secession—some even earlier. His brother, for instance, had enlisted as a private in the First Virginia Infantry, a crack militia regiment, one week after the firing on Fort Sumter; when assigned to staff duties against his wishes, Charlie had transferred to an artillery unit in hopes of seeing action more quickly. That spirit, so representative of the "Fighting Picketts of Fauquier County," contrasted sharply with George's nonchalant approach to enlisting. "So bitter is the feeling here," he supposedly commented, "that my being unavoidably delayed so long in avowing my allegiance to my state has been most cruelly and severely criticized by friends—yes, and even relatives, too."[28]

He tried to make amends. The day after his arrival he repaired to the Confederate War Department and placed himself at the disposal of the authorities. By some accounts, he waived his claim to a commission and enlisted as a private soldier in a Richmond company. Such self-effacing behavior—rather out of character for a soldier who had attained a certain celebrity by 1861—is not borne out by the records, which indicate that on September 14 Pickett was appointed a captain of infantry in the Provisional Army of the Confederate States of America. Such an appointment—to the same grade at which he had long served—surely disappointed him. He realized, however, that in the unsettled, dynamic state of affairs then obtaining, higher rank might be only days or weeks away.[29]

He remained at home for nine days, until the government decided where and how to employ him. During that time he made the rounds of government offices, seeking to learn where field vacancies existed; visited tailors and military purveyors to outfit himself for active service; and renewed acquaintances with army friends he had not seen in months or years—some not since West Point, the last time each wore the gray uniforms they were sporting once again. Most of his Southern-born colleagues were miles away from Richmond, with the troops holding the line above Manassas. In those positions the Confederate Army of the Potomac—still excited about its great victory on July 21—waited patiently for the defeated Yankees to leave the defenses of Washington and again offer battle.

In seeking an assignment, Pickett may well have written to the commander at Manassas, General Joseph Eggleston Johnston, a Virginia-born veteran of infantry, cavalry, and staff service in the old army, most recently as its quartermaster general, and whose family Pickett knew well. He almost certainly corresponded with those of his friends serving under Johnston. These included James Longstreet, who had resigned his commission in the Eighth Infantry to accept appointment as a brigadier general of Confederate forces and who had won acclaim for his handling of a brigade during the preliminary stages of the recent victory. Doubtless Pickett was happy for "Old Pete" but he must have envied the high rank and suc-

Library of Congress
Joseph E. Johnston

cess the Georgian had attained in the early going.[30]

He would have been more envious still of the station his Academy classmate George McClellan had assumed in the Union ranks. From news accounts Pickett was aware that the officer whom the Northern press was already calling the "Young Napoleon" had succeeded to the command of the army routed at Manassas. McClellan's appointment also drove home the possibility that Pickett would soon be fighting against friends from West Point and the old army. This unsettling prospect he came to view as a tragic but inevitable consequence of a brothers' war.

Some of the letters Pickett wrote soon after he reached Richmond went to Lynchburg, where thirteen-year-old Sallie Corbell had entered a female academy. He had continued to correspond with the precocious little girl throughout his tenure in the Northwest; according to her account they met on at least one occasion during that period, probably during a six-months' leave that Pickett took shortly before his initial assignment to San Juan Island. In her memoirs, La Salle Pickett writes of meeting her soldier at Greenbrier White Sulphur Springs, a watering hole favored by well-to-do Virginians. There they danced in the resort's ballroom, walked the well-manicured grounds, and with water colors sketched the local scenery. Before parting, she gave him a keepsake to repay him for the locket and ring he had placed in her hand at Fort Monroe. In a letter written four days after reaching Richmond he spoke of wearing one of her "long, silken ringlets next [to] his heart." He ended the letter with a romantic flourish: "Now, little one, if you had the very faintest idea how happy a certain captain in the C. S. A. (My, but that 'C' looks queer!) would be to look into your beautiful, soul-speaking eyes and hear your wonderfully musical voice . . . I know that you will have mercy on your devoted."[31]

The letter produced no reunion, for it failed to reach Sallie before Captain Pickett received his first duty assignment in the Confederate service. On September 23 he was ordered to the Fredericksburg vicinity, there to assume "temporary command on the Lower Rappahannock," including militia and volunteer outfits on both sides of the river. The news was exciting in itself, but even more so was the fact that the assignment elevated him to the provisional rank of colonel.[32]

At first he could not believe his good fortune: even in his most ambitious dreams he had not expected to move up in rank so quickly. It may have been a temporary appointment to a position outside the mainstream of military activity in Virginia, but it confirmed his belief that he was living in a time of unbounded opportunity. A general's wreath—all the power and authority he could ever have imagined—might lay just ahead. He seemed well along the path to ultimate professional fulfillment. On the way, he might even help his state throw off the yoke of Yankee oppression.

FIVE — *Leader of the Game Cocks*

As soon as able, Pickett bade family and neighbors farewell—already he could see a changed attitude in their proud, approving faces—and repaired to the Richmond, Fredericksburg & Potomac Railroad depot. After an overly long ride aboard cars crammed with soldiers and civilians he alighted at the Brooke's Station headquarters of Brigadier General Theophilus Hunter Holmes, commander of the Department of the Rappahannock. Holmes, who was only days away from gaining a second star, was a fifty-six-year-old West Pointer with more than thirty years service in the old army; as a major he had served with Pickett in the Eighth Infantry. Although he had commanded a brigade at Manassas, Holmes was to prove himself a lackluster combat leader; as a desk general, however, he was proficient and solicitous of his subordinates—a good man under whom to begin one's war service. At the outset he appeared happy to have Pickett at his side, a sentiment that boded well for their renewed relationship.[1]

After briefing Pickett on the local situation, Holmes sent him to take command of forces along the Northern Neck, an assignment that returned the new colonel to ancestral territory. But this link with his family's past proved to be the only agreeable feature of Pickett's service along the Rappahannock. His district, which encompassed Lancaster, Northumberland, Richmond, Westmoreland, Essex, and Middlesex Counties, had been stripped of its manpower base to fill the army at Manassas, to garrison the defenses of the capital, and to man various outposts in the northeastern part of the state. From his headquarters at Tappahannock, Pickett commanded an on-paper force of several thousand. The majority of these troops, however, were militia and with the exception of the well-appointed Fifty-fifth Virginia, a volunteer outfit, none of his regiments consisted of more than 300 men, barely 30 percent of authorized strength. This undesirable situation threatened to leave a strategic section of Virginia—which offered a northeastern approach to Richmond, only fifty miles away—vulnerable to attack by land or sea.[2]

Barely a month after Pickett entered upon his duties—while still attempting to gain a reliable count of his troop strength—rumors of pending enemy invasion assailed his peace of mind. On October 27 Acting Secretary of War Judah P. Benjamin relayed to General Holmes (now commanding the Aquia District) a report that a fleet of transports in Hampton Roads was ready to deposit upwards of 25,000 Yankees along the Rappahannock line, "with the view of executing a flank movement upon your command." Simultaneously, Confederate Adjutant and Inspector General Samuel Cooper wired the news directly to Pickett at Tappahannock, authorizing him to call out all available defenders.

Caught off-balance, Pickett—with or without General Holmes's approval—went directly to the War Department with a plea for reinforcements as well as for rifled cannon and other weaponry critical to the defense of his district. Secretary Benjamin promptly sent the guns but explained that no troops were available to bolster Pickett's meager force.

Left to his own resources, the harassed colonel attempted to round up enough soldiers and civilians to counter the threat but came up well short of the number he considered necessary. He was shocked, then incensed, to find so many able-bodied citizens unwilling to contribute to the local defense; a certain number appeared pleased rather than terrified at the prospect of invasion. Pickett won General Cooper's permission to use his own judgment in deploying the manpower at his disposal, but it was so limited that even the most judicious placement of troops would have left the river accessible to the foe.[3]

Fortunately, the invasion report lacked substance; over the next few days Holmes's scouts detected no unusual activity along the water line between Union-held Fort Monroe and Fredericksburg. By the first week in November it had become apparent that the enemy was not coming—this time. But even as Pickett's heart resumed its normal beating, anger and indignation caused his blood pressure to rise. His difficulties in raising a defense force of the local citizenry showed that the Northern Neck contained a large disaffected element—men in uniform as well as in mufti—who would give aid and comfort to the enemy. To complicate the situation, many loyal secessionists had been demoralized by rumors that Confederate troops were to be withdrawn from the region because the authorities in Richmond considered it virtually impossible to safeguard.

Early in December Pickett informed General Holmes of the state of affairs locally, sought advice, offered some suggestions of his own, and theorized that the problem had socio-economic as well as military and political roots. He began by praising the "greater portion of our loyal men, the chivalry and high-toned gentlemen of the country, [who] have volunteered, and are far from their homes." He condemned the rest of the population, who, when called on in a crisis, had displayed an alarming tendency "to be non-combatants or to fall back under the old flag."

As a descendant of the planter aristocracy, Pickett was disposed to be suspicious of the loyalty and dependability of poor whites and non-slaveholding citizens of any social class—such people appeared to lack a personal stake in the success of the Confederate experiment. "We have to fear them most," he warned Holmes. "All during a war like this must suffer, but for the good of the general service it will not do to yield to those persons who have refused to volunteer, while the proprietors of the country are actually in the field, and who plead poverty and would join the enemy should an occasion occur." To neutralize the effect of the disloyal and the faint-hearted, he suggested placing the militia under stronger, more committed officers, then hauling it far from home. Meanwhile, to calm the fears of the loyal folk, he called on Richmond to reaffirm its intent to maintain their armed protection.[4]

It appears unlikely that Pickett's words of wisdom had the intended effect. A trip to Richmond in mid-December "to report to the War Department in person what I have already done by letter" left him doubtful that his warning had been heeded. Even a later, much less sweeping proposal for strengthening the local defenses—emplacing a battery on bluffs overlooking the strategic port of Urbana, thirty miles downriver from Tappahannock, to forestall any amphibious incursion—failed to win the approval of his superiors. By the end of the year Colonel Pickett must have been chafing at his general inability to influence the local situation. No doubt he was casting about for a more rewarding position with the forces near Washington.[5]

Meanwhile, through no especial fault of his own, Pickett found himself not only without influence but virtually without a command. By year's end General Holmes was informing the War Office that while the colonel had "managed his command on both sides of the Rappahannock admirably well," that command was no longer sizable enough to support an officer of his rank. At least partially in response to Pickett's earlier plea for reinforcements, the day before Christmas

Holmes dispatched Colonel J. M. Brockenbrough, with his Fortieth Virginia Infantry and a battery of light artillery, to the Northern Neck. Since Brockenbrough was senior to Pickett by date of commission, the latter had become a supernumerary. Holmes was forced to relegate him to command of troops in Essex and Middlesex Counties, an assortment of infantry and cavalry companies aggregating less than a full-size regiment.

The demotion may have been a deliberate act by Holmes; Brockenbrough's assignment to Pickett's district was not an unavoidable necessity. Nor did Holmes attempt to soften the blow by exerting himself to find Pickett another job; he merely suggested to the War Department that the colonel "may be usefully employed elsewhere." One wonders if Pickett's habit of dealing directly with the authorities in Richmond may have played a role in his superior's decision to supersede him.

A colonel without a regiment, a district commander without much of a district, Pickett was very much at loose ends. On December 28 he begged General Cooper to place him in "any post that the Department may think me competent to fill." When no reply was forthcoming, he appears to have returned to Richmond to expedite the reassignment process, preferably to secure a position with Johnston's army. At first the search produced no results, but then he met his old friend James Longstreet, recently promoted to major general in command of a division of infantry in the Army of the Potomac.[6]

Their reunion proved a boon to Pickett, although it coincided with personal tragedy. According to some historians, Pickett was at his friend's Richmond home late in January 1862 when an outbreak of scarlet fever took the lives of three of Longstreet's children. While this may be so, there appears to be no basis to the contention that Pickett joined with Sallie Corbell to supervise funeral arrangements when Longstreet and his wife, prostrated by grief, proved unable to assume that responsibility. It does seems likely that Pickett, who took seriously the obligations of friendship, provided a shoulder for the Longstreets to lean on during their ordeal. In his bereavement, Old Pete would have been grateful for the younger man's material and emotional support.[7]

Whether out of gratitude, because of their long and cordial association, or for some unrelated reason, Longstreet put in a strong word for Pickett with General Johnston, who was casting about for experienced and enterprising subordinates. The army leader would have known of Pickett's old army exploits, of his reputation as a fighter; for this reason, perhaps, he appears to have been receptive to Longstreet's suggestion. On February 13, 1862, eight days after Longstreet returned to the army, the War Department notified George Pickett that

Library of Congress
General George E. Pickett, ca. 1862

he had been appointed a brigadier general—to rank, for purposes of seniority, from January 14. The effect of this stunning piece of good news on Pickett's frame of mind was eclipsed only by word, received on the last day of the month, that he had been assigned command of a brigade of Virginians in Longstreet's division.[8]

In his third uniform of this young war, he reported to the army near Manassas, intent on proving that he was worthy of his high station. He found that he had been assigned a command that was becoming known throughout the army as the "Game Cock Brigade" for its plucky service at Manassas, and possibly as a play on words derived from the name of its first commander. The brigade, which consisted of the Eighth, Eighteenth, Nineteenth, and Twenty-eighth Virginia Infantry, had originally belonged to Brigadier General Philip St. George Cocke, "a high-minded and gallant soldier, a devoted patriot, and a gentleman of cultivation and refinement." The brigade had been leaderless since the day after Christmas, when the sickly and despondent patrician committed suicide at his home in Powhatan County.[9]

Under Cocke the quartet of regiments had been well organized, well trained, and well staffed with regimental commanders: Colonels Eppa Hunton, R. E. Withers, John B. Strange, and Robert C. Allen. While none of these officers was a professional soldier, Hunton and Strange had militia experience, while Strange and Allen were graduates of the Virginia Military Institute. Moreover, Captain James Dearing, Jr., who commanded the light battery attached to the brigade, the Lynchburg Artillery, had spent a couple of years at West Point, resigning a few days after Fort Sumter. The education and experience of these officers, and the generally strong soldierly material among the rank-and-file, told Pickett that he had landed a plum assignment.[10]

As the brigadier inspected his command, his new comrades inspected him in turn. Some liked what they saw: Colonel Withers of the Eighteenth Virginia pronounced Pickett "a handsome man" who seemed born to command. Others were similarly impressed by the general's appearance, especially the hirsute portion thereof. One of Longstreet's aides, later his chief of staff, Captain G. Moxley Sorrel, described the new brigadier as "a singular figure indeed! A medium-sized, well-built man, straight, erect, and in [a] well-fitting uniform, an elegant riding-whip in hand, his appearance was distinguished and striking. But the head, the hair were extraordinary." Sorrel asserted that upon meeting Pickett for the first time he found the general's hair in "long ringlets," hanging below shoulder length and "highly perfumed; his beard likewise was curling and giving out the scents of Araby." It should perhaps be noted that this reference, which has inspired so many impressions and depictions of Pickett, is the only recorded claim that the general wore his hair so long and doused it with perfume.[11]

Other first-time observers were less concerned with Pickett's looks than with the circumstances behind his coming. Colonel Hunton, a lawyer from Prince William County who had been a militia general before the war and had entered the Confederate service months earlier than Pickett, appeared to regard him as an interloper who had usurped Hunton's own claim to command. Although Hunton admitted that the new brigadier carried an exalted reputation, he suspected that Pickett's rise was due more to old army contacts than to proven

Valentine Museum
Eppa Hunton

merit. Captain Sorrel shared Hunton's view, stressing that Pickett "had been in Longstreet's old Army regiment, and the latter was exceedingly fond of him." Sorrel claimed that his boss "looked after Pickett" like an older brother, giving him preferential treatment over subordinates who were not Longstreet's favorites.[12]

Early on, the rank-and-file expressed mixed opinions of Pickett. Some soldiers, who had heard of his exploits in Mexico and on the Northwestern frontier, expected that he would quickly prove himself a worthy successor to General Cocke. Beneath the flowing curls and the gilt-spangled uniform, they saw a mature, experienced, self-confident soldier. Others suspected Pickett was a textbook-bound martinet with no heart. Private Randolph A. Shotwell of the Eighth Virginia scrutinized Pickett as he conducted his first inspection of Hunton's regiment and disliked what he saw:

"He is an old West-Pointer, and conducted himself accordingly. Taking up my gun, he rubbed his white glove over the barrel, and lo! a rusty streak on the glove!" Pickett reacted caustically to this display of neglect, whereupon Hunton interceded on Shotwell's behalf, pleading leniency on the ground that the private was a raw recruit from a good family: "General, this young man left college at the North to come South and fight with us." Unimpressed by Shotwell's credentials and unconcerned that he might have hurt his feelings, Pickett "whipped out his handkerchief and blew a nasal blast," then moved on to the next man in line.[13]

While in camp at Manassas, Pickett selected promising young men to serve on his staff. As the staff comprised a military family of sorts, it is not surprising that he turned to his brother for help, persuading him to leave his artillery company to accept the position of aide-de-camp and the rank of lieutenant. For another aide-de-camp slot, Pickett tabbed Lieutenant Edward R. Baird in fulfillment of a pledge to Confederate Secretary of State Robert M. T. Hunter, a friend of the Baird family. From the lower Rappahannock he brought his adjutant general, Captain Charles Croxton, and his chief quarter-master, Captain R. P. Archer. In later months Pickett would add a second relation—his cousin, Lieutenant W. Stuart Symington—to his staff along with a youngster from an old-line Williamsburg family, Lieutenant Robert A. Bright. Other staff members would come and go, but the quartet of subordinates with whom Pickett enjoyed the closest relationship—Charlie, Baird, Symington, and Bright—would remain to serve him throughout the war.[14]

* * *

He was accorded the briefest of periods in which to acclimate himself to his command before the army resumed active campaigning. At the end of the first week in March, barely ten days after Pickett arrived at Manassas, General Johnston ordered a withdrawal to the Fredericksburg vicinity. His army numbered barely 50,000 troops; more than twice as many Yankees under George McClellan had begun an advance south from Washington, threatening to swarm over the works in their path. Johnston was not about to offer up his command as a sacrifice; he wished to place the broad and deep Rappahannock River between him and the foe.

Thus it was that by March 25 Pickett's brigade lay in camp four miles east of Orange Court House along the plank road that ran to Fredericksburg. Pickett was destined to spend even less time in that vicinity than he had at Manassas. At the latter place, McClellan had halted his overland advance, frustrated at finding his enemy gone and at being forced to plan a new campaign. The plan he adopted—an amphibious movement down the Potomac River and Chesapeake Bay to Fort Monroe, then an overland advance up the Peninsula toward Richmond—forced Johnston's army into a blocking movement south. By early April the Confederates were moving toward the old Revolutionary War battlefield of Yorktown, the initial objective of McClellan's mighty army. Disappointed by Johnston's refusal to stand and fight at Manassas, Pickett now looked forward to meeting his old classmate in battle on the Peninsula.

The route south took Pickett back home. On April 13 he marched his brigade to Hanover Court House and from there to Richmond. Passing through the capital late that day, Pickett's command stepped in time to the cheers of a vast throng. "Judging from the crowds upon the sidewalks," Private Shotwell estimated the city's population at

100,000—all of whom must have turned out to greet them. To make the greatest possible display, Pickett formed his command in column of half-companies, "so that as it marched down Main street the line seemed more than a mile in length, with music, banners, mounted officers, artillery, etc." Riding grandly at the head of his brigade, cap raked at a jaunty angle, curls fluttering, Pickett basked in the favor of the multitude like a sun-worshipper soaking up golden rays.[15]

A day or two later his troops, along with the bulk of Johnston's army, were filing into the works around Yorktown—many of them built eighty years before by the armies of Washington and Cornwallis, others thrown up recently by Brigadier General John B. Magruder's Army of the Peninsula. McClellan's initial contingent had already debarked at Fort Monroe and had pressed up the Peninsula to Johnston's new position, which the Union commander had decided to besiege. The prospect of a long, enervating investment had little appeal for George Pickett, but the brigadier was in a good mood nonetheless: as the recent movement had demonstrated, his command marched well, and he had no reason to doubt that it would not fight as well. His assigned position, astride the Warwick River a few miles west of Yorktown, appeared a strong one—and he still luxuriated in the memory of a recent reunion with Sallie Corbell.

The girl who was occupying his thoughts with increasing frequency had come up from her family's plantation at Chuckatuck in mid-month, probably meeting him in Richmond as he passed through the city at the head of his brigade. They could have enjoyed only a few hours, if that long, in each other's company and by now "two long, weary weeks" had passed "since I drank comfort from those bright eyes." Still, the lingering effect of their encounter—the first since his return from the Northwest—gladdened his heart and quickened his step.

Other concerns vying for his attention would provide less pleasant memories. Within a day or so of arriving outside Yorktown Pickett moved south with a part of his command in support of a reconnaissance-in-force by a Virginia brigade under another new brigadier, Lewis Armistead, whose heroics at Chapultepec Pickett remembered well. Encountering the enemy sooner than expected, both forces butted up against an artillery emplacement along McClellan's siege line. According to La Salle, Her Soldier blithely informed her that "we got under a concentrated fire of about sixteen guns and had as jolly a little time of it for about fifteen minutes as I ever saw. Parrot[t] and round shots were about as thick as the ticks are, and their name is legion. However, the object was effected, and we have lost only about seventy-five men. . . ."[16]

Library of Congress
James Dearing, Jr.

Back on the Warwick line, Pickett experienced new troubles with artillery, this time within his own army. On the morning of April 24, McClellan's siege guns began to blast away at one of the earthen dams General Magruder had constructed to make the Warwick River a formidable barrier to enemy advance. When some batteries stationed along Pickett's front failed to reply, the general, accompanied by Captain James Dearing, rode out to learn the reason why. To Pickett's surprise and displeasure, the officers of the silent units explained that Magruder's chief of artillery had forbidden them to return fire unless the Yankees tried to capture the dam.

Pickett's response convinced Captain Dearing that the general was "not noted for keeping his temper." Dearing listened, half-shocked and half-amused, as his superior "ripped out with a whole handful of pretty strong words and told them that he ranked Col. Brown and was in command down here just then and if they did not fire they had better leave." His tirade might appear an overreaction, but soon afterward General Longstreet reached the scene to support his subordinate and lecture the artillerists all over again. A few days later he replaced the quiet cannoneers with a section of Dearing's battery, which opened against the Yankees each day, early and often.[17]

Writing during the last days of April, Lieutenant Thomas J. Goree of Longstreet's staff predicted that the siege of Yorktown would soon reach a violent climax. The outcome was of the greatest import: "I feel that the fate of Va., if not the Confederacy, depends on the result of this fight." For a time, however, it appeared that the campaign around Yorktown had already been lost. When May came in, McClellan put the final touches to an awesome array of siege batteries with which he expected to blast his enemy into surrender. Instead of remaining and fighting in Yorktown, however, his ranking adversary again decided to clear out. On May 3 the leading elements of Johnston's army, now augmented by the addition of Magruder's compact command, began to file out of their trenches and breastworks and took to two thoroughfares—the Yorktown Road and the Lee's Mill Road—that led to Richmond via Williamsburg. Only when outside the capital—protected by a triple line of intricate works—would Johnston make a resolute stand.[18]

A portion of his army was destined to be brought to battle well short of its objective. On the morning of the fourth, finding his enemy streaming north, McClellan sent his cavalry, under Brigadier General George Stoneman, another member of the West Point Class of '46, to overtake Johnston; infantry hastened to close up in Stoneman's rear. Trying to keep in front of their pursuers, Johnston's evacuees—the divisions of Longstreet, Daniel Harvey Hill, Gustavus W. Smith, and Pickett's and Stoneman's classmate David R. Jones (today leading Magruder's troops)—moved as quickly as muddy roads choked with artillery and wagons would permit. Those roads converged two miles short of Williamsburg, Virginia's colonial capital; from that point, the withdrawal assumed an excruciating pace, enabling Stoneman's troopers to overtake the Confederate rear outside town late on the fourth. There they squared off against not only Rebel infantry but also their natural enemy, the cavalry of Brigadier General James E. B. Stuart.

When Stoneman dosed his rear with carbine- and horse artillery-fire, Johnston realized that the main body could clear the area and reach safety only if the rest of his army bought it time. He pushed on with the troops of Jones, Smith, and Hill while directing Longstreet's division to occupy a line of earthworks south of Williamsburg, the northernmost of three defense cordons that Magruder had built across the Peninsula, from the York River on the east to the James on the west, during the early days of the conflict. Longstreet filled the works with a few guns and the brigade of his senior subordinate, Richard Heron Anderson, keeping the remainder of his division, including the men of Pickett and those of yet another of his Academy mates, Cadmus Wilcox, southwest of town where they could assist Anderson as needed.[19]

By late on the fourth, Pickett's regiments had grouped in and about Williamsburg, some of the soldiers bivouacking on the campus of the venerable College of William and Mary. Early the next morning—cool and damp from intermittent rain—the brigadier called his troops into line and had them fall in behind Wilcox's command as it countermarched toward Fort Magruder, the largest earthwork in the local defense line.

Near the earthwork Pickett and Wilcox parted ways, Pickett reporting to General Anderson, who placed the Game Cock Brigade in a holding position well to the west of Fort Magruder. In that area Pickett's men had a clear view of Stoneman's operations; they took the opportunity to fire "at any horseman who made his appearance." Within about a half-hour, however, heavy musketry and the booming of numerous batteries astride the roads leading south indicated that Union infantry—it proved to be part of the division of Brigadier General Joseph Hooker—had come up on the Lee's Mill Road in Stoneman's rear to put pressure on Anderson's troops. It appeared only a matter of time before the Game Cocks would be sent out along the battle line.[20]

As if on cue, about midmorning a courier from Anderson appeared out of the mist and directed Pickett to hasten to Anderson's support by way of a belt of woods not far from the Lee's Mill Road. Then the courier rode off, leaving Pickett to find his way as best he could—a tedious, uncertain process until he encountered "Jeb" Stuart, who was kind enough to show him the most advantageous route. Continuing onward with greater confidence, Pickett was nevertheless sobered by the sound of small-arms and artillery, which grew alarmingly close with every step he took.

Doubting that the timber in his front would furnish a good position for artillery, Pickett had sent Dearing's battery to the rear. When he finally reported to Anderson, however, he learned that the Yankees had disabled some of the guns placed inside Fort Magruder, and so Pickett sent back for a two-gun section of Dearing's battery to restock the work. Then, at Anderson's direction, Pickett pushed his column, spearheaded by the Eighth Virginia under Lieutenant Colonel Norborne Berkeley (Colonel Hunton being absent, sick), toward another stretch of timber, this leading to the left flank of the enemy line. En route, Berkeley's people came under a heavy shelling that provided a first glimpse of carnage for many a raw recruit. Private Shotwell was "horrified at seeing a man running, struck by a shell and his head blown square off at the neck, and tumbling before the corpse as it staggers and falls!"

Pickett's involvement in the expanding battle temporarily ended at the tree line, where, at about ten o'clock, he received a recall message from Anderson. As per his instructions, he left the Eighth Virginia in its present position and conducted the Eighteenth, Nineteenth, and Twenty-eighth to the support of that part of Longstreet's division closely engaged with the foe.[21]

As the troops advanced, sights and sounds gave them more than an inkling of the reception awaiting them. Lieutenant William Nathaniel Wood of the Nineteenth Virginia recalled that "shells were bursting and solid shot was ploughing [*sic*] mother earth just where we had to go. In front and to the left clouds of dust [marking Hooker's position] gave some indication of the danger into which at a double-quick we were rushing." Nevertheless, "marching forward in line for the first time as Pickett's brigade, we felt strong and hoped our very appearance would cause the enemy to fly."[22]

The brigade's resolute advance soon brought it to the precarious position held by Wilcox's brigade. The Alabama and Mississippi troops under Pickett's cadet companion had absorbed a rough beating; many were now on the run, wounded and demoralized and streaming to the rear, cheering Federals in warm pursuit. Staking out a line in Wilcox's rear, Pickett had barely formed to meet the Yankees before they were upon him. Suddenly a portion of the Eighteenth Virginia, under Lieutenant Colonel Henry A. Carrington, unleashed a volley that cleared the front. When the smoke curled away, Hooker's assault had become a retreat, his troops scrambling eastward to take cover behind an extensive slashing of felled trees.

To retain his new-won foothold, Pickett brought up Colonel Strange's Nineteenth Virginia and formed it in line of battle to the left of the Eighteenth, where it linked with the right flank of Wilcox's command; meanwhile, he established Colonel Allen's Twenty-eighth Virginia in the rear as a reserve force. At West Point and on the frontier Pickett had learned the vital importance of field works; thus, he ordered his Virginians to dig in, improving their position as much as time permitted.

It was well they did, for within minutes Hooker's reinforced line lurched forward, his men advancing to within thirty or forty yards of the Virginians' position. At that point Pickett's soldiers opened what their leader pronounced "a most severe, well-directed, and determined fire along the front of the Eighteenth and right of the Nineteenth Regiments." Fortified by the effect of their firepower, the Game Cocks refused to give ground; their determination eventually persuaded the bluecoats to pull back, form a new line, and stay there. They reopened upon their opponents and the Virginians returned their fire round for round. "This furious, close, and deadly work," wrote Pickett, "was kept up some half an hour without cessation or giving way on either side."

The impasse continued so long and appeared so difficult to break that the brigade commander began to fear his men were wasting ammunition. For some reason Pickett took it on himself to ride along the battle line, passing the word to conserve powder and cartridges. Barely had he started on his errand, however, when he found his troops, from right to left, falling back in response to someone's order (he never learned whose), thus "abandoning our dearly-bought position." Only through great exertion and the hearty cooperation of his regimental commanders and staff officers was he able to halt the movement "in time to save a great disaster."[23]

After regaining its position at the front, the brigade—just as its general had feared—began to run low on ammunition. The shortage was most acute in the ranks of the Eighteenth Virginia, so Pickett ordered it to the rear and replaced it with Colonel Allen's reserves. At the same time he sent a galloper to inform Longstreet that, unless supported, his people would have to retire, this time at his order. A concerned Longstreet sent him part of an Alabama regiment from Brigadier General Roger Pryor's brigade. Grateful for even small-scale assistance, Pickett led the Alabamians toward a position along his far right threatened by Yankee sharpshooters—only to see the newcomers exposed to enemy view and shattered by a volley that killed their commander and several other officers and men, and sapped the survivors' will to fight.

Once again bereft of support, running perilously low on rounds, Pickett may well have considered ordering a retreat—a most undesirable option, especially in one's first fight. Thankfully, he did not have to; through fortuitous timing, heavy reinforcements reached his side: additional elements of Pryor's brigade, plus the Virginia and North Carolina troops of Brigadier General Raleigh Colston.

Their coming signaled a general advance, in which Pickett joined with his entire command. From its detached position, Lieutenant Colonel Berkeley's regiment, supported by one of Pryor's outfits, fired at that part of the enemy line opposite Pickett's right—held by New Jersey troops under Brigadier General Francis E. Patterson—and swept it clean. As the Jerseymen turned to flee, the Eighteenth and Nineteenth Virginia scrambled forward in pursuit, performing an early rendition of that eerie, spine-tingling keening later famous as the Rebel Yell. Their dismounted general took the lead, racing across the soggy earth while twirling his Ames dragoon saber and snapping his Smith & Wesson .22 at the backs of the fugitives.[24]

The articulate Lieutenant Wood recorded what happened when "Pickett's brigade made its first charge. . . . Pell-mell we went over logs, through the laps and limbs of the fallen trees, yelling and shooting! on! on! each [man] trying to be a little in advance of the other." Coming upon the original line of the enemy, Wood and his comrades surged over some abandoned artillery pieces; farther on they began to overtake the demoralized enemy, gathering up prisoners.[25]

While the Eighteenth and Nineteenth Regiments charged, the Twenty-eighth, which had become separated from the main body of the brigade and had come under General Wilcox's control, launched a charge of its own that drove other enemy units into retreat. A Union counterattack inflicted several casualties and temporarily made a prisoner of Colonel Allen, but the Twenty-eighth kept its composure, repulsed the effort, and put the finishing touches to the rout. When the Yankees had moved beyond easy pursuit, Pickett recalled his troops. He found the ground in front of his original line "literally covered" with blue-clad bodies.

Satisfied that the enemy was retreating to a remote position from which they could easily be held in check, Pickett happily rode to the rear and reported to Longstreet. The division leader instructed him to bring off his dead and wounded (a total of 164 officers and men) and, as soon as darkness came on, to withdraw up the road to Richmond, guarding the army's rear as it cleared the field.

Then and later, Longstreet commended Pickett for the outstanding service he and his Game Cocks had rendered in their first engagement together. Their timely reinforcement of Wilcox's brigade and their staunch defense of the Confederate right flank had not only prodded the enemy into retreat but had negated gains by McClellan's troops on other parts of the field. In his after-action report Longstreet called attention to Pickett's "distinguished" service in the pre-war army, while lauding him for having employed "his forces with great effect, ability, and his usual gallantry."[26]

Such praise may sound excessive. Perhaps Longstreet's report was colored by his long-standing affection for Pickett. And yet the plaudits were not disproportionate to those the division commander bestowed on other subordinates. In truth, Pickett deserved credit for engineering a major part of the successful defense effort at Williamsburg. In his first battle as a field commander, he had earned the wreathed stars that adorned his collar.

SIX — *Battle Laurels and Battle Wounds*

With McClellan blocked at Williamsburg, Johnston's army was home free on the road to Richmond. Dirty, weary, famished, his troops plodded up the Peninsula, crossed the Chickahominy River, and on the south side, almost within sight of Richmond and out of reach of their enemy, dropped down to enjoy a deserved rest.

Their respite lasted nearly a month. For much of that time the Federals moved northwestward at a glacial pace, seemingly more interested in establishing supply bases on the Pamunkey River than in reestablishing contact with the forces of the Confederacy. Such deliberation permitted the victors at Williamsburg to hunker down behind the river, strengthening a defense line they knew would eventually be tested. Jefferson Davis, his cabinet, the Confederate Congress, the press, and the common citizenry agreed that the capital must be held at all costs; given its political and economic significance, its fall might mean the demise of the Southern nation and the political assumptions and code of values it represented. To Johnston the message was powerfully clear: he must make a last stand along the Chickahominy; no further retreating would be tolerated.[1]

Because of McClellan's timid advance, for weeks the armies came to blows only occasionally and without the wholesale commitment of resources. Rather than seeking a quick confrontation, the Young Napoleon appeared content to maneuver, pushing one segment of his army after another in an effort to gain a foothold astride the Chickahominy. Such a foothold would enable him to plant the heavy guns that had failed to capture Yorktown but which, he was certain, would spell Richmond's downfall. A showdown was in the making east of the capital but how long the preliminaries would last, perhaps no one but McClellan himself could say.

George Pickett, for one, believed he understood why his enemy was moving so tentatively toward battle. Having known McClellan since West Point, he considered the Pennsylvanian both militarily and politically conservative. Unlike his civilian overlords, McClellan was not disposed to view the war as an apocalyptic struggle between good and evil; he had many friends such as Pickett on the other side and he admired and even shared many of the values that made up the Southern ethos. McClellan, like Pickett, considered the abolitionists and other Northern fanatics as much to blame for the conflict as the most frenzied South Carolinian.

Library of Congress
George B. McClellan

His overriding concern, Pickett believed, was to halt the fighting short of a massive bloodletting on the doorstep of Richmond.

Whether or not his assessment of his old friend's motivations was accurate, Pickett entertained at least a faint hope that time remained to reverse the engine of war. In letters to Sallie from the Chickahominy line he begged the leaders of the North to listen to reason before it was too late: "All that we ask is a separation from people of contending interests, who love us as a nation as little as we love them." The problem, of course, was that each side held his interest to be sacred and thus worthy of great sacrifice, including the ultimate sacrifice. Doubtless thinking of McClellan, he mused that "all the men I know and love in the world—comrades and friends, both North and South—are . . . fighting for one side or the other, and each for that which he knows to be right." Pickett realized that both sides could not possibly be right, although both could be tragically wrong.[2]

* * *

When not writing to Sallie, the general passed the time in trying to prepare his troops for a battle he hoped would not come but feared would take place any day. He saw to it that ammunition depleted at Williamsburg was replenished, that gaps torn in the ranks were patched as effectively as limited manpower allowed, and that the men's morale was kept high by the regular issuance of rations and the occasional replacement of clothing and supplies. He took pains to ensure that the fieldworks his troops occupied, constructed at the outset of the war, were continually improved and that their occupants received exercise on the drill plain. At the same time, he strove to prevent native Richmonders from availing themselves of the opportunity to visit home without official sanction. As Lieutenant Wood of the Nineteenth Virginia noted, those caught "running the block" to the city were punished with a heavy dose of extra duty.[3]

In the last days of May, the advance guard of McClellan's grand army shuffled up to the Chickahominy crossings, signalling that a confrontation was near. Fearing the consequences of absorbing a blow, General Johnson determined to strike first. He saw an opening in his opponent's questionable placement of the various elements of his army: by the thirtieth, two of McClellan's five corps were ensconced south of the Chickahominy, one of them—Major General E. D. Keyes's IV Corps—having moved up to a location known as Seven Pines, only three miles in front of the Confederate right flank. The rest of the invading army lay on the north bank, beyond easy supporting range of their comrades.

The temptation to interpose between McClellan's forces was compelling, but Johnston did not act until learning that a sixth Union corps, left to guard Washington when the main army sailed to Fort Monroe, was moving overland to join McClellan. Already enjoying a great numerical advantage, the Union leader would become virtually invulnerable if allowed to absorb these reinforcements.[4]

After Johnston briefed his division commanders on his plan, much of the army left its works on the drizzly morning of the thirty-first and advanced eastward along roughly parallel routes, the Williamsburg Stage Road and the Nine Mile Road. Johnston hoped to move smoothly and stealthily, taking the Yankees unawares, but from the first his advance was a study in error and confusion. Surprisingly, the usually steady-going Longstreet, in command this day of the army's right wing, was the source of most of the trouble. In violation of oral instructions from Johnston, he moved out along the road

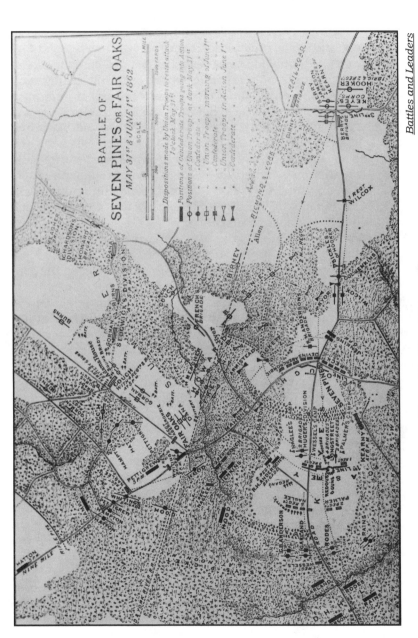

Map of Battle of Seven Pines

from Williamsburg instead of the Nine Mile Road. In altering his commander's plan of operations Longstreet upset its delicate timing by blocking the advance of other elements of the army, ensuring they would get into attack position well behind schedule.

To compound his erratic performance, Longstreet started forward with only part of his force; he detached several components of his wing to sectors that would see little action. Early in the afternoon he shoved Pickett's infantry north of the main battlefield to cover a remote area north of Seven Pines, below the line of the Richmond & York River Railroad. His thinking was that Pickett would block any effort to interfere with the main assault, but no Yankees ventured near and the men spent that rainy day engaged in long-distance skirmishing. Only Dearing's battery, which Longstreet retained for service with his main force, saw heavy action, the captain and his cannoneers "behaving most heroically" in support of the offensive, which did not get under way till midafternoon.

Through the rest of that day sounds of heavy fighting drifted in from many directions and hectic activity lapped around Pickett's position (William Wood recalled seeing "orderlies riding rapidly, the generals looking solemn and wise, regimental and company officers very strict"), but the Game Cock Brigade was not sent toward the scene of action. Thus it missed the chance to participate in the furious attack up the Williamsburg Road by D. H. Hill's division that overran a redoubt-defended outpost under Brigadier General Silas Casey, Pickett's superior on San Juan Island.[5]

Hill's assault appeared a decisive triumph, but McClellan, shocked at being caught with the bulk of his army far from the scene of danger, hustled his most reliable corps across the high-rising Chickahominy over a creaking, swaying bridge and placed enough troops on the south bank to halt the Rebel drive and recover much of his lost ground. After dark, when the fighting tapered off, the initiative seemed to lie with the Yankees, although Johnston wished Longstreet to renew the offensive come morning. Pickett could not determine if his brigade was to have an integral role in the next day's fighting. He feared the prospect of another day of inactivity while the rest of the army was heavily engaged all around him. His instinct was to be in the thick of things if only to avoid giving the impression that his command was fit only for reserve or support duty.[6]

To aggravate his concern, early in the evening a staff officer from Longstreet's headquarters led his troops to the edge of a swamp not far from Seven Pines. This did not appear an auspicious position; furthermore, it was an inhospitable place in which to bed down. Lieutenant Wood "broke off small pines and piled them up until I had a superb bed in the middle of muck and mud." Not everyone was so fortunate: "Very few found a place on which to build a fire large enough to set a tin cup in which to make coffee."[7]

Pickett's worries about gaining a rear-guard reputation eased early on the clear, warm first day of June, when his brigade was permitted to move toward the front. Soon after daylight on that Sabbath morning he was instructed to report to General Hill, along with elements of three other brigades from Longstreet's division: Pryor's, Wilcox's, and Colston's. Hill advised the four leaders that the troops McClellan had rushed down from north of the river were preparing to seize the rest of the ground lost by Casey around Seven Pines. To meet the attack, Hill wished the brigadiers to reel in their extended pickets, assume a defensive posture, and dig in north and west of Seven Pines.[8]

Instructions imparted, the conference adjourned. Pickett went back to his brigade and, accompanied by one of Hill's aides, led it to a position about 400 yards north of Casey's captured redoubt. There and nearby, his men helped themselves to a cache of rations and supplies that Pickett's old superior had left behind in his flight. As Randolph Shotwell recalled, hungry troops broke ranks to partake of "meats, crackers, canned fruits, desiccated vegetables, 'Sanitary Commission' stores, lemons, raisins, wines, etc. . . . piled here, there and everywhere—a prize too tempting to be resisted. . . ."[9]

While his troops gorged themselves, Pickett rode ahead to get a better view of his new position and those of his supports. Scanning the terrain, he could see Pryor and Wilcox digging in on his right flank, while off to his left Colston's men and two brigades of Hill's division—Lewis Armistead's and Brigadier General William Mahone's— did the same. Pickett felt comfortable in knowing that veteran troops were shielding him on both sides, but he was distressed by his inability to discern the position of the Yankees. General Hill had told him only that "they were some distance in advance—in fact, I had no definite idea where, as I saw no one and had not had time to examine the nature of [the] ground. . . ."

If still in the dark as to what lay ahead of him, Pickett must have greeted warily Hill's next instructions: to place himself in communication with Brigadier General John Bell Hood, whose Texas Brigade had taken up a position well to the north and west, near the railroad. With brother Charlie and Captain Archer, Pickett started out on his errand, riding for about a quarter of a mile through thick foliage that considerably slowed his progress.

Short of the railroad, the riders encountered a foraging party of Louisiana Zouaves "rushing past me," Picket reported, "at a most headlong speed." He collared one of the fugitives and demanded to know the reason for his haste. The man whipped out a pistol, threatening to shoot his captor unless he was let go: the Yankees were advancing just behind him and he had no intention of becoming a prisoner of war.

Surprised to silence, the general released his captive, turned about, and raced his aides back to Hill's field headquarters, where he breathlessly relayed the news. It was quickly decided that the Confederates would strike before struck. Historians criticize Pickett for assuming the offensive, without scouting the position or size of the enemy. In his after-action report he claimed that the decision was not his: Hill "ordered me to attack, and I supposed [the] same order was given to other brigade commanders." Even Hill's biographer appears to agree that the division leader ordered an offensive.[10]

Immediately Pickett rejoined his brigade north of Seven Pines. In response to a torrent of shouted instructions, the command filed into line of battle, facing northeastward. Supposing that the brigades on his flanks were advancing in concert with him, Pickett led the way toward the assumed location of the enemy.

His sense of direction did him credit: after moving a short distance the head of his line absorbed what Private Shotwell called "a wild rattling volley of musketry. . . . The storm of bullets raked the field like a hurricane. . . ." After recovering from some initial confusion that Shotwell feared would end in panicky retreat, the Game Cocks closed ranks, returned fire, and drove the nearest enemy troops— skirmishers of Brigadier General David Bell Birney's brigade of McClellan's II Corps—back upon their main body. With Pickett afoot at the head of his line, the brigade struck the Union vanguard, turned it about, and chased it beyond an abatis that it had been holding. Raising a triumphal yell, Pickett's troops cleared the barrier, hastening "through sharpened pine limbs, through patches of briars," toward a second slashing. It seemed like Williamsburg all over again, screaming Confederates putting the foe to ignominious flight.[11]

But the Federals were not the only ones to break for the rear. As he poised before the second abatis, covered in front by what Lieutenant Wood called "an immense frog-pond," Pickett glanced to the left and watched open-mouthed as Armistead's brigade disintegrated under a Yankee counterattack, the majority of its troops "leaving the field pell-mell." Soon Pickett's left was guarded by a mere handful of Virginians including "the gallant Armistead himself." Unwilling to press on with his flank uncovered, he recalled his brigade, added to it Armistead's remnant, and went over to the defensive, dropping down behind the captured abatis. As he did, he dispatched two couriers to Hill, seeking flank supports, then reinforcements. Neither request received a reply.

Library of Congress
Lewis A. Armistead

As Pickett feared, once the Game Cocks halted, the enemy regained the initiative, moving against their exposed left. Pickett refused the flank by positioning the Nineteenth Virginia at a right angle to the regiments on the front line. This tactic secured the threatened sector, while the abatis protected his men so well in front that they easily repulsed a series of attempts to dislodge them.

The fighting had been raging for some hours when, in mid- or late morning, Pickett discovered that his right flank was now also in the air, uncovered by the withdrawal, at Hill's order, of Pryor's brigade. Again Pickett sent for help, this time going so far as to promise General Hill that if properly supported he would shove the Federals back across the Chickahominy. Hill never tested Pickett's boast, and the brigadier waited in vain for a renewed offensive. He would complain that "a most perfect apathy seemed to prevail" at division headquarters.

In high disgust, Pickett took it upon himself to ride back to Hill, where he "laconically" explained the state of affairs in his front. Instead of agreeing to reinforce him, his superior merely asked if Pickett could withdraw from his present position. Pickett said he could but not without abandoning his wounded and without suffering losses when pressed by the enemy. After some argument, Pickett claimed, he persuaded Hill to place on his left flank a part of Colston's brigade and on his right the whole of Mahone's brigade, which early in the day had supported Pickett only to be prematurely withdrawn by its commander.[12]

Before Colston could take position, however, the enemy made a strong effort against Pickett's left. The Unionists charged to within small-arms' range of the Nineteenth Virginia before Colonel Strange's regiment and part of Colonel Withers's Eighteenth Virginia "rose up in the abatis and fired a withering volley into them, killing their commanding officer and literally mowing down their ranks." Upon the appearance of Colston's command minutes later, the bluecoats drew off.

Their retirement closed the morning's action. At about one o'clock, Pickett received Hill's positive order to fall back to a less exposed position. In concert with its supports, the Game Cock Brigade left its abatis and retired to a point some 400 yards from the scene of the engagement. Pickett proudly recorded that "we withdrew in perfect order . . . bringing off all our wounded," something he could not have accomplished earlier.[13]

The wounded were a concern because there were so many of them; with its fatalities added in, the brigade had suffered 350 casualties this day, slightly more than 20 percent of its number engaged. Like Williamsburg, Seven Pines had furnished Pickett with a battle performance he could be proud of. Again Longstreet lauded his leadership and the steadfastness of his troops, while in his report General Hill portrayed Pickett as holding his ground "against the odds of ten to one for several hours longer, and [he] only retired when the Yankees had ceased to annoy him." Pickett and his soldiers won additional praise in General Johnston's report of the fight.[14]

The heroics of Pickett and his men may have added another stripe to his battle-standard, but it had been won at fearful cost— almost twice as many losses as the brigade had suffered in its first action. Simple mathematics warned that the Game Cocks could not stand many more fights of such deadly proportions.

* * *

The night after the second day's battle Pickett's troops bivouacked beside the same swamp that had furnished them such a soggy slumber the previous evening. The following morning they helped cover the withdrawal of the army along the stage road toward Richmond. While the Confederates had won a tactical victory, holding the field despite heavy pressure, their commander's gamble had failed. The enemy had not been sent reeling from the gates of the capital; now, in fact, McClellan's siege guns would enjoy even closer positions from which to pound the city to its knees.[15]

Along with his strategic defeat, Joe Johnston had suffered painful wounds of the arm and chest during the first day's fight at Seven Pines. While the fighting on June 1 had been under the nominal supervision of Gustavus Smith, late that day army command had passed to General Robert E. Lee of Virginia, heretofore chief military advisor to Jefferson Davis. Once he saw that stalemate was inevitable, Lee had elected to press the attack no longer; his had been the decision to withdraw westward on the morrow, returning the army to its old post in the Richmond suburbs.

For George Pickett, who had never served with Lee in the prewar army, the new commander was an unknown quantity. To be sure, Lee's prewar record as an engineer officer, Mexican War hero, cavalry commander, superintendent of West Point, and captor of John Brown was the stuff of legend. Even so, the white-haired patrician who had taken over what was now known as the Army of Northern Virginia had gained a reputation as a plodder (and the derisive nickname "Granny Lee") during the conflict's first year. Although La Salle Pickett claimed that her husband referred to Lee, immediately after Seven

Library of Congress
Robert E. Lee

Pines, by the more respectful appellation "Marse Robert," it would take time before Pickett or any of his comrades believed that their new commander had earned such a title.[16]

As McClellan's army closed in on Richmond and Lee developed his strategy for dealing with it, the Game Cock Brigade settled back into the routine of holding breastworks that ran south from the Williamsburg Road toward the roads leading to Charles City and Darbytown. As he had after Williamsburg, Pickett attempted as best he could to augment his depleted ranks. This time he got help from above; on June 17, as Lee implemented a large-scale reorganization of Johnston's army, adding some commands, breaking up others and shifting about their components, he bolstered Pickett's force with Colonel William D. Stuart's Fifty-sixth Virginia. This regiment had recently arrived in Richmond after a long train ride and an even longer overland trek from Middle Tennessee. On February 16 the Fifty-sixth had been among the lucky garrison troops to escape capture at Fort Donelson on the Cumberland River—a victory that had won national acclaim for one of Pickett's oldest friends, along with the nickname "Unconditional Surrender" Grant. If Stuart's newcomers fought as hard as they marched, they would compensate, in more ways than one, for the casualties Pickett's command had suffered on the bloody route from Yorktown to Seven Pines.[17]

During the three-week lull that followed the army's return to Richmond Pickett had time for interests apart from his brigade. He may well have gone into the city to visit Sallie, who had taken up temporary residence at the home of family friends. She had nowhere else to go: the Lynchburg Academy had closed for the summer and her home in Chuckatuck lay behind enemy lines, the Yankees having overrun Nansemond County. Although safely ensconced in the capital, she remained the object of Pickett's concern, he hoping that "your beautiful eyes and tender heart have been spared the horrors of war which this battle [Seven Pines] must have poured into sad Richmond." According to Sallie, by this point Her Soldier had begun to shower her with prose heavy with noble thoughts and professions of love. She even has him writing her from the battlefield of Seven Pines, hopeful that "the last shot that will ever be heard was fired on June first, 1862. What a change love does make! How tender all things become to a heart touched by love—how beautiful the beautiful is and how abhorrent is evil! See, my darling, see what power you have—guard it well."[18]

This portrait of Pickett as love's plaything is of dubious accuracy. Like her claim that Pickett ranked among the earliest believers in Lee's greatness, Sallie is rushing things a bit here. George Pickett was not yet sure that he was in love—indeed, that he could be in love—with a girl well less than half his age. That assessment would change, however, as the result of his next battle and its aftermath.

During the last week in June, with the Yankees slowly but inexorably closing in, Lee's army bestirred itself. On the twenty-third a part of Pickett's brigade conducted a reconnaissance along the Darbytown Road, probing toward the Federal left flank. The operation ended without a clash of arms or a casualty list, although Pickett suspected both were in the offing when three days later Lee issued marching orders for the entire army. Like Joe Johnston almost a month ago, Lee had resolved to force a showdown with his opponent before McClellan could invest Richmond and condemn the city to a death quick or slow.[19]

In common with the rest of Longstreet's division, on the morning of the twenty-sixth Pickett led his troops westward, then northward through Richmond and out of the city via the Mechanicsville Turnpike. As it moved, the Game Cock Brigade could hear plainly the sounds of battle near Mechanicsville, which some of the troops knew to be the location of McClellan's upper flank. That night—unaware of the day's outcome but ever hopeful of success—the command crossed the Chickahominy and moved eastward toward one of its boggiest tributaries, Boatswain's Swamp, behind which lay the isolated right flank of the Union army, Major General Fitz John Porter's V Corps. After weeks of erratic maneuvering, McClellan still permitted the Chickahominy to split his army. Unlike weeks ago, when Johnston had attacked below the river, the vulnerable link in the Union battle-suit now lay on the north side of the stream. Lee had struck there on the twenty-sixth, pressing Porter back to Boatswain's, and he proposed to strike there again, this time in the hope of utterly routing him.[20]

When Lee's attack rolled forward on the hot, humid morning of June 27, it consisted of disparate segments, principally the division of D. H. Hill, which struck Porter's right and center, with support from Longstreet on the south flank as well as from the command of Major General Thomas J. Jackson, at present the Confederacy's brightest star. In the years since Pickett had shared West Point experiences with him, the gangly, bookish farmboy from the Virginia hill country had risen to high station as an instructor at V. M. I. and more recently in the Confederate armies in the East. His heroics at Manassas, where he gained the enduring nickname "Stonewall," had been eclipsed by his recently concluded campaign in the Shenandoah Valley during which, at the head of a small army, he outmaneuvered, outfought, and outsmarted not only a cordon of outposts but three separate corps sent to run him to earth. His mission in the Valley accomplished, Jackson had been called on to help deliver a knockout blow to Academy classmate McClellan.[21]

Jackson might have been brought in to help, but for a time it appeared that Pickett had not. Throughout the morning and well into the afternoon of the twenty-seventh, Lee's forces attacked toward Boatswain's Swamp and an adjacent landmark, Gaines's Mill, but the Game Cock Brigade remained in its support position along the north bank of the Chickahominy. There was a reason for its inactivity: Longstreet was aware that Pickett's command had suffered heavily

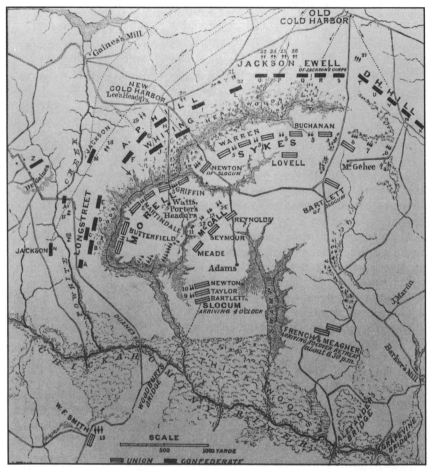

Map of Battle of Gaines's Mill

in its first two battles and he did not wish to commit it today unless bereft of alternatives. Twice during the afternoon he sent other elements of his division to batter Porter's left, held by the brigades of Brigadier Generals Daniel Butterfield and John H. Martindale, but although he made little headway against the strong Union works in that sector he did not turn to Pickett.

While Longstreet met stalemate, Confederate fortunes were running no higher elsewhere. As at Seven Pines, delays and poor coordination hampered a succession of assaults against the Union right and center, preventing Lee from driving Porter's soldiers from their swamp-lined works despite an unusual Confederate advantage in manpower. By six P.M., with his opportunity to crush McClellan's unsupported wing slipping past, Lee edged toward desperation. Gambling everything on a final effort, he ordered Longstreet and his other commanders to attack all along the line.

As part of this effort, Longstreet sent three brigades under Cadmus Wilcox angling toward the Federal south flank. To ensure that this thrust hit home, Longstreet believed he must support Wilcox's left with a parallel advance. However, the terrain ahead—a low rise, beyond it the mucky bottoms of Boatswain's, beyond them a slashing, and in rear of all a line of breastworks atop a tall, wooded hill— looked foreboding. Afterward Colonel Hunton would write that "in the Brigade it was said and insisted upon that when General Lee called on Longstreet for a brigade that would carry this formidable position, Longstreet said, 'I have a brigade that will carry it, but it has been in the thickest of all the fights and has lost heavily. I don't like to send it in.' Lee said, 'This is no time for sentiment. I must carry the place'."[22]

Whether or not this exchange occurred as reported, Longstreet acted reluctantly in sending forward Pickett as well as the brigade of Richard Anderson, which had also been held out of the fighting thus far. At the same time, Longstreet had the Virginia brigade of James Lawson Kemper—formerly the division leader's own command—leave a sheltered position and move up in rear of the advancing units.[23]

As soon as he received Longstreet's order Pickett moved out in the gathering twilight with speed born of pent-up tension, hurling his men at the Union line. Again his actions would generate controversy. Critics would contend that he had been ordered to make a diversionary attack to draw pressure from Wilcox's provisional division and that Pickett—either through misinterpretation of his instructions or discontent at being assigned to conduct a feint—went ahead with a full-fledged assault. In his battle report Colonel Strange implied that Pickett attacked merely because he was tired of waiting for an enemy offensive. In his memoirs, however, Longstreet asserts that the only diversion he ordered was assigned to Wilcox and that he sent forward Pickett and Anderson "as assaulting columns."[24]

Pickett advanced with three of his regiments—the Nineteenth, Twenty-eighth, and Fifty-sixth Virginia—in front, and with Hunton's and Withers's regiments in skirmish order along his right flank. As he topped the rise and descended to the creek bottom, however, he brought all of his regiments together in a double-line formation, hoping to land the heaviest possible blow. His 2,000-plus troops made a formidable sight. A neighboring staff officer watched Pickett's skirmishers wheel into formation, then sweep ahead: "A moment's pause, and then the long line streamed forward, descending the slopes leading into the wide bottoms of the stream, and as they entered and disappeared into the woods and thickets their ranks were fringed with the curling white smoke of musketry fire."[25]

Pickett directed the charge on horseback although he must have suspected he would have a difficult time negotiating the broken ground in his front. He took the first slope without difficulty and, against a rain of rifle balls, splashed through the creek bottoms. In good order he started up the hill toward the abatis, cheering his troops onward. About seventy-five yards from the Yankee entrenchments he heard a thwacking sound like boards slamming together, felt a fiery pain in his right shoulder, and toppled from his mount.

As aides rushed up to minister to him, he regained his feet, examined the wound, and tried to keep pressure on it to prevent the flow of blood. Quickly regaining his presence of mind, he sent word to Colonel Hunton, his senior regimental leader, to take charge. (Minutes after assuming command, Hunton, himself weak from previous illness, collapsed from exhaustion, passing command to Colonel Strange.)

With or without a leader, Pickett's troops rushed onward, screaming the Rebel yell, then pounded up the fire-swept slope toward the summit. Despite the searing pain spreading through his body, their general watched with pride and admiration as they topped the rise, surmounted the barricades there, and gradually but steadily drove the troops of Butterfield and Martindale from their impregnable-looking position. Pickett may not have been with them at the moment of their triumph, but in a sense he was, for his leadership and training had been instrumental in gaining success.[26]

Two writers, one who supposedly watched Pickett fall, the other who heard the story second-hand, offered differing accounts of the general's reaction to his wound. Artillery Major John Cheves Haskell claimed to be passing by when he found Pickett "standing by his horse in a deep small hollow, almost like a well, bewailing himself. He called to me to send him a litter as he was mortally wounded, but I had none and was busy with my men. He was very slightly wounded and perfectly able to take care of himself." For her part, La Salle Corbell Pickett would always insist that her husband argued with a surgeon who suggested he quit the field at once, protesting that "my men need me!"[27]

Doubtless the truth lies somewhere between these extreme characterizations. While he may have mouthed them, the words Mrs. Pickett attributes to her husband smack of false bravado; they probably constitute yet another effort to embellish his image. Haskell's account appears similarly overdrawn, but for other reasons: he appears to have been animated by a desire to discredit Pickett, whom he personally disliked. Haskell strains credulity by asserting that "a perfectly able" officer, repeatedly cited for courage and determination, would claim to a passing stranger that he lay at death's door. Then, too, Haskell went out of his way to downplay the severity of a wound which, while not life-threatening, would keep its victim out of active service for three months—three long, tedious months far from the fields of fire that held such an attraction for George Pickett.

SEVEN — *Division Command*

Part of the way by train, part of the way by horse-drawn ambulance, the general was conveyed to the Richmond home of his sister, Virginia, now the wife of Doctor Blair Burwell, assistant surgeon of the Eighth Virginia of Pickett's Brigade. In the good doctor's house, he received the best of care; still, it would be a long time before the swelling in his right shoulder and arm, and the pain that accompanied it, subsided—longer still before he regained full use of the injured limb.[1]

He had better things to do than concentrate on his discomfort. When he had passed the crisis stage and could sit up in bed he had the newspaper read to him so he might follow in as much detail as possible the movements and engagements of his Game Cocks. Whenever visitors called, he pumped them for news that reporters would overlook or editors would neglect to print.

In the main, the news was very good. Despite suffering heavily in its successful strike across Boatswain's Swamp, Pickett's brigade had failed to break Fitz John Porter's left—some critics would judge the strike a needless waste of manpower for which they unfairly held Pickett responsible. In fact, General Lee had failed to land his hoped-for knockout on any part of the battlefield. Even so, he had the great satisfaction of seeing McClellan pull back from his forward position for fear that his scattered army was being beaten in detail. Thus, in a strategic sense, Gaines's Mill had been the success that the Confederate commander had so desperately needed.

To cap Lee's good fortune, four successive days of clashes atop the Peninsula—the last occurring on July 1 at Malvern Hill, within sight of the Pickett estate on Turkey Island—had pushed McClellan's army even farther from the gates of Richmond. On the day after Malvern Hill, in fact, the demoralized Federals were huddling along the James River near Harrison's Landing, more than a dozen miles from their original objective—too far to pose an immediate threat to the continued existence of the Confederate government. For now, at least, the Southern nation had been spared.[2]

Three days after its commander's wounding at Gaines's Mill, Pickett's brigade had played a conspicuous role in another of the so-called Seven Days Battles. At Frayser's Farm (White Oak Swamp), June 30, the Game Cocks, first under Colonel Hunton and then under Colonel Strange, won new plaudits by standing firm while supporting troops fled, then charging and capturing a battery. Once again, however, the brigade had purchased success at high cost; at the end of the Seven Days, the butcher's bill approached 600, more than a quarter of the brigade's effective strength.[3]

The roll of casualties included many good men whom Pickett knew well, but none stirred his concern more than that of his brother, severely wounded at Frayser's Farm while still serving on the brigade staff. His leg broken by an enemy round, Charlie was at first in such poor shape that he was evacuated to Fredericksburg rather than invalided home. Only after a long stay in a field hospital would he be sent to Richmond to complete his recuperation, and nearly a year would pass before he would be sufficiently recovered to retake the field.[4]

The elder Pickett would not be out of action that long, but his enforced visit to the Burwell home proved to be a greater ordeal than he had anticipated. In fact, he did not appear to recover until Sallie Corbell cut short her studies and rushed to his side. After her arrival, the formerly restive, ill-tempered patient appeared more "gentle; amiable, good-humored, affectionate and hospitable." Two years later Pickett recalled how her appearance had speeded his recuperation by "blessing and cheering me. I can feel now the soft touch of your little white hands, as you gently stroked and soothed my wounded shoulder and swollen arm and hand."

Her ministry took many forms. When not changing his dressings or seeing that he lay comfortably, she read to him, sang to him, sewed for him, and guarded his privacy. Only occasionally would she permit well-wishers to call on him. No less a personage than Jefferson Davis dropped by to monitor his recovery. On another occasion, Sallie claimed, Stonewall Jackson came to see the patient and to pay his respects to his nurse, he having served on the V. M. I. faculty with her uncle, Colonel J. J. Phillips. Sallie may have embellished or even invented the story of Jackson's visit, for neither at West Point nor after-

ward had he and Pickett been close. Her version of their conversation
is especially fanciful, Pickett bewailing the loss of so many good men
at Gaines's Mill and his visitor admonishing him for being softhearted
("General Pickett, we are fighting to save the country, not the army. I
fight to win, no matter how many are killed").[5]

When well enough to move about, Pickett gingerly negotiated the
grounds of the Burwell home on Sallie's arm. They sat and talked
quietly under the trees on the lawn—planning, she claimed, a life
together. Slowly, gradually, strength began to return to his shoulder,
although not till the latter part of summer did he feel sufficiently recovered to consider rejoining the army.

By then he had missed two major campaigns, one a dramatic
victory for the Southern cause, the other a strategic draw. In July Lee
went on the offensive, leading the army from the suburbs of Richmond toward the environs of Washington, D.C. On the last days of
that month he, Longstreet, and Jackson combined to fool, frustrate,
and throttle McClellan's successor, Major General John Pope, on portions of the old Manassas battlefield.

Riding the tide of victory that had drowned Pope and brought
McClellan back to the surface, Lee then ranged into western Maryland. On September 17 outside the village of Sharpsburg he and
McClellan combined to create a day of horrific violence that left both
armies drained and weak and persuaded Lee, head held high, to re-
cross the Potomac to refit and plan anew.

The army had much to show for its travels during Pickett's recuperation, but virtually every element of it, including the Game Cock
Brigade, had suffered terribly. To its heavy losses on the Peninsula
the command had added almost 150 casualties under Colonel Hunton
at Second Manassas and nearly 200 at Sharpsburg—including the
death of the fiery Colonel Strange—under the temporarily assigned
Brigadier General Richard Brooke Garnett.[6]

When he learned of the carnage in Maryland, Pickett resolved to
return to his command without further delay. He made his decision
against the strident protests of Sallie, who was concerned by his inability to flex his injured arm enough to draw on a coat sleeve.

At their parting, they embraced in a heated rush of affection that
heightened the sense of loneliness Pickett felt the moment he rode off.
Now—quite possibly for the first time—he must have realized he was
falling in love with La Salle Corbell of Chuckatuck, Nansemond County,
Virginia.[7]

* * *

Richard Garnett had done a fine job of leading the Game Cocks at Sharpsburg; Pickett believed that under his leadership the brigade "has sustained its old reputation for fearlessness and endurance." Pickett knew and admired the military talents of the Garnett clan of Essex County, having served under Richard's cousin, Robert, in the Ninth Infantry. Himself a veteran of the prewar army, Richard Garnett had carried a record of courage and high competence through the early months of the conflict until running afoul of his superior, Jackson, under controversial circumstances during the Valley Campaign.

Richard B. Garnett

Removed from brigade command and court-martialed after Jackson faulted his performance and impugned his courage at the battle of Kernstown, Garnett sagged under the weight of those charges until assigned to Longstreet's division in early September. Doubting the validity of Jackson's accusations—the man could be myopic and harsh in judging his subordinates—Pickett considered Garnett a "fine fellow, a brave, splendid soldier," and hoped one day to serve with him. He would get his wish sooner than he expected.[8]

When Pickett caught up with Lee's army outside Martinsburg in the lower Shenandoah Valley, he was pleased beyond words to find himself assigned temporary command of a division in James Longstreet's newly constituted First Army Corps (a second corps had been organized under Jackson). The command included Pickett's old brigade, now led by Colonel Montgomery Dent Corse of the Seventeenth Virginia, who had been transferred to the post when, after Sharpsburg, Dick Garnett was assigned to provisional command of another brigade under Longstreet. At first Pickett was uncertain whether he would gain permanent command of the division, but to his great satisfaction the appointment came through in late October and with it his elevation to major general. The date of promotion is uncertain; although most sources give it as October 10 or 11, on the twenty-seventh Lee was writing Secretary of War George W. Randolph recommending Pickett for the position and the appointment was not announced until November 6.[9]

The army grapevine advanced several theories to explain Pickett's lofty rise, the most prevalent being that Longstreet, Lee's senior subordinate, had lobbied his boss in Pickett's behalf just as he had promoted Pickett as a prospective brigade commander to Joe Johnston. Critics of later date would claim that Lee elevated Pickett without knowing much about his capabilities and because at this stage in the war he lacked a large pool of talent from which to choose division leaders. There is a measure of validity in this assertion, but it is likewise true that at Williamsburg, Seven Pines, and Gaines's Mill Pickett had established a reputation as a courageous and hard-driving, if rather impetuous, combat leader able to employ his troops to advantage against great odds. Those qualities would stand any man in good stead when vacancies occurred at the higher levels of command.

In addition to his Game Cocks, Pickett's new force consisted of three brigades culled from the divisions of D. R. Jones and Richard Anderson. Pickett was pleased to find that two of them were composed exclusively of regiments from the Old Dominion. The brigade of James Kemper—lawyer, V. M. I. student, Mexican War veteran, former speaker of the Virginia House of Delegates—comprised the First, Seventh, Eleventh, and Twenty-fourth Virginia. The other Virginia brigade was Lewis Armistead's; its combat record was somewhat less distinguished than that of Kemper's command, the majority of its men having fled Yankee counterattack at Seven Pines. Pickett nevertheless considered its regiments made of good material commanded by an officer of high merit: the Ninth, Fourteenth, Thirty-eighth, Fifty-third, and Fifty-seventh Regiments. Pickett's third new acquisition consisted of a half-dozen units under as promising a young brigadier as the army possessed: Micah Jenkins's First, Fifth, and Sixth South Carolina Infantry, the Second South Carolina Rifles, the infantry portion of the famed Hampton Legion, and a regiment of marksmen known as the Palmetto Sharpshooters.[10]

To Pickett's infantry additions General Lee initially assigned Dearing's Lynchburg Artillery—which had served so staunchly at Seven Pines and had continued to distinguish itself throughout the Seven Days—while temporarily attaching Captain Robert M. Stribling's Fauquier Artillery. In December Stribling's battery would be permanently assigned to the division, while Captain Miles C. Macon's Richmond Fayette Artillery would be brought over from Major General Lafayette McLaws's division of Longstreet's corps to give Pickett a third battery. By virtue of seniority as well as demonstrated ability, James Dearing, whom Pickett considered one of the ablest artillerists in the army, took command of the battalion, eventually with the rank of major.[11]

For a time, General Lee toyed with the idea of assigning Roger Pryor's infantry brigade to Pickett's new command as well. Eventually the army leader changed his mind, breaking up the politician-general's force and assigning its regiments to other units; in the shuffle Pryor's Third Virginia joined Kemper's brigade. Even without the bulk of Pryor's troops, Pickett enjoyed a command substantial both in terms of size and combat potential. At the time he took over, it boasted an aggregate present and absent total of 10,317 officers and men—the cream of his state's contribution to the fight for Southern independence.[12]

To help him effect day-to-day control over so many troops, Pickett enlarged his staff. Until brother Charlie could return to duty as chief of staff at the rank of major, Pickett installed in his place Colonel Robert Johnston, an old regular who had lost a line command during the reorganization that accompanied Lee's assumption of the army. Pickett also added to his military family Major Walter Harrison (assistant adjutant general and inspector-general of the division), Major Charles W. Chancellor (division surgeon), Major Robert Taylor Scott (chief quartermaster), Major Horace W. Jones (chief commissary), and Lieutenant Samuel G. Leitch (chief ordnance officer). To serve his new command he retained his trusted aides-de-camp, Captain Baird and Lieutenants Bright and Symington.[13]

* * *

Less than a month after assuming his new position, Pickett and his troops were in motion. On October 28, only a few days after General Lee held his first review of Pickett's division, the command trudged southeastward in common with thousands of comrades to counter the movements of the Army of the Potomac, now under Major General Ambrose E. Burnside.[14]

The long march was a painful ordeal for many of Pickett's men, who may have been made of sturdy material but who suffered from insufficient clothing and inadequate equipment. Despite the approach of winter, almost 2,100 of Pickett's troops were barefoot—more than 30 percent of the army's total of shoeless men. While their plight distressed their new commander, he could do little about it, at least until the division settled into a permanent position. At least one of his

Battles and Leaders

Map of Battle of Fredericksburg

subordinates, however, improvised to ease the problem: Lewis Armistead provided the needy with footwear fashioned from the hides of cattle killed to feed the army. A veteran of the Ninth Virginia recalled that "these moccasons [*sic*], or whatever you may call them, were . . . [put on] while green, and in a few days they dried, and there was no getting them off without cutting them."[15]

Pickett attempted to tend to his men's needs at the army's next port-of-call, Culpeper Court House in the Rappahannock-Rapidan River basin, but the nine days his division spent there proved insufficient to address the problem. If unable to improve the quality of life of his division, however, he did something about its quantity. By November 25 a large part of the army continued the march to Fredericksburg, toward which Ambrose Burnside was heading from the north, the direct route to Richmond. The following day, as the move ended and Pickett's veterans began to construct winter quarters along the Orange Plank Road west of the city, Longstreet assigned the division a fifth brigade, thus placing it on a par with what had hitherto been the largest component of his corps, Anderson's division.[16]

Pickett's new addition, which he appointed Montgomery Corse to command, consisted of Corse's own Seventeenth Virginia (formerly of Kemper's brigade) plus the Fifteenth and Thirtieth regiments; later the Thirty-second Virginia was added as well. In assuming command Corse received a deserved promotion to brigadier general. Meanwhile, as Corse left the Game Cock Brigade, Dick Garnett returned to lead it. While happy to avail himself of the man's services, Pickett admitted to mixed emotions when his old command went to Garnett on a permanent basis. He told Sallie of "a little 'kind of curious' feeling within when I hear it called 'Garnett's Brigade,' even though he has . . . won for it distinction and from it love and respect."[17]

Ironically, after assembling such a mighty force of foot soldiers and cannoneers—the new additions raised his manpower level to perhaps 9,000 effectives—Pickett brought only a fraction of his command to bear on the enemy during the army's next battle. Early on December 11, Burnside began to push across the Rappahannock from his base at Falmouth, opposite Fredericksburg. That evening Pickett, whose command held a position in rear of the Confederate center below the city, was informed that his men would be kept in reserve for use as needed at any point along Lee's perimeter. They were still in that position two days later, east of the old Telegraph Road along the summit of an eminence later known as Lee's Hill, when Burnside launched a series of assaults north and south of their part of the line.[18]

Made across a wide stretch of open ground sloping upward to artillery-covered crests, the Union advance consisted of roughly equal parts of senselessness and valor. Throughout the afternoon of the thirteenth and well after darkness descended, wave after wave of attackers, spearheaded by the Irish Brigade of the Army of the Potomac, made futile efforts to drive the Confederates from the high ground behind and below Fredericksburg. From their impregnable positions, Confederate riflemen and gunners could only stare at the tragic perseverance of their opponents. A captain in Armistead's Thirty-eighth Virginia reported seeing "the enemy advancing on our right and left, moving up their heavy columns in grand style . . ." Then, noted a South Carolinian of Jenkins's brigade, the Federals absorbed a staggering one-two punch: "The artillery would thin them some and then they would break . . . when the Infantry fire reached them."[19]

On most parts of the field, the attackers did not get close enough to absorb musketry; artillery shells cut them down long before. A member of the Eleventh Virginia observed cannon north and south of Pickett's position "belching forth shot and shell, grape and canister the while, and each time upon receiving a deadly fire, [the attackers] halted and then began to waiver [sic], give back, scatter and finally disappear over the rise in the ground, out of sight and out of range, leaving many dead and wounded behind." An enlisted man in the Seventeenth Virginia remarked that each time a wave of attack receded, "such a shout went up along the whole line as almost to drown out the roar of the musketry." A man in the Fifty-seventh Virginia summarized his impressions succinctly: "I never saw such carnage in all my life."[20]

Only a portion of one of Pickett's brigades saw action on this bleak and bloody day. Late in the afternoon, shortly before the last wave of assaults began, Longstreet ordered Pickett to strengthen the line atop Marye's Heights, one focal point of the ill-advised offensive. In response, Pickett dispatched Kemper's and Jenkins's people to report to General McLaws and Brigadier General Robert Ransom, Jr., whose divisions held the high ground between the Orange Plank Road and an unfinished railroad line just above Pickett's left.

About seven P.M. Kemper's brigade filed into position along a sunken road beneath the heights, while Jenkins's men moved to reinforce one of McLaws's brigades. The support forces dug in as well as the hard ground would permit, then hunkered down beneath their makeshift defenses. But they had arrived too late to help repulse Burnside's forlorn last attack; they inflicted few casualties and took few—a total of forty-six—in return. Throughout the night they held their position despite falling temperatures and frigid winds, guarding against a bayonet attack that never came and wishing they were back in the snug cabins they had left behind.[21]

If the Confederates had a difficult time keeping warm that night, the hundreds of wounded Federals lying on the plain before Marye's Heights and elsewhere along the front experienced immeasurably greater discomfort. The scene in front of the sunken road at Marye's Heights beggared description; Colonel John Bratton of the Sixth South Carolina wrote his wife that "I have never seen or conceived of such havoc." Immediately east of Bratton's position lay upwards of 500 dead Federals, "actually counted." Yet these made up a small portion of the 13,000 casualties Burnside's criminal stubbornness had cost his army as against fewer than half as many Confederate losses.[22]

Many of the Yankees who littered the field were alive but badly wounded and in great pain. Decades after the battle, a member of Kemper's brigade could not erase from his mind the sounds they gave off: "the crys [sic] and groans and prayers of these poor fellows in the death like stillness of the night . . . awakened within us thoughts like . . . the glories of war one gained at a dreadful sacrifice." This man and his comrades "thought we were hardened veterans having just returned from the bloody fields of 2nd Manassas, Boonsborough Gap and Sharpsburg, but those groans that night was the most horrid experience of our life."[23]

Similar sentiments—comments about war's mingled horror and glory—found their way into a letter Sallie Corbell claimed her beau wrote her from the battlefield. "Your Soldier's heart almost stood still," he told her, "as he watched those sons of Erin fearlessly rush to their death. . . . we forgot they were fighting us, and cheer after cheer at their fearlessness went up all along our lines." Pickett added a condolence to the highest-ranking victim of the day's carnage, yet another Yankee he could not bring himself to consider his enemy: "I can't help feeling sorry for Old Burnside—proud, plucky, hard-headed old dog. I always liked him. . . ."

In the same letter Pickett mentioned an incident that highlights his military capacity at the expense of a more celebrated colleague. This incident calls into question the sense of commitment of John Bell Hood, whose division had been positioned on Pickett's right, connecting with Jackson's line farther south. When giving both division leaders instructions early on the thirteenth, Longstreet had prepared them for the assaults he knew to be coming, while cautioning them to be alert to an opportunity to strike the exposed flank of the Federal columns. Only Pickett seems to have understood. In the formative stage of the day's fighting, when attacks on Jackson's front appeared to leave the Union line opposite Hood's heretofore-uncommitted command vulnerable, Pickett galloped to Hood's headquarters and urged the division leader "to seize the opportunity." Hood, however, appeared "afraid to assume so great a responsibility and sent for permission to Old Peter. . . . Before his assent and approval were received, the opportunity, alas, was lost!"

Some critics believe that Pickett overstated his claim of an opening and unfairly blamed Hood for failing to capitalize on it. Longstreet, however, shared Pickett's view, believing that had Hood acted as instructed, a crushing Union defeat might have been turned into panic-stricken rout. Looking back long after the war, Longstreet praised Pickett's foresight while regretting that he had not court-martialed Hood for his critical lapse.[24]

* * *

Two days after the bloodshed on Marye's Heights, Pickett's men looked out across the frozen plain and found no living men. Litter-bearers had carted off the few wounded who had survived their injuries and the weather; burial teams had interred many of their dead comrades; and the rest of the Union army was gone, Burnside having recrossed the river in abject defeat. Late that morning Randolph Shotwell was "surprised to see General Pickett and staff galloping across the valley where the Yankee sharpshooters had been the night before!"[25]

Over the next two weeks Pickett moved successive portions of his division a mile or two south of Fredericksburg and encamped them in a wooded area near Guiney's Station on the Richmond, Fredericksburg & Potomac Railroad. There, for a second time in less than a month, his men built winter cabins. In that vicinity they also stood picket duty, drilled when weather allowed, and when it did not engaged in snowball fights that pitted whole regiments against one another.[26]

For once, Pickett did not have to spend his time after a battle trying to make good heavy losses. He did, however, have to work long and hard to provide his troops with even a minimum of rations; like the rest of the army, his Virginians suffered not only from bare feet but from empty stomachs. Again, however, there seemed no help for it; food and forage were not abundant in the Fredericksburg vicinity, which Pickett referred to in a letter to Sallie as "that miserable, eaten up country." Moreover, a change of venue appeared unlikely.[27]

Organizational and manpower concerns also attracted the general's attention. While at Guiney's Station his division received another addition when, shortly before Christmas, it assimilated a new regiment. The Twenty-ninth Virginia, an aggregation of mountaineers short on discipline and soldierly bearing but with a high tolerance for privation and discomfort, was assigned to Corse's brigade to give it the same complement of regiments—five—as the other brigades under Pickett. According to Major Harrison, the Twenty-ninth was an unusually large regiment; the resulting manpower increase, however, would be more than offset if a rumor then making the rounds proved true: the transfer of Jenkins's brigade to Hood's division. While such a move would give Pickett's command an all-Virginia orientation that appealed to him, it would reduce the division to fewer than 7,500 officers and men present for duty.[28]

★ ★ ★

Late in January 1863 Ambrose Burnside activated Lee's vigilance when he commenced his ill-timed if not ill-conceived Mud March around the Confederate left flank via Banks's Ford on the Rappahannock. On the twentieth, under a cold rain, Pickett obeyed Longstreet's order to guide a part of his command along riverbank roads due west of Fredericksburg toward Burnside's suspected crossing-site. In that vicinity the troops entrenched where the frozen, rutted earth permitted and built works against the anticipated advance. By the quiet morning of the twenty-sixth, however, it became evident that the weather had forced Burnside to curtail his operation and return to his cheerless camps at Falmouth. On that day a relieved Longstreet sent Pickett's men a little more than a mile to the south, where they took up a position on the plank road near Salem Church. There, with extra entrenching tools borrowed from Hood's division, they fashioned what Colonel Sorrel of Longstreet's staff described as "an important line of defense." Although Longstreet had informed Pickett that his men would be stationed near Salem Church "permanently," on the twenty-ninth the division was abruptly ordered out of its important works and returned to the old camp at Guiney's Station.[29]

Beaten by Lee outside Fredericksburg and by the weather on the road to Banks's Ford, luckless Burnside lost command of the Army of the Potomac, being replaced by Major General Joseph Hooker. Instead of going into enforced retirement as had McClellan, Burnside eventually accepted a demotion to lead the IX Corps. Even before he took over, that command was on the move. In mid-February General Lee heard reports that the corps was making an amphibious movement down the Potomac, heading for any number of possible objectives including Fort Monroe. The news created alarm in Richmond, where President Davis and his new secretary of war, James Seddon, suspected that the move heralded a change of base by Hooker's army. For weeks government authorities had feared the capital to be in danger of attack from southeastern Virginia as it had been the previous spring. Even if Burnside's command did not menace the city, Yankee troops south of Hampton Roads, particularly the heavy garrison at Suffolk, might be planning a movement on Richmond.[30]

To calm the government's anxiety, on the fifteenth Lee ordered Longstreet to detach Pickett's division for service in the vicinity of the capital. That same day, the troops left their camps near Salem Church and marched toward the Chickahominy River. As the movement began, Lee attempted to assure Secretary Seddon that "Pickett's division can meet and beat it [Burnside's corps] wherever it goes." When the government continued to act skittish, however, Lee decided to have Hood's troops follow Pickett's. Finally, to lend the proper air of importance to the mission, especially in the event Pickett and Hood served apart from his army for a lengthy time, Lee directed Longstreet to take personal command of both divisions.[31]

Before the month was out, Longstreet was named commander of the Department of Virginia and North Carolina with headquarters at Petersburg. The "Cockade City" lay close enough to Suffolk as well as to the enemy outposts in the Tarheel State to cover the major approaches to Richmond from the south and to guard the railroads that brought rations and forage to Lee's army from the Confederate interior. For Longstreet, Pickett, and Hood, the move toward Richmond began three and a half months of detached duty. By the time they rejoined Lee's army it would be the middle of spring and Lee would have conducted another major campaign.

The operation took Pickett back to familiar territory. On the seventeenth, as the general's troops marched toward the Chickahominy, Secretary Seddon altered their destination. In response to alarming reports of Union reinforcements at Suffolk, he suggested to Lee that Pickett cross the James and place his command between the capital and Petersburg; Lee quickly concurred. Pickett's formal orders, issued on the eighteenth by General Cooper, directed him to guard not only Petersburg but Drewry's Bluff and Chaffin's Bluff below Richmond, and to repel any advance from the line of the Blackwater River around Suffolk.[32]

On the twenty-first Pickett marched his infantry through Richmond; the artillery under Dearing would follow four days later. The occasion conjured up memories of his first triumphal march through the city when leading his Game Cocks to the defense of Yorktown. This day no reunion with Sallie was possible; following his return to the field, she had gone back to the Lynchburg Academy, where she was in her last year of study. While not on hand, she was very much on Pickett's mind; aboard his favorite mare, Lucy, he rode on ahead of his men, pulled up in front of the family home, "ran into the garden and gathered for my darling some lilies of the valley, planted by my sweet mother, which I knew were now in the full glory of their blossoming."[33]

Reaching Falling Creek, about eight miles from the city, early that evening, he wrote Sallie to suggest that, being unable to meet him in Richmond, she come to Petersburg, which he supposed to be the ultimate objective of the expedition. On that occasion, presumably, he would present her with his little bouquet. He closed his letter with the sort of romantic flourish becoming more and more a part of his correspondence, signing himself "Your (and nobody else's) George."

At times such prose and the sentiments behind it left him feeling self-conscious and a bit foolish. He realized that some in the army thought it ridiculous that he should act like a lovesick swain half his age. Even the gentle kidding of fellow commanders amused by his youthful antics sometimes embarrassed him. Increasingly, however, he did not care what kind of reaction the June-December relationship provoked in those about him. Every day he was finding it harder and harder to live apart from the girl who crowded his thoughts. And the idea that field operations were carrying him ever closer to her home left him positively giddy with anticipation.[34]

EIGHT – From Suffolk to Gettysburg

The mission that had brought Pickett's and Hood's divisions to Richmond underwent a fundamental change in early March. Once fears about threats to Richmond from the Peninsula began to ease, the Confederate War Department shifted its attention from local defense to a campaign in southeastern Virginia and northeastern North Carolina, areas largely untouched by the heavy hand of war. The several counties straddling the boundary between the two states contained some of the most abundant farmland east of the Shenandoah Valley. An army foraging in that region might in a few weeks obtain enough grain, livestock, eggs, and poultry to sustain Lee's underfed army throughout the winter. The Yankee garrison at Suffolk—which the IX Corps appeared to have reinforced—would have to be neutralized, but Longstreet had enough troops to hold the enemy in check while scouring the countryside for food and forage.

The operation that the War Office, Longstreet, and Lee began to develop early in March involved an advance not only against Suffolk but toward some coastal and inland outposts in North Carolina. The latter mission would temporarily cost Pickett two of his brigades and would cause the permanent loss of a third.[1]

As overall field commander of the operation, Longstreet ordered D. H. Hill, now senior Confederate officer in the Tarheel State, to attack the enemy garrison at New Bern, by the mouth of the Neuse River. For the operation he had Pickett, on March 9, send Dick Garnett's brigade to Hill via Tarboro, North Carolina. A week later, when Longstreet heard what turned out to be an erroneous report that the enemy was heavily reinforcing New Bern, he considered sending Pickett there with the rest of his division; ultimately, nothing came of the scheme.

For various reasons Hill's movement against New Bern was unsuccessful. At Longstreet's direction, he then moved thirty miles northward to attack the outpost of Washington, on the Tar-Pamlico River. To augment his force, on the twenty-first Longstreet ordered Kemper's brigade to Washington via Goldsboro and Kinston. Again, Longstreet mulled the notion of sending Pickett himself to the scene of action but at the last minute thought better of it. To crack the works at Suffolk, he would need all the division-level expertise he could obtain.[2]

The siege of Washington would also prove a failure, although the investment force, including Garnett's and Kemper's commands, gathered huge quantities of foodstuffs from the surrounding region with which to provision Lee's army. At the end of their foraging operation, those brigades would return to Pickett. As part of the project planned for southeastern Virginia, however, Longstreet also detached Jenkins's brigade, sending it to the Suffolk vicinity to guard the line of the Blackwater River. There it became part of the local forces under Major General Samuel Gibbs French, which had been operating unsuccessfully against Suffolk for many months. Jenkins, in fact, was appointed to head both his own and another brigade, under French's titular command. Neither Pickett nor Longstreet realized it when Jenkins went on ahead to Suffolk, but his brigade would never rejoin the division it had been a part of for the past six months.[3]

Soon after Hill and his supports moved against Washington, Longstreet made the decision to operate against Suffolk with Hood's and Jenkins's divisions and what remained of Pickett's. Lee was wary about letting Longstreet's main force get involved in such a large operation so far from the main army; he feared that if "Fighting Joe" Hooker moved against him he would find Hood and Pickett beyond quick recall. On March 17, when a Union cavalry force crossed the Rappahannock at Kelly's Ford, Lee wondered if the movement presaged an advance by Hooker's main army. Just in case, he called on Longstreet for help. Before the attack could be identified as an isolated strike, Pickett, with his truncated command, was sent to his old bailiwick at Tappahannock on what he aptly termed a "wild goose chase."[4]

Finally, early in April, when he learned that the greater part of the IX Corps had left southeastern Virginia to join Burnside in the Department of the Ohio, Lee urged Longstreet to proceed with his two-fold operation in and around Suffolk. Already Pickett had sent Corse's brigade in that direction; now, in concert with Hood's division, he moved toward Suffolk with the soldiers of Lewis Armistead.

Meanwhile, Longstreet called on General Hill to return Garnett's and Kemper's brigades as soon as possible. Kemper left immediately for Suffolk, rejoining Pickett in time to advance against Suffolk, but Garnett remained with Hill until the siege of Washington ended in mid-April.

While his forage wagons fanned out to gather up the spring crops of the countryside, Longstreet considered his options for neutralizing Suffolk. Initially he wished to attack and take the garrison by storm, although, protected as it was by fifteen miles of works manned by 15,000 troops under Major General John J. Peck, the outpost constituted a formidable objective. Once he learned that he could expect no help from the Confederate States Navy in neutralizing Union gunboats in the Nansemond River, Longstreet revamped his thinking. At length he decided upon a siege. Pickett, Hood, and Jenkins would construct investment lines running down from the banks of the Nansemond, circling westward around the town and, below it, extending as far east as the Dismal Swamp.[5]

Early on April 11, the Confederates crossed the Blackwater River—Pickett's division, preceded by Jenkins's, at South Quay, Hood farther north at Franklin—and closed in on their target. While Hood and Jenkins pushed north and west, Pickett advanced up the Somerton Road south of the Yankee garrison, then fanned out toward Dismal Swamp, en route crossing the Edenton (or White Marsh) Road.

Pickett reached his assigned position early on the twelfth. That same day two-thirds of his troops got into action, Corse on the Edenton Road, Armistead along the Somerton Road—Kemper's brigade holding the rear. On both thoroughfares Pickett's men drove in blue-clad skirmishers until heavy artillery-fire from three large redoubts south of the town forced the Confederates to pull back. When subsequent advances were also turned back by gunners and sharpshooters inside the works, Longstreet saw that the garrison was invulnerable on that side.[6]

For the duration of the siege, while Hood's and Jenkins's men maneuvered north, west, and southwest of Suffolk, Pickett's troops spent most of their time building and holding a line of earthworks and entrenchments paralleling those of their enemy. They remained in those defenses south of town for the next three weeks, preventing the Federals from striking Longstreet's right flank but virtually powerless to take the offensive themselves.

While Pickett's infantry dug in, the guns of Dearing's battalion—now augmented by the addition of Captain William H. Caskie's Hampden (Virginia) Battery, which made good the recent loss of the Louisiana Guard Artillery—were parceled out to various points along the siege line, some far removed from Pickett's reach. Longstreet, in fact, assigned all of his guns to General French, who, preferring an infantry command, tried to fob them off on uncaring subordinates. Thus French was primarily to blame when, on the evening of April 19, a picked force of Federals, transported into position by gunboats in the Nansemond, landed below, and launched a surprise attack on, Fort Huger, an earthwork at the opposite end of the siege lines from Pickett's headquarters. Through the laxity of infantry assigned to protect the fort, the Yankees seized the five guns and 130 men of Stribling's Fauquier Artillery, which had manned the fort. The captors spirited away the cannoneers and by great exertion carted their guns into freshly dug rifle-pits. The success of the raid embarrassed the Confederate high command, touched off a feud between Longstreet and French, and led Longstreet to reassess his intentions outside Suffolk. Having lost a key defensive position in his fight against the enemy's fleet, Pickett's friend and superior began to doubt that he could accomplish anything of value at Suffolk except through foraging.[7]

The only major action in Pickett's sector during the balance of the siege occurred on the rainy afternoon of April 24, when General Peck launched a reconnaissance-in-force south of town. A 5,500-man contingent of infantry and cavalry, backed by ten field guns, trooped down the road from Edenton toward Corse's brigade, while 1,200 foot soldiers demonstrated against Armistead's position on the Somerton Road. The attackers ripped apart the picket screens along both roads, then rushed onward to strike the main position of Corse. They ran into a force prepared to meet them, a provisional brigade that Pickett had placed under Colonel John Bowie Magruder of the Fifty-seventh Virginia to guard his far right flank. Pickett's vigilance was validated when this force stopped the Yankees like a brickbat to the skull. A blast of musketry tore into the oncomers, followed by a shelling from Macon's battery that one Union officer called "remarkable for its precision and accuracy." Before Colonel Magruder's infantry could advance, Macon's gunners placed so many shells in the enemy's midst that the Yankees scattered, retreated, and refused to return to the fight. In his report of the action, Pickett observed that the enemy officers "had great difficulty in making their men come up to the mark" once Macon started in. Further shelling sent the Yankees into headlong flight and caused them to abandon a large number of weapons and supplies that their adversaries greedily appropriated. Sobered by the carnage and confusion farther east, the supporting force on the Somerton Road turned back to its works without a fight. General Peck, as if chastised for having had the temerity to test Pickett's lines, launched no more sorties south of town.[8]

If the remainder of the siege furnished Pickett with no further opportunities for military glory, it did enable him to visit his Sallie, who was home between school terms. Because her hometown remained accessible to combatants—during the siege cavalry clashes occurred almost in the streets of Chuckatuck—she had gone to stay with an uncle who lived near Ivor Station on the Petersburg & Norfolk Railroad; there she met Her Soldier at the outset of the campaign. Once the siege began, Sallie moved in with an aunt at Barber's Crossroads, ten miles northwest of Suffolk and fifteen miles from Pickett's headquarters. Undaunted by the distance between them, Pickett rode out to see her at frequent intervals. Before the campaign ended, he was making the thirty-mile circuit almost every night. Each visit was necessarily brief, for he had to be back in camp come morning, but he could not keep away; as for Sallie, "these short visits were glimpses of heaven to me."[9]

At first, he sought Longstreet's permission each time he wished to visit Barber's Crossroads. When Longstreet approved the trips with increasing reluctance and seemed about to forbid the practice, Pickett tried to circumvent him by obtaining the permission of Colonel Sorrel. In his memoirs, Longstreet's adjutant general—one of those who disapproved of Pickett's wartime romance, fearing it would interfere with his military duties—huffed that "I don't think his division benefited by such carpet-knight doings in the field." He told Pickett so at the time, but he could not counter the general's anguished protestations that "I must go, I must see her. I swear, Sorrel, I'll be back before anything can happen in the morning."[10]

Sorrel was not the only critic of Pickett's frequent comings and goings. Colonel Stuart of the Fifty-sixth Virginia complained in letters to his wife that the general "was continually riding off to pay court to his young love, leaving the division details to his staff." Presumably, Pickett's absences also disturbed others in the command. In the end, however, all fears proved groundless; Pickett's attentions to his beloved failed to jeopardize the operations around Suffolk. It appears that only good came from his nocturnal visits, for by the time the siege of Suffolk ended he and Sallie were engaged.

He wanted to marry as quickly as possible, even in the midst of a field campaign, but she—influenced by "the rigid system of social training in which a girl of that period was reared"—could not countenance the thought of being wed "by the wayside in that desultory and unstudied fashion." Finally they agreed to wait at least until the summer, after Sallie's graduation from the Lynchburg Academy. Then they would have a wedding complete with all the trappings a wartime economy would allow.[11]

* * *

Late in April General Lee became increasingly alarmed that the Army of the Potomac was about to advance against him. He began to importune Longstreet to complete his campaign in the countryside as soon as possible and return to him ready to fight. Lee's concern not only persuaded his subordinate to lift his siege somewhat sooner than intended but effectively quashed a plan hatched by the Richmond authorities to send either Pickett's or Hood's troops to reinforce General Braxton Bragg's army in Middle Tennessee on the eve of an important campaign against the Union forces of Major General William S. Rosecrans.[12]

On the twenty-eighth Lee's fears became acute: that day Hooker began crossing the Rappahannock upstream from Fredericksburg as if he intended to gain the Rebel rear. The following day Lee sent a peremptory order for Longstreet to rejoin him with Pickett and Hood. Longstreet hustled to comply but it took days to recall his foragers and their heavily laden wagons. Only after dark on May 3 could he put his command in motion toward the Blackwater. Gingerly, Pickett and his four brigades—Garnett had rejoined him from North Carolina two weeks earlier—disengaged and made for the river crossings. Not till the next morning did the Federals find their opponents gone, a testimonial to the swiftness and stealth with which they had departed. "Retreat successfully made," one of Longstreet's staff officers noted in his diary. "Never one more so."[13]

On May 5, en route to Petersburg and points north, Pickett's column heard some good news that also told them they were too late to aid General Lee against Joe Hooker. In the first days of the month Lee had engaged his adversary in the Wilderness, a heavily timbered region below the Rappahannock and west of Fredericksburg. Near a crossroads known as Chancellorsville Lee had thrashed the heavier Army of the Potomac into retreat. "This announcement acted like a charm upon the men," remarked a member of Corse's brigade, "almost annihilating all thought of physical inconvenience arising from the toils of the day's march." Not for another day or so would the men hear early rumors of the May 2 wounding of Stonewall Jackson, and not till the eleventh, while laying over at Falling Creek, would they get positive word of Jackson's death from complications arising from his injury. The intelligence was sobering to the division as a whole, although Lieutenant Colonel Powhatan B. Whittle of the Thirty-eighth Virginia wrote his brother that "there seems to be very little despondency, on account of the loss of the brave & heroic Jackson. The men believe in the leaders which are left behind, and they will now fight under almost any man of gallantry."[14]

Even if speed was no longer of the essence, Pickett kept his men moving north. They passed through Petersburg on the seventh and eighth, only to learn that Longstreet wished them to encamp "for a few days" along the Williamsburg Road a couple of miles south of Richmond. On the thirteenth, while Pickett's main body lolled in camp on the outskirts of the capital, two of his better-attired, better-accoutred regiments, along with the gunners of Macon's battery, accompanied General Longstreet to Richmond to take part in the funeral procession that would conduct the remains of the deeply lamented Jackson to the state capitol.[15]

Three days later the northward march resumed, Pickett's troops again passing through the streets of the capital. On the other side, by order of Secretary Seddon, they were marched toward Hanover Court House, where the railroad from Richmond to Fredericksburg intersected the westward-leading Virginia Central. South of that depot, around Taylorsville—almost thirty miles short of Fredericksburg and Lee's army—Pickett's men were again placed in camp as though the Confederate authorities could not decide where they could be used to greatest profit.

At Taylorsville Pickett passed the time distributing to his troops some of the recent abundance gathered from the farmlands to the south. In his free time he wrote letter after letter to Sallie—so many "that I am ashamed of myself and you must be tired of reading my musings, but I can't help it, tis a pleasure to me (the only one I have). . . ." He asked her to meet him at Fredericksburg when he reached the main army, something he expected to occur sooner rather than later. Until then he could only anticipate their meeting and curse dragging time: "Hours seem days . . . to me now. I live only under the hope of once more being with you."[16]

* * *

Despite Pickett's prediction of an early march to Fredericksburg, the War Department seemed content to leave the division along the railroads of Hanover County. This was not Lee's doing; through late May and into early June the army leader sought the return of Pickett and Hood as well as the reattaching of Jenkins's brigade, which the Richmond authorities had left on the Blackwater line after Longstreet's exodus. Anticipating the feelings of both Pickett and Jenkins, Lee declared that the latter's command "is much wanted with its division." He also corresponded directly with D. H. Hill, who had replaced Longstreet in command on the Blackwater, to expedite Jenkins's return. On May 29, however, President Davis wrote Lee to explain that to detach Jenkins from his present position would be to "abandon the country" around Suffolk to the tender mercies of General Peck. The President was under the impression that another North Carolina-based command had been sent to Pickett to compensate for the loss of Jenkins. Even after Longstreet and Lee set him straight on the matter, Davis refused to release Jenkins.[17]

The protracted estrangement of Jenkins's sorely missed command was vexing enough, but for Pickett worse luck lay ahead. During the first days of June, with Longstreet and Hood finally en route to rejoin Lee's army, which rumor had on the verge of another major campaign, Pickett learned that he was being left behind. On the second, Lee had acceded to Jefferson Davis's wish that Pickett's command be retained in the Taylorsville-Hanover Junction area along with the North Carolina brigade of Brigadier General J. Johnston Pettigrew, which had recently come up from North Carolina and the unhappy foray against New Bern. Pickett's enforced stay was the result of another outbreak of jitters in Richmond, again perceived as threatened from the Peninsula.

Early in May more than 5,000 enemy troops had sailed up the York River to West Point, about forty miles southeast of Hanover Junction. This movement, a feint conducted in distant cooperation with Hooker's offensive, had ended in the invaders' quick withdrawal. Now, however, Richmond officials had learned that another, albeit smaller, expedition was afoot in the same area. Perhaps this would turn south against Richmond or north to smite Lee's line of communications with the capital.

By June 5, Pickett and Pettigrew learned that this new Yankee force had moved by ship up the Mattapony River to land at Walkerton, well above West Point and within striking range of Hanover Junction. The invaders were reported to be burning houses, barns, and crops in Prince William County. Accordingly, Richmond directed Pickett to counter the expedition; another command, Brigadier General Henry A. Wise's Virginia brigade, would be sent via White House to assist.[18]

Rather nonchalantly, it seems, Pickett went about the task of trying to locate the Yankees—a 400-man party from the corps of E. D. Keyes—and curtail their depredations. Slowly he led part of his force down the north side of the Mattapony, while Wise moved up the opposite bank, hoping to catch the enemy in between. Cooperation proved lacking, however, and neither force overtook the enemy. Keyes's troops continued to scorch the earth around Walkerton until the job was done to their satisfaction, whereupon they returned to their transports and sailed away.

An apoplectic General Wise—a political general who considered most professional soldiers obtuse, incompetent, or both—blamed his colleague for the enemy's escape, asserting that Pickett had advanced no farther than five miles from Walkerton before turning back to Hanover Junction. Learning of Pickett's failure to "go far enough" toward bagging the raiders, on or about June 7 Robert E. Lee wired him to return to Walkerton, find the Yankees, and this time "drive them back." By the time he received Lee's cable there were no raiders to drive, but Pickett, who had a long-standing hypersensitivity to criticism, may have taken offense at the army commander's directive. If so, it constituted only one of several incidents that had begun to harm their relationship.[19]

Already, of course, Pickett was unhappy about the detaching of Jenkins's brigade, a mistake that Lee may not have worked hard enough to prevent or to remedy. Pickett was more than a little miffed at having been left in Hanover County while the rest of the army started on a campaign without him: Lee's second invasion of the North in nine months. Pickett's detaching appeared to raise questions about the value Lee attached to him and his command. Pickett's frame of mind may have had something to do with his halfhearted pursuit of the raiders around Walkerton, an assignment one might consider beneath the dignity of a combat commander.

When Pickett finally got the word from Longstreet to leave Hanover Junction and rejoin the First Corps there occurred another flap for which he seems to have held Lee at least partially responsible. Because Secretary of War Seddon demanded that a brigade remain at the junction to secure Lee's communications, Pickett departed only after agreeing to leave Corse's troops behind—temporarily. Once other forces from the Department of Richmond arrived to secure the area, Corse would rejoin Pickett's main body on the march. The promised reunion did take place: Corse started north as intended three days after Pickett left and covered twenty miles on the route before being recalled to the junction on the twelfth. The Richmond authorities had changed their minds; even with additional troops in the area, they did not feel comfortable letting Corse evacuate that strategic depot in Lee's rear.[20]

Pickett, of course, was furious. Losing Jenkins was bad enough, but he calculated that Corse's loss had reduced his division to fewer than 4,800 effectives (the true count was closer to 6,000). When he rejoined Lee, Pickett protested what he considered a gross injustice, lecturing his commander that "it is well known that a small division will be expected to do the same amount of hard service as a large one, and, as the army is now divided, my division will be, I think, decidedly the weakest." At the very least, until Corse's return he should be compensated by the temporary addition of a brigade.

Though Pickett claimed his intent was not to accuse, there is an accusatory tone to the letter, as though he suspected Lee of being a party to Corse's detaching—which was not true—or of failing to fight Richmond for Corse's return—also untrue, as was the case with Pickett's earlier suspicion that Lee had failed to push for Jenkins's return. Through his adjutant general, Major Walter H. Taylor, the army commander acknowledged Pickett's disgruntlement and apologized for his inability to make things better. As for Pickett's suggestion of temporary reinforcements, "there is no other brigade in the army which could be assigned to the division at this time."[21]

Even after Pickett caught up with the army and accompanied it into Maryland, his attitude toward Lee had a rough edge. Entering Hagerstown on a rainy day in late June, Lee, riding alongside Longstreet and Pickett, encountered a bevy of female admirers. When one asked for a lock of his hair, Lee politely declined but suggested that "General Pickett would be pleased to give them one of his curls." A bystander noted that Pickett, whose auburn ringlets "were not particularly becoming when the rain made them lank," did not appreciate the joke at his expense. The little incident probably signified nothing more than Pickett's brittle pride and his tendency to take himself too seriously. On the other hand, the jest may have further alienated him, personally and professionally, from Marse Robert.[22]

★ ★ ★

Once on the march toward the Mason-Dixon Line, Pickett's attitude appeared to improve; trading inertia for momentum had much to do with the adjustment. On June 13, two days after catching up with Longstreet's column at Culpeper Court House, he wrote Sallie of his conviction that "we shall have a *successful* campaign and think 'twill go far towards bringing about a termination of difficulties." By now he was privy to at least the general outline of Lee's plan of invasion, which had as its near-term objective the country above the Susquehanna River near Harrisburg, Pennsylvania. Although he did not divulge details, he hinted to his betrothed that it was a bold yet calculated scheme to end the war with a major victory on enemy soil. The campaign promised hard fighting, but "should I be fortunate enough to get back, my first step shall be to reach out and *claim my own Sallie. . . .*"[23]

Having been so concerned that he would have to march long and hard to overtake his comrades, Pickett must have felt a bit sheepish when the army lay over at Culpeper for several days as Lee's advance—Jackson's old corps, now led by Lieutenant General Richard S. Ewell—cleared outposts in the Shenandoah Valley from the path of invasion. Lee used the stopover to mass his scattered forces, including his new third corps, under Pickett's West Point friend A. P. Hill, which had initially been left to cover the rear at Fredericksburg.

By the fifteenth, Longstreet's command hit the road, heading for the upper Valley. Despite marching through sometimes-stifling heat and omnipresent clouds of dust, Pickett's troops made good time on their northwestern jaunt. Two days after departing Culpeper they were crossing the line of the Manassas Gap Railroad and route-stepping through the villages of Gaines's Cross Roads, Markham, and Piedmont. By the nineteenth they had reached Paris and Middleburg, along the eastern rim of the Blue Ridge Mountains. That day Stuart's cavalry, screening the flank of the invasion column, tangled at Middleburg with Yankee cavalry seeking to ascertain Lee's whereabouts and divine his intentions. As the horsemen grappled farther east, Pickett's men held the line between Ashby's and Snicker's Gaps in support of Hood's division, then blocking the latter defile to the Federals.

The following day, most of Pickett's command forded the Shenandoah River to Edgemont and Berryville, although the tag end of the column, Garnett's brigade, did not cross till the twenty-second. Perhaps Old Dick's men were moving slowly in sympathy for their commander's lameness, he having been severely bruised when kicked by the horse of Pickett's aide, Lieutenant Bright. On the twenty-third, with the division poised to cross the Potomac, Colonel Whittle wrote home that "our cause is bright, our men are in high spirits and confident, and have unbounded trust in Genl. Lee."[24]

Spirits began to decline when, on June 26, the division crossed the river that marked the barrier between North and South, Rebeldom and Yankeeland. Passing through Williamsport and Hagerstown, Pickett experienced what his men had encountered when entering Maryland the previous September: an icy reception from cities and towns supposedly inhabited by large numbers of Confederate sympathizers. Not surprisingly, cold stares and angry silence also greeted the troops as they pushed across the Mason-Dixon Line into southern Pennsylvania. Major Dearing noted that the men began to cheer for themselves to compensate for the "welcome they were not receiving in the enemy's country. . . ." From Greencastle, his first stopover in Pennsylvania, Pickett wrote Sallie that he had saved a local girl from trouble at the hands of his men, whom she had been taunting by conspicuously waving an American flag. The incident, which portrays Pickett as sensitive and courtly, is a crowd-pleaser, but its stagy, set-piece character suggests that it sprang, like so many dramatic vignettes involving Pickett, from the fertile imagination of his widow.[25]

On the evening of the twenty-sixth Pickett made his headquarters a few miles from Chambersburg along the western ledge of South Mountain. Next day his division closed up on the town, where the army's supply and ambulance wagons were parked; it remained in camp there, guarding the rear, for the next four days. Meanwhile, Longstreet's main body forged eastward, accompanying Lee across the mountains toward Cashtown and the rail hub of Gettysburg.

At first Pickett did not fret over his detached status; covering the rear in the midst of enemy territory was an honorable assignment. But as June came to an end, vagrant rumors drifted in to suggest that a major confrontation was in the making near Gettysburg. Then a trickle of wounded men, stragglers, teamsters and the other refuse an army throws off reached Chambersburg to confirm the early reports. The slow-footed Army of the Potomac, now under Major General George Gordon Meade, had overtaken Lee at last, bringing him to battle on Northern soil. Suddenly rear-guard duty lost its value. If a battle was shaping up beyond South Mountain, Pickett and his men should be there in case needed. Their orders, however, were clear: they must remain with the trains until relieved by the slowly approaching cavalry and mounted infantry of Brigadier General John Imboden.[26]

Imboden's somewhat ragtag command finally reached Chambersburg late on the first. To its commander Pickett happily entrusted the supply vehicles and the rear-guard community he had been safeguarding. From that point, he anxiously awaited the order to move. Thus, when a courier from Longstreet reached him in the small hours of July 2, Pickett scanned his dispatch and called to his subordinates in a voice high with excitement: "We must move at once to Gettysburg! Order the men into line and lead the movement!"[27]

As he led the march out of Chambersburg astride his big black charger, Pickett was looking forward to what lay ahead. As a year's worth of battles had shown, he was a fighter—his whole life had centered around his ability and his readiness to fight—and he had been held out of action too long. Not since the opening hours at Gaines's Mill had he smelled the acrid, invigorating stench of battle smoke.

Like him, his men were ready for a scrap. Held in reserve at Fredericksburg, they had seen no action at Chancellorsville and precious little outside Suffolk. More than once during the past month it looked as though they would be kept out of this coming fight as well. Fortunately, that was not to be the case: very soon, Pickett's command would have the chance to show what it could do when unleashed against the Yankee army.

NINE — Grand But Fatal Day

General Pickett and his division spent morning and afternoon crossing the mountains, tramping through Greenwood and Cashtown past glowering civilians, closing up on Gettysburg. En route they were able to form a graphic picture of the carnage toward which they were advancing. The story was told in the corpses that lay scattered in fields to right and left, bloating under the summer sun; overturned wagons and shattered limbers and caissons; and the column of crowded ambulances that passed them, going the other way. The tide of vehicles and refugees heading toward the rear was not large enough to place the army on the verge of retreating or changing position. The conclusion was that although it had missed the opening act of this bloody struggle, time remained for Pickett's division to take the stage before the tragedy reached finale.[1]

As the march continued, the division began to gain a picture of this battle still raging at white heat, pieced together from the accounts of stragglers, walking wounded, teamsters, and provost guards. The previous morning a part of A. P. Hill's corps, the division of Pickett's cousin and West Point partner-in-crime, now-Major General Harry Heth, had tangled with Union cavalry, the advance of Meade's army, northwest of Gettysburg. What began as a skirmish on the outskirts of a quiet little town grew into an epic struggle. Casualties ran high— Cousin Hal taking a stunning but not fatal blow to the head—and the fight continued to expand as elements of both armies flooded the field, Lee's from the west and north, Meade's from the south.

Fighting on unfamiliar terrain, a bit unsure of their footing, the Confederates threatened to uproot the enemy before the latter dug in, but their attacks faltered at critical moments. Late in the day they pushed the smaller Federals below the village but there they squandered more than one opportunity to clear the field; no mistake would loom as large as General Ewell's failure to take a vulnerable eminence along the enemy's right as Lee intended. The day ended in stalemate, with the Army of Northern Virginia holding a ridgeline southwest of Gettysburg on which sat a Lutheran seminary, their opponents a parallel ridge roughly one mile to the east that held the town's burial ground: Cemetery Ridge.

By the start of July 2, both armies were on the field in full force. If the first day's fight had featured quick footwork, a flurry of blows, and probing for a knockout punch, the second would provide an old-fashioned slugging-match along the length of the Union line. As Pickett tramped to the scene, his corps commander was moving slowly into position to hammer the lower end of Cemetery Ridge, while Ewell struck at Meade's north flank, Cemetery Hill and Culp's Hill. Lee's margin of error had dwindled since the first day, but he still held the initiative. The outcome of the battle, of the invasion, hinged on whether his subordinates, Pickett included, could exploit that initiative to the fullest.[2]

A successful outcome seemed assured late in the afternoon when Pickett's troops, fatigued by their twenty-two-mile, fourteen-hour march, came up the Cashtown Road in rear of Lee's line about three or four miles from Gettysburg. While Pickett halted along a stream named Marsh Creek, dispatching Lieutenant Bright to report his near-arrival to corps headquarters and Major Harrison to carry the same news to General Lee, Longstreet was driving the enemy from successive positions in front of Meade's left. In the end, however, the First Corps would fall short of decisive success, quite possibly because Longstreet had attacked slowly and reluctantly—disliking to commit himself to battle, as he confided to General Hood, "with one boot off"— that is, without Pickett. Meanwhile, Ewell's ongoing assault would also fall short of the breakthrough Lee needed to prolong his presence in the enemy's country.[3]

Despite the frustrating outcome, Lee's army had fought well on all parts of the field; by evening it held strategic positions from which it might yet land a devastating blow. "These partial successes," the army leader later wrote, "determined me to continue the assault next day." Until then, however, Pickett would not be needed; Lee instructed him to remain along Marsh Creek until called upon. Pickett's troops bedded down for the night south of the road from Cashtown. They were permitted a long sleep, not being called up until well after sunrise on July 3.[4]

The belated wake-up call was not the intention of Lee, who believed he had reached an understanding with Longstreet to renew the offensive—this time adding Pickett's command—at sunrise on the third. He had expected Longstreet to have Pickett up with the army before dawn. As when sent into the fight the previous afternoon, however, Longstreet was less than enthusiastic about his assigned task. Rather than continue to attack Cemetery Ridge head-on, as Lee desired, Old Pete wished to conduct a wide circling movement around the enemy's left. His lack of heart for Lee's offensive may have resulted in Pickett's idling in the rear till too late to join a morning assault. When Lee learned of Longstreet's laxity, he did not upbraid his trusted subordinate, but he did take steps to ensure that Pickett lost no further time in reporting at the front.[5]

What Lee had in mind this day was a much wider and deeper assault than on the previous afternoon—a thrust against not only Meade's flanks but his center as well. The Confederate commander believed his opponent had weakened the midpoint of his line to reinforce those sectors struck by Longstreet and Ewell; doubtless the Union center was still thinly held. The day before, a limited assault on that part of the line by the Georgia brigade of Brigadier General Ambrose R. Wright, part of Anderson's division of the Third Corps, had penetrated some 100 or so feet inside Meade's defenses before a lack of support forced its withdrawal. Lee believed that a larger, fresher command such as Pickett's, the only previously uncommitted component of the army—especially if well supported on both flanks—would succeed where Wright had failed.[6]

Lee's plans for supporting Pickett would involve Longstreet and him in controversy. Initially Lee expected that the other divisions of the First Corps, Hood's and McLaws's, would advance toward the Union line alongside Pickett. Concerned that both commands had been worn down by severe fighting and that they must remain in their present positions to protect the right flank against envelopment, Longstreet persuaded his superior to refrain from using them. Others privy to the meeting of minds between Lee and Longstreet, including the army commander's adjutant, Major Taylor, would forever contend that Lee agreed to no changes in his original plan, but evidence suggests that he did.[7]

If not Hood and McLaws, then who to go in beside Pickett, guarding his flanks as he crossed the mile-wide valley under fire? Lee and his senior lieutenant finally agreed to substitute Heth's division of Hill's corps, which held a convenient position along the line north of the point from which Lee planned to launch Pickett. The generals also decided to add to the assault, on Heth's left, two brigades from the Third Corps division of Major General William Dorsey Pender. Both divisions had seen hard fighting earlier in the battle and had lost their commanders to wounds. Neither Lee nor Longstreet, however, appeared to have been aware of the extent of their common weakness.

To replace the still woozy Heth, Lee selected General Pettigrew, whose North Carolina brigade, just up with the army, would form a part of the attack column. To spell General Pender, who had been invalided back to Virginia, the army leader tabbed Major General Isaac R. Trimble, a supernumerary officer travelling with the army in the hope of landing just such an assignment as this.[8]

Pickett's left flank taken care of, Lee and Longstreet planned how to shield its right. Again they selected a segment of Hill's corps—Richard Anderson's division—to play a role in the assault. Unlike the commands of Heth and Pender, Anderson would not advance in line with Pickett but would cover his advance with musketry and artillery-fire. Anderson's division—more specifically, the Alabama brigade of Cadmus Wilcox and three Florida regiments under Colonel David Lang—would move toward the Yankee line only "if necessary" to ensure a breakthrough, an unconscionably vague directive apparently intended to cover all contingencies. Finally, it was supposed that Dearing's batteries—then hurling hot metal at the Union lines from a close-in position nearly midway between the lines—would go forward at the outset of the charge, keeping pace with their infantry comrades and protecting their exposed flank.[9]

If certain aspects of the attack plan might have appeared unclear or open-ended, at least that plan would be carried out by a fair-sized force, comprised roughly of a third of the army. All told, Pettigrew's four brigades, the pair assigned to Trimble, and the two commanded by Wilcox and Lang would add perhaps 15,000 effectives to the 6,200 veterans in the fifteen regiments under Pickett. That many troops, if properly led and fortified by an artillery barrage to neutralize as many of the Yankees in their front as possible, might form a battering-ram hefty enough to pierce the enemy line. After a breakthrough, the attackers could turn to right and left, sweeping the length of Cemetery Ridge and prying Meade out of his strategic position. Should that occur, Lee would find an open road before him—one he might take, surrender demand in hand, to Washington, D.C.

* * *

Pickett shook his men out of their bedrolls at three A.M. on Friday, July 3. After permitting them a quick breakfast, he returned them to the road. He pushed them only a short distance toward Gettys-burg before shunting them onto a farm road that Lee's or Longstreet's staff must have directed to his attention. A little more than half a mile along this road, the column turned left and followed a mill path that brought it to an intersection along a wooded rise, Herr Ridge. Turning right yet again, the men headed due south across the Hagerstown Road, forded a stream known as Willoughby's Run, then veered south-eastward toward Seminary Ridge, three-quarters of a mile away.

Reaching the high ground at about five-thirty, the division fell out to bivouac in a small valley west of Lee's main line, where the trees of Spangler's Woods sheltered them from enemy view. In this place Pickett conducted an inspection of arms and ammunition, then climbed the ridge to study the land in front. At once he and his staff saw that the narrowness of the position assigned them would require one of their brigades to advance in rear of, rather than in line with, the other two. The order in which the division had marched from bivouac that morning dictated that when the advance began, Kemper would form the right flank, Garnett the left, while Armistead would move in rear of one or the other.[10]

As soldiers fell out of formation in rear of Seminary Ridge, many walked about until gaining a view of the valley that stretched toward the Federal line. Not a man liked what he saw. Even at that distance it was clear that the Yankees occupied a formidable position, bristling with artillery pieces whose barrels gleamed in the sunlight. Those guns, if properly handled—and Union artillery was almost always prop-erly handled—would wreak havoc in the ranks of an assaulting force long before it could reach their position. Shot and shell would do damage even before the moving column crossed the Emmitsburg Road, which intersected diagonally the wheat-and clover-filled plain stretch-ing between the lines. Contemplating the prospect of crossing that open space—with or without close support—many men decided that "a very bloody battle" lay ahead. Some used stronger language: a member of the Eighteenth Virginia, Garnett's brigade, shook his head and told his comrades: "This is going to be a heller! Prepare for the worst!"[11]

Completing his inspection tour of the ridge, Pickett located Gen-eral Longstreet; taking seats beneath one of Mr. Spangler's apple trees, they talked strategy. Despite facing a long, unobstructed approach to the enemy line, Pickett expressed the belief that he could put enough troops on the far ridge to drive Meade's people away. Longstreet was not so sure. As he had been on the previous day, the corps leader entertained strong doubts that he could accomplish what Lee was asking of him. Suddenly Lee himself rode up, whereupon Longstreet made bold to speak his mind, stressing that though his corps would make a supreme effort, "no troops could dislodge the enemy from their strong position."

Curiously, Lee turned to some of the soldiers resting nearby and asked if they felt the same way. Anyone could have predicted the response; not a man in the division would ever admit that he might fail Marse Robert. An enlisted man of the Eleventh Virginia, typical of Lee's audience, declared to his comrades: "Boys, many a one of us will bite the dust here today but we will say to Gen. Lee if he wants them driven out we will do it."[12]

* * *

It is difficult to characterize Pickett's state of mind in the hours prior to the charge. To the account of his optimistic prediction under the apple tree may be added the claim of Colonel E. Porter Alexander, Longstreet's acting chief of artillery—whose pre-attack barrage would largely determine when Pickett's men would start forward—that Pickett was in "excellent spirits & sanguine of success." Still another who spoke to Pickett in the hours before the charge—his sometime West Point friend B. D. Fry, now commanding a brigade under Pettigrew and on whose right flank Pickett's command would dress—testified that the division leader "expressed great confidence in the ability of our troops to drive the enemy after they had been 'demoralized by our artillery'."[13]

The impression of confidence that Pickett presented this day may have represented genuine conviction—or it may have been a pose. Like those of his troops who responded to Lee's query, he would not have wished to give his superiors the impression he lacked the heart or the will to carry out his assigned orders. Nor would he have wanted his soldiers to see him downcast or nervous for fear his attitude might infect them, choking off the remote possibility of success. But Pickett had eyes at least as sharp as theirs and his capacity for self-delusion was no greater than any other man's.

In the hours of waiting that preceded Alexander's cannonade, Pickett conversed with comrades seemingly less confident of success than he. The concerns they expressed would have given him cause to revise any sanguine opinions he might have entertained initially. One to whom he spoke was Lieutenant Colonel G. T. Gordon of the Thirty-fourth North Carolina, an outfit assigned to General Trimble. Gordon, a former officer of British marines whom Pickett had wined and dined on San Juan Island in 1860, doubted the feasibility of reaching, let alone taking, the Yankee position. He was frank in telling Pickett that his regiment hoped to avoid taking part, although "I will go as far with you as any other man, if only for old acquaintance sake. . . ."[14]

Even without such warnings, Pickett ought to have seen that what lay ahead was a formidable if not an impossible task. His first sight of the gun-crowned ridge would have told him that even if Alexander could provide his column with a covering fire every step of the way, those cannon and the riflemen that surrounded them would cut down an attacking force with the ease and precision of a thresher chewing wheat. Indeed, just before the charge started, two officers in the Eighth Virginia heard Pickett advise General Garnett to move as rapidly as possible across the field, "for in my opinion you are going to catch hell."[15]

It seems unlikely that Pickett believed his men could take—could even reach—Cemetery Ridge without substantial loss. He must have carefully considered the prospect that the attack would end a bloody failure. To be sure, there were grounds for hoping otherwise, and while unwilling to describe Pickett as confident Longstreet did characterize him as "quite hopeful."[16]

If the enthusiasm others believed they saw in Pickett represented play-acting, another, more cynical explanation must be considered. Pickett's attitude may have stemmed from the knowledge that he was not going to face the same consequences that awaited his men. Well before his troops went forward, he appears to have made a decision to direct them not from the front line but from a position well to the rear, out of harm's reach.

Alexander's cannonade—conducted by more than 120 guns atop and in front of the ridge, in some places crowded hub-to-hub— began at approximately one P.M. By this point Pickett had moved his brigades to the east side of the high ground and had informed Longstreet of his readiness to advance whenever directed. Some indication of the reception awaiting his division was already available, for the barrage drew a furious counterbattery fire from Cemetery Ridge as well as from flanking positions to north and south. With a deafening roar the Yankee artillery hurled shot and shell so far across the valley as to make it clear they could savage the Confederates well short of the high ground.[17]

The return fire was physically as well as emotionally damaging. It created havoc among the regiments of Kemper and Garnett, whose men had been directed to lie down so as to minimize the targets they would make of themselves. This precaution availed them little; as Kemper later recalled of his troops, "the enemy's hail of shot pelted them and ploughed [*sic*] through them, and sometimes the fragments of a dozen mangled men were thrown in and about the trench left by a single missile." To show his concern and share their danger, General Longstreet rode "slowly and alone immediately in

Library of Congress
James L. Kemper

front of our entire line," a gesture of fearless composure that Kemper considered "the grandest moral spectacle of the war." Pickett, it may be noted, made no similar display then or later.[18]

While not himself under fire, Pickett appears not to have taken the barrage too calmly. Aware that Longstreet had asked Alexander to recommend "the most opportune moment for our attack" based on the enemy's response to his cannonade, Pickett at least twice sent couriers to ask the colonel if the men should go in. Although he had originally intended to give an early go-ahead, Alexander both times replied in the negative. For almost two hours, as his guns and howitzers pounded away without noticeable effect on Union retaliatory fire, the artillerist grew dejected about what he was accomplishing and pessimistic about the effectiveness of an infantry assault.[19]

At about two-thirty, doubting that any diminution of return fire was possible, Alexander sent a message to Pickett: "If you are to advance at all, you must come at once or we will not be able to support you as we ought, but the enemy's fire has not slackened materially & there are still 18 guns firing from the cemetery." Only a few minutes after his messenger galloped off, Alexander suddenly perceived a slackening of fire from Cemetery Ridge and upon closer look, found that the cannon had been withdrawn from the graveyard. When another five minutes passed without replacements coming up, he sent a second, fateful summons to Pickett: "The eighteen guns have been drawn off. For Gods sake come on quick or we cannot support you. . . ." By then Pickett, holding Alexander's first communique, had ridden up to his corps commander to ask if his men should move out. He carried Longstreet's mute but unmistakable reply to his men, formed them into a column, tried to align their left flank with Pettigrew's right, then led the way forward.[20]

After Pickett left his side, Longstreet mounted and rode to the far left flank of the artillery line where he found Alexander. When the colonel bewailed the unavailability of several guns promised him by Lee's headquarters and the paucity of long-range ammunition that would keep Dearing's battalion from advancing on Pickett's right as originally planned, Longstreet seriously considered recalling Pickett before it was too late. But by then the division leader was coming up at the head of the troops he had just exhorted to do their duty as Virginians. Longstreet hesitated, struck by the appearance of his favorite subordinate. Many years later he would recall with brilliant clarity Pickett riding "gracefully, with his jaunty cap raked well over on his right ear and his long auburn locks, nicely dressed, hanging almost to his shoulders. He seemed rather a holiday soldier than a general at the head of a column which was about to make one of the grandest, most desperate assaults recorded in the annals of wars."[21]

* * *

Pickett's conduct during the charge has ever been a matter of dispute. For many years after the war many of the survivors of the attack, along with Pickett's staff, his widow, and his friends, would maintain that the general had done his duty nobly, accompanying his men into the muzzles of the Yankee guns. Other veterans claimed to have seen him cowering in the rear, drunk or otherwise acting in a manner deserving of court-martial.[22]

Neither of these contentions appears valid. While it is true that Pickett failed to share in the dangers and the glories of the attack on July 3, he did not skulk off into a safe haven under circumstances that support charges of cowardice. Pickett seems to have conceived of his role as that of a directing hand, not as a leader making a conspicuous display of courage to inspire and hearten the troops; his elected role need not have been played out on the front line. Even by

the battlefield customs of his day, which stressed personal leadership, his was an entirely defensible stance: mid-nineteenth-century
tactics did not dictate that a division leader go in with his assaulting
troops—rather, that he position himself in such a way as to supervise
the movement, save it from error, and ensure that it delivered maxi-
mum power against its objectives. This is just what Pickett did.

Regardless of the fact that his name would attach itself to the
assault as a whole, Pickett's actions throughout July 3 are consistent
with the view that he considered himself responsible for the conduct
of his division alone. No one, then or afterward, heard him speak of
himself as commanding the entire attack force. Before the charge, he
did not confer with Pettigrew, Trimble, Anderson, or anyone else with
whom an overall commander would have worked out support arrangements. Neither did Lee, Longstreet, or any other superior ever suggested that Pickett had charge of any force besides that which bore
his name.

Justifiably, in view of Pickett's limited jurisdiction, he placed himself in the rear and on the flanks of his command, where he had a
wide, deep, and virtually unobstructed view of its operations. Once
the columns swept past him, he confined himself to sending information and instructions to his brigade leaders, to recommending changes
of direction as needed, and to warning of threats to flanks and rear
that only he could clearly discern.[23]

The most detailed, objective, and credible description of Pickett's
whereabouts during the attack comes from his orderly and courier,
Private Thomas R. Friend, who was at his side for the duration of the
assault. Friend reported that when the column began its advance
Pickett and his staff moved forward in close accompaniment, taking
position between the ranks. Pickett kept pace with the division almost until its head struck the Emmitsburg Road. Since the Union
guns had never stopped shelling, he would have come under their fire
well before this time. To spare his troops as much as possible from
the leaden hail, near the road he called on them to double-quick to
the front, adding, "Boys, give them a cheer!"

At about this point Pickett must have passed to the far right of
the column, for Friend recalled riding with him to the edge of a peach
orchard in which a part of Longstreet's corps had seen hot action the
day before; the grove lay not far from the right flank of Kemper's initial path of advance. From the orchard, Friend noted, Pickett "rode off
from his staff in a left obliqed [oblique] direction," heading toward
Kemper's rear. "He then dismounted, and walked some distance, and
then remounted and rode towards his division. . . ." After getting a
close-in view of his troops as they neared Cemetery Ridge under a
barrage of rifle fire as well as a torrent of shells—again, presumably,

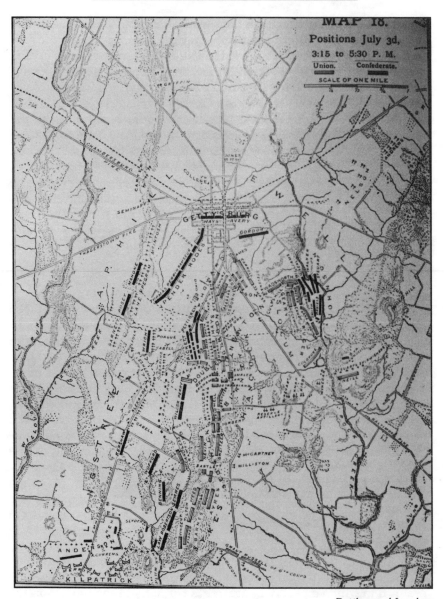

Map of Battle of Gettysburg—Third Day

making a target of himself—Pickett wheeled back to the flank and rode out of the line of fire.[24]

Although the orderly is not specific about Pickett's subsequent movements, based on the accounts of those who saw or claimed to have seen Pickett at some point in the latter stages of the charge (including more than one officer who wished to indict Pickett for cow-ardice), it appears that while his men closed with the Federals, Pickett and his aides gathered on the Wentz farm, near the intersection of the Emmitsburg Road and the road from the Wheatfield. In this position along the right flank of the artillery line supporting the assault, the general could view his command along its length, monitoring its progress and the degree of precision with which it was coordinating its movements with the men of Pettigrew and Trimble. He may have accompanied his troops less than halfway toward the Union line but Private Friend made a valid point when he wrote that his boss "went as far as any Major General, commanding a division, ought to have gone. . . ." Friend's assertion was seconded by Major Edmund Berke-ley of the Eighth Virginia, who after the war told anyone who asked that as far as he knew, Pickett was not with the men during the at-tack and "if he had been [it] would have been out of his proper place."[25]

Nevertheless, once the question of Pickett's position in regard to the attack came under scrutiny, his historical stature was bound to suffer, for the final assault of July 3 would play a major role in setting the standards of Confederate iconography. From the very first, those who suspected that Pickett had not gone in with his troops condemned him for his behavior. At the height of the assault, couriers from Lee failed to find Pickett up front with his men. One messenger finally reported to Colonel Alexander and asked him if he knew Pickett's whereabouts. "I don't know where General Pickett is," the artillerist replied angrily, jabbing a finger toward Cemetery Ridge. "I know where he *ought* to be. He ought to be there!"

Regardless of the propriety of his taking position in rear, he would always come off badly in comparison with the fate of his fellow-com-manders. Both Pettigrew and Trimble ranged far afield of their proper positions in the assault and ended up taking wounds. Pickett's repu-tation might have made it through the century intact had he acquired his own red badge of courage.[26]

* * *

From his vantage point on the fringes of the attack, Pickett did what he could to influence events, but he found himself a mere by-stander, an impotent witness to tragedy. At a fairly early stage of the attack, before his men reached the Emmitsburg Road, he and his aides advised brigade and regimental commanders in making the series of left and right obliques necessary to direct their advance to the proper sector, the copse of trees that staked out the center of the Union line. At intervals Pickett sought to bring Dearing's guns into support range of his troops. At one point, he and his staff prevented a group of demoralized soldiers from disrupting the momentum of the charge. As the attackers closed in on their objective, Pickett tried to warn them of threats to their left flank by a portion of the Union division of Brigadier General Alexander Hays, coming down from its position astride the ridge; and to the right, where the well-posted Vermont Brigade of Brigadier General George J. Stannard blasted Kemper's unsuspecting troops as they passed the Codori farm.[27]

When resistance grew too heavy and Pettigrew's troops began to waver, uncovering Pickett's left, he tried desperately to hold the line together. He sent Captain Baird and Lieutenant Symington to try to rally the North Carolinians. They failed to do so, whereupon Armistead's brigade passed to the front around and through Garnett's troops in a futile attempt to plug the gap. Armistead spearheaded a small-scale penetration of the Union line, but not enough able-bodied troops remained to help him keep his advantage.[28]

Minutes later, with his own people beginning to give ground, Pickett sent Lieutenant Bright to inform Longstreet that his command might take the ridge but could not possibly hold it without reinforcements. Longstreet authorized the staff officer to ride to Wilcox's position and order him to advance with his own and Lang's brigades. When he got the word, Wilcox moved forward, if rather slowly, but then, blinded by powder smoke, went tragically awry. Instead of obliquing left to conform his movements to Pickett's, Wilcox led his would-be supports straight ahead into the fire of the guns on the ridge and Stannard's sharpshooters. His misdirected thrust ensured that his column would be shredded while Pickett's men were left to face their fate alone.[29]

By the time Wilcox's and Lang's brigades fell back, bleeding, Pickett's division was reeling with mortal wounds. Too late to save it, its commander ordered a retreat. From that point on he could only watch in wide-eyed horror as his men disengaged as best they could and made their way back across the valley in pain, shock, and defeat.

Undoubtedly Pickett felt those same sensations. He may have expected failure, even if he did not voice it, but nothing could have prepared him for the sights and sounds that beset him as this "grand but fatal day" came to an end. His once-mighty division had been reduced to incoherent clumps of leaderless men. As reports filtered in, he learned that all of his brigade commanders were down—Garnett missing and later reported dead, Kemper supposed to be mortally wounded (he would slowly recover but would never return to field command), and Armistead in the hands of the enemy, where he would die early on July 5. All but one of the field-grade officers involved in the assault had been killed or wounded. Although a true estimate would not be quick in coming, eventually army headquarters would determine that Pickett's division had suffered almost 2,700 casualties out of fewer than 6,300 troops engaged; in some outfits manpower losses approached 90 percent. At the regimental level, at least, Pickett's command had virtually ceased to exist as a fighting force.[30]

It was all too much for Pickett, who, upon making his way back to Seminary Ridge, gave way to anguish and despair. One of the first to meet him upon his return was an English-born artillerist. "With tears in his eyes," the man recorded, Pickett stared at the line of guns through which his men had passed at the start of the advance, then exclaimed to their crews: "Why did you not halt my men here? Great God, where, oh! where is my division?"[31]

Stumbling to the rear, Pickett found Longstreet, to whom he cried: "General, I am ruined; my division is gone—it is destroyed." The corps leader tried to assure him otherwise, but Pickett would have none of it. When Lee cantered up minutes later, Pickett had yet to regain his composure. Observing him wandering along the ridge, alone and disheveled, Lee gently admonished him to regroup his division farther to the rear. Looking up abruptly, as though startled by the absurdity of the order, Pickett replied in a low, halting voice that he no longer had a division.[32]

TEN — The Department of North Carolina

For several hours after the great battle Pickett went about his duties slowly and awkwardly, as though dazed by a fall. He could scarcely credit his eyes as he collected what remained of his brigades behind Seminary Ridge and stared at their formless ranks, literally riddled with holes. For a time nothing could bring him up from the depths of melancholy, not even the sympathetic praise of his superiors. In his battle report Longstreet lauded Pickett and his men for the "determined manner" in which they struck the Federal line. The night after the battle, preparing to withdraw from Pennsylvania, Lee remarked to General Imboden, commander of the retreat column: "I never saw troops behave more magnificently than Pickett's division of Virginians did to-day in that grand charge upon the enemy. And if they had been supported as they were to have been . . . we would have held the position and the day would have been ours."[1]

The matter of the promised supports that never reached him furnished Pickett with an opportunity to purge away, at least in small measure, his grief and bitterness. In the immediate aftermath of Cemetery Ridge, before the searing pain of the tragedy could lessen, Pickett wrote a report of his division's operations that ascribed defeat to unconscionable negligence on the part of his support forces. His accusations probably fell hardest on Wilcox, who could never satisfactorily explain his failure to find his way to Pickett's aid, but Pickett may also have taken aim at Pettigrew, Trimble, A. P. Hill, and even Lee.

The latter, who already had drunk too deeply from the cup of suffering, did not wish to see grievances and recriminations finish off his wounded army. He returned Pickett's report with a soft-spoken rebuke: "You and your men have crowned themselves with glory, but we have the enemy to fight, and must carefully, at this critical moment, guard against dissensions which the reflections in your report would create."

Lee asked Pickett to submit a new report but to confine it "to casualties merely," leaving out his opinions as to why so many had occurred. Apparently, Pickett obeyed only to the extent of destroying the original; he never wrote a second. His wife claimed that the criticism that prompted Lee to suppress the first report made its way into a letter her husband wrote her just after the battle, the contents of which she refused to make public. Her assertion to the contrary notwithstanding, it seems unlikely that Pickett's caustic commentary on his colleagues' failure to assist him in his hour of need survived his merciful act of destruction.[2]

* * *

In its wretched condition, Pickett's division would be of little use in any continued campaigning in the North. Once he resolved to withdraw across the Potomac, however, Lee assigned to the survivors care of some 4,000 prisoners of war. In advance of the general withdrawal, Pickett's men would escort the captives to Staunton, Virginia. From that point, Lee later decided, the mounted troops of General Imboden would convey the Yankees to Richmond via Winchester.[3]

Pickett's men spent most of July 4, like the rest of their battered army, waiting for a counterattack none believed Meade would launch. That night, once it had become obvious that the Union commander was not going to copy his enemy's mistake, the retreat began. As Imboden started the supply wagons and ambulances toward the mountains, Pickett and his tattered ranks took to the roads leading west and south, their downcast, dirty, famished-looking prisoners in tow. Despite their own debility, some of the guards expressed sympathy for their charges. "I felt sorry for the poor fellows," wrote a member of the Eighteenth Virginia, "they were nearly starved. . . . I gave them all I had to spare." He added pointedly: "I know what it is to be hungry too well."[4]

The march to the Potomac was long and hard, now that the thrill of invasion and the lure of victory were gone. Pickett did not like his assignment at all; he appeared to consider it a demeaning gesture by

Lee. The latter either heard of or sensed his attitude; on the ninth, the day Pickett ferried many of his men and prisoners across the rain-swollen Potomac, the army leader sent him a detailed explanation that should not have been necessary—a humane gesture on Lee's part as well as a deserved tribute to a veteran command that had bled itself white for the cause:

"It was with reluctance that I imposed upon your gallant division the duty of conveying prisoners to Staunton. I regretted to assign them to such service, as well as to separate them from the army, though temporarily, with which they have been so long and efficiently associated. Though small in numbers, their worth is not diminished. . . . I still have the greatest confidence in your division, and feel assured that with you at its head, it will be able to accomplish any service upon which it may be placed. . . . No one grieves more than I do at the loss suffered by your noble division in the recent conflict, or honors it more for its bravery and gallantry." He closed by promising Pickett an opportunity to recruit his command toward some semblance of its pre-Gettysburg strength.[5]

Pickett should have been mollified by these sentiments. At about the time Lee penned them the division leader seemed finally to emerge from his post-battle depression, regaining something of his old confidence, his hopefulness, even his jauntiness. Returning to Virginia and ridding himself of the prisoners provided some relief as did the return of Corse's brigade, which, finally relieved of its duties at Hanover Junction, rejoined what remained of the division at Winchester on the thirteenth. Not even the news Pickett received en route to Winchester—that Ulysses Grant had forced the surrender of strategic Vicksburg, bagging almost 30,000 Confederates—derailed his spiritual renewal.[6]

For one thing, he had a wedding to look forward to, and a life of bliss with his beloved. Late in July, by which time his command had waded the Shenandoah River to hold the gaps in the Blue Ridge against Meade's advance, Pickett wrote to Sallie in eager anticipation of "that blissful hour" of their union as man and wife. But when would that hour come? "Darling we can not tell, but let us cheer ourselves with the idea that it may not be very far off."

Despite his brightening mood, he could not refrain from dwelling on the ruined hopes his division had left behind in the wake of its "short but terrible" invasion. Nor could he suppress a nagging regret over opportunities lost or squandered: "If the charge made by my gallant Virginians on the fatal third of July had been supported, or even if my other two Brigades had been with me, we would now have been in Washington, and the war ended." But since God had willed otherwise, "would that we had never crossed the Potomac. . . ."[7]

The "blissful hour" awaited the army's return to at least a semi-permanent camp, a goal it attained in the last week of July when Longstreet's corps, followed by Ewell's and Hill's, put down stakes along the Rappahannock near Culpeper Court House. Soon afterward Meade's army took up a fixed position farther north around Warrenton. Reconnaissances and small-unit maneuvers consumed the next two months; during that time, officers left the army on recruiting duty while many enlisted men went home on furlough. The general inactivity provided Pickett with the opportunity Lee hoped he would have: to recruit and reorganize his command. It also gave him time to plan his wedding.

Late in August and early in September Pickett firmed up nuptial details, at long distance, with his betrothed, who after completing her studies had returned to her parents' home in Chuckatuck, slipping inside the Yankee lines. They set a date of September 15 and selected for the site an Episcopal Church in Petersburg that her family had attended. According to Sallie, Longstreet for some reason was unable to grant Pickett a leave during which to marry so he detailed his subordinate to "special duty" in Petersburg on the appointed date.[8]

In actuality, much of Pickett's command was being sent to southside Virginia—the region below the James River—and Pickett was merely accompanying it. While the tempo of activity in Virginia had diminished, events were heating up in the western armies, especially in East Tennessee where Braxton Bragg was heading toward a confrontation with the forces of Rosecrans near Chattanooga. To reinforce Bragg in time for the showdown, the War Department had decided to send Longstreet to him with Hood's and McLaws's divisions. Neither Longstreet nor Lee considered Pickett's division in any shape to accompany the others; at their suggestion, President Davis authorized most of its troops to move to Richmond, Petersburg, and the country in between, relieving other forces earmarked for Longstreet. In its new bailiwick Pickett's command could not only guard important sections of Virginia but also recruit from a fairly large population base. With a wedding on the horizon, the timing could not have been more fortuitous.[9]

The nuptial arrangements were complicated and their implementation entailed no small amount of danger. Fearing her husband-to-be would be captured trying to cross the lines, Sallie would not permit him to claim her at Chuckatuck; she would come to him. On the day before the wedding she set out for Petersburg in company with her father and her uncle, a local physician whose travels between the

Eleanor S. Brockenbrough Library,
The Museum of the Confederacy

General and Mrs. Pickett, 1863

armies Yankee sentinels did not regard as suspicious. Disguised as a farmer, her father drove a wagon full of fodder that concealed her wedding trunks. (Sallie's mother was forced to remain behind to care for her youngest son, who was ill.)

At Waverly Station on the Petersburg & Norfolk Railroad, just inside the Confederate lines, the trio was met by Charles Pickett—

himself a recent groom—and Andrew and Olivia Johnston (the prairie lawyer had returned to Richmond upon the outbreak of war). Under military escort Sallie and her family continued on to Petersburg, where she and Her Soldier were reunited for the first time since the close of the Suffolk Campaign.

Next morning the couple were pronounced man and wife by the Reverend Doctor Platt, rector of Saint Paul's Church, before what Sallie described as "congregated thousands, for soldier and civilian, rich and poor, high and low, were all made welcome by my hero." The bride wore white satin and lace; like Sallie herself, the gown, sewn by a friend of Sallie's grandmother, had been smuggled through the lines. After the ceremony bride and groom entrained for Richmond "amidst the salute of guns, hearty cheers, and chimes and bands and bugles."

According to Sallie, the reception was a gala affair, attended by a small army of Confederate officials including Jefferson Davis and his cabinet. Notable for his absence, however, was the man who had made the wedding possible, James Longstreet having entrained for Tennessee only the day before. The wedding feast was spare, in keeping with wartime austerity; it featured turkey, and terrapin soup. Some of the guests provided additional courses; among the wedding gifts was a fruit-cake baked by Mrs. Robert E. Lee. Another wedding gift highly prized by the guests of honor was a brace of servants from the Pickett estate on Turkey Island. They would augment the couple's small staff of slaves including Jachin, the body-servant who had attended Pickett in camp and field since the earliest days of the war.

The happy couple honeymooned on Turkey Island. They strolled the grounds hand in hand, signing ballads and hymns including the groom's favorite selection from the Book of Common Prayer, "Guide Me, Oh Thou Great Jehovah." They hunted birds and rabbits, "more for the meat," Sallie admitted, "than the sport." The days they spent on the old plantation—miles from Yankee occupation and a world away from the horrors of Gettysburg—created memories they would treasure till the end of their lives.[10]

* * *

One of the most thoughtful wedding gifts came eight days after the ceremony, in the form of a directive from the War Department assigning Pickett to command the Department of North Carolina. His new domain embraced territory and troops between the James and the Cape Fear Rivers, with headquarters at Petersburg. Not only did the assignment mean he would not have to leave his bride and return to Lee's army, it provided the couple with a five-story house for their private use. Thus they would not share the fate of so many wartime marrieds—a long and lonely separation.[11]

Unfortunately Pickett's new duties were so many and the affairs of his vast realm so complicated and taxing that for the next eight months he and his bride had relatively little time together. Often he spent all day and part of the night at his headquarters; at frequent intervals he was called to far-off corners of his department on inspection tours and for strategy sessions. During such times La Salle would see her husband only when she accompanied the family slaves who carried him his meals.

Being kept apart from his young bride was bad enough, but the demands made on Pickett's time by his new job threatened to prevent him from accomplishing a task of paramount importance: the rejuvenation of his division. Upon taking up the post, he had obtained from the War Office assurances that once active campaign resumed he and his command would return to Lee's army. In the interim, he must piece the division back together, assimilating not only recruits but conscripts, released prisoners, and detached and wounded men returning to their regiments.

To do all this, he needed to keep his division intact and readily accessible. Instead, soon after reaching Petersburg he saw his division fragmented and moved beyond his reach. Garnett's old brigade, under now-Brigadier General Hunton, and Kemper's brigade, now led by Colonel William R. ("Buck") Terry, had been sent to the fortified camp at Chaffin's Farm, below the capital, where both commands had become part of the Department of Richmond. To counter anticipated Federal advances, the government later dispatched Terry's men to Hanover Junction while sending Corse's brigade toward the Tennessee border where it temporarily became part of Major General Samuel Jones's Department of Western Virginia. Of Pickett's organic division only Armistead's much-depleted brigade had accompanied its division leader to his new station. In late September the War Office assigned the brigade to Brigadier General Seth Barton, a Virginia native with an uneven combat record who had been captured at Vicksburg and subsequently paroled.[12]

Compensation for Pickett's losses came in the guise of two North Carolina brigades, under Brigadier Generals Matt W. Ransom and Thomas L. Clingman. At least on paper, Pickett's departmental force was a substantial one: as of the end of the year, it numbered more than 7,300 foot soldiers, 1,350 cavalrymen, and 2,000 artillerists, the latter including Dearing's trusted battalion. The troops, however, were spread thinly to cover the cities of Petersburg, Weldon, and Kinston as well as dozens of outposts, supply depots, and rail stations stretching toward Wilmington.[13]

Despite Pickett's fears, his division's rebuilding program appeared to make some progress throughout the autumn of 1863. Colonel Charles C. Flowerree of the Seventh Virginia, stationed at Chaffin's Farm, noted that by October Hunton's and Terry's brigades "had grown comparatively strong" from a fairly steady influx of enlistees and conscripts. The quality of the newcomers was, however, a matter of conjecture. The historian of the First Virginia, also encamped on the James, noted of the new additions: "Some of them made excellent soldiers, but many were of no use at all, and should not have been sent into the field." Because the Confederacy had raised the age limitations on drafted men and enlistees, many were so old they "looked like they had been resurrected from the grave, after laying therein for twenty years or more."[14]

Pickett himself was certain that much remained to be done if the division were to regain its old strength. Early in October he heard a report that Longstreet, still in the West, was about to call the division to his side. Pickett interceded with General Cooper for more time to rebuild his ranks, then containing fewer than 4,000 men: "The plan of reorganizing this shattered division is in fact but just commenced." Until detachments had been returned and large numbers of new men absorbed, "it will not be the crack division is was, and I decidedly would not like to go into action with it."

His plea to keep his scattered command out of the field "till it is fit for service" was only partially effective. While the division was not dispatched to the West, General Cooper decided to send Barton's brigade to Kinston, then under threat of Union attack, and later to Weldon. No sooner had Barton returned to Petersburg in late November than the War Office wanted a large part of his command to join Hunton and Terry below Richmond to counter a move by Meade's army at the outset of the Mine Run Campaign. Pickett did what he could to help but he was pained by the prospect of a long estrangement. In exasperation he wired Seddon that "if I am to take my division into the field, I wish to take the whole division, and not a portion of it, as I did at Gettysburg, and I beg of you not to split it up when going into action. If I am to keep command of this department, do not entirely denude it."[15]

Repeated detachments from his old division were bad enough, but through fall and winter Pickett experienced difficulty in hanging onto other elements of his assigned force. At frequent intervals well into the new year Cooper and Seddon ordered elements of Ransom's and Clingman's brigades out of their department. While most of the

losses were of short duration, Pickett occasionally found himself trying to hold Petersburg with a scratch force.[16]

Pickett was also concerned by the War Department's inability or
unwillingness to address the weaknesses of the works along the northern and southern approaches to Petersburg. Not even face-to-face
meetings with the authorities resulted in fortifications or obstruc-
tions being erected in the lower James. Without such protection enemy forces in North Carolina might be tempted to cross into the Old
Dominion and attack Pickett's headquarters.

His fears about the lower reaches of his realm were justified.
Troops operating out of Plymouth, Washington, Newport Barracks,
the recently reinforced garrison at New Bern, and other coastal and
inland posts raided through his department with impunity, tearing
up railroad track, downing telegraph lines, harassing secessionists,
and burning and looting with abandon. Occasionally he travelled to
the most threatened areas, hoping personally to supervise a defense
effort, but usually got there too late to stop the depredations or bag
the raiders.[17]

Library of Congress
Benjamin F. Butler

Most of Pickett's secu-
rity problems in the Tarheel
State were the work of a
notorious politician-gen-
eral, Major General Ben-
jamin F. Butler, who in
early November took com-
mand of the Union Depart-
ment of Virginia and North
Carolina. From his head-
quarters at Fort Monroe,
Butler—whose hard-war
policies when commanding
captured New Orleans in
1862 had won him the ap-
pellation "Beast" and had
prompted Jefferson Davis
to brand him a war crimi-
nal—launched an unend-
ing series of raids throughout Pickett's department
during the winter of 1863-64, the most destructive taking place in
northeastern North Carolina.

Early in December an expedition under one of Butler's subordinates, Brigadier General Edward A. Wild, a one-armed abolitionist
from Massachusetts who commanded a brigade of United States Col-

ored Troops, did a particularly effective job of laying waste to Camden and Pasquotank Counties, burning, confiscating, liberating slaves, and overwhelming bands of Confederate regulars and militia. Outside Elizabeth City Wild capped his terroristic spree by hanging a Rebel soldier, one Daniel Bright, whom he accused of guerrilla activities.[18]

Pickett took Wild's raid personally, as though physically outraged and violated. "It makes my blood boil," he wrote, "to think of these enormities being practiced, and we have no way of arresting them." Upon reflection, however, he came up with a few ideas. As he informed General Cooper, to stop "these fiends, backed, or rather instigated, by such a beast as Butler is . . . there is but one resource [recourse]—to hang at once every one captured belonging to the expedition, and afterward any one caught who belongs to Butler's department." Without awaiting official approval, he took his own advice, hanging a black soldier captured during Wild's expedition and describing the act as retaliation for the execution of Private Bright.

Pickett's action only spurred General Wild to further atrocities. To safeguard other captives in Rebel hands, he took hostages including the wives of two prominent Confederate citizens, one of whom was aged and unwell. This was too much for Pickett, who considered men like Butler and Wild—guilty of looting, turning slaves against their masters, and violating Southern womanhood—to be devils incarnate. "Let us come to a definite understanding with these heathens at once," he advised General Cooper. "Butler cannot be allowed to rule here as he did in New Orleans. His course must be stopped," even if it meant stooping to his level of warfare.

While Pickett felt great antipathy for opponents such as these, he hated another class of enemy even more. His problems in defending his large domain with limited resources were immeasurably worsened by the hostility and treachery of a large portion of the citizenry of his department. North Carolina had long been a haven for "tories" who openly supported U.S. troops. What was worse, hundreds of local Unionists engaged in the most violent guerrilla activities, shooting and burning out their secessionist neighbors, waylaying Confederate supply trains, attacking outposts. It was Pickett's Northern Neck experience all over again, but with an added helping of brutality.

Pickett had always entertained a great distaste for turncoats, those who would be disloyal to their state, their government, their cause. But he developed an especial enmity toward the North Carolina breed, whom he came to regard as a kind of sub-species of humanity. Though he had recommended the hanging of raiders in uniform, that seemed too kind a fate for these cutthroats and plunderers who continually thwarted Pickett's plans to bring order and stability to what should have been a quiet corner of the Confederacy.[19]

* * *

Early in January 1864 General Lee proposed to President Davis that an advance be made on New Bern by forces from Pickett's department. That garrison on the Neuse and Trent Rivers, which since 1862 had threatened Confederate communications and furnished raiding parties to devastate the countryside, "has been so long unmolested, and experiences such a feeling of security, that it is represented as careless." Lee's plan, which he would furnish troops to help implement, called for a naval force to descend the Neuse at night, capturing Yankee gunboats and chasing the enemy from their riverside works, while large land units attacked the post in front and rear. Success would bring the Confederates "a large amount of provisions and other supplies . . . much wanted for this army, besides much that is reported in the country that will thus be made accessible to us."

Distressed by the deteriorating situation in North Carolina, the President readily assented to the plan, subsequently expanded to include a simultaneous movement against nearby Newport Barracks. Late in January Lee detached the infantry brigade of the young and highly capable Brigadier General Robert F. Hoke, a North Carolina native. Lee recommended Hoke to command the expedition, but when the Richmond authorities decided that an officer of higher rank should lead, Pickett became the consensus choice. Well in advance of the mission, he familiarized himself with Lee's strategy, studied the best means of cooperating with the naval contingent of Commander J. Taylor Wood, and made the logistical arrangements to bring to Kinston, the jumping-off point of the expedition, Hoke's column and the other forces that would take part, including Terry's and Barton's brigades.[20]

In the last days of January, Pickett bade farewell to his young bride, now three months pregnant, and with his staff rode off to oversee what he considered the most important operation assigned him since last July 3. His elation did not last. A few days later, the mission at an end, he wrote Sallie that "it seems an age, my darling, since we rode away, leaving you . . . standing in that wonderful grove of maiden trees. I veil the annoying, disappointing scenes since then and see again the beautiful picture of my own bride, clothed in white. . . ."[21]

"Annoying" and "disappointing" failed to do justice to the bungled operation outside New Bern, which produced frustration, defeat, recrimination among its leaders, and black marks against Pickett's name in the ledgers of Confederate officialdom. At bottom, that project had failed through a lack of adequate reconnaissance and a want of resolution on the part of General Barton, who commanded one of the three columns that converged on New Bern on the morning of February 1. Then and there Barton confirmed Pickett's long-held suspicions as to his reliability.

The other elements of the expedition did their job well. On the first, Commander Wood's naval forces ran down the Neuse to surprise the enemy's gunboats, capturing one. Meanwhile, Pickett, with the brigades of Hoke, Corse, and Clingman and supporting units of all arms, moved against New Bern from the north, crossing Batchelder's Creek and routing outlying forces of substantial size.

After penetrating to within a mile of the garrison, Pickett and Hoke halted their drive till they could confirm Barton's success on the opposite side of the town. After long hours of waiting, however, they learned that Barton, at the head of a strike force composed of his own brigade, Terry's, and most of Matt Ransom's plus 600 cavalry and fourteen cannon, had failed to cross Brice's Creek and take a line of fortifications along the Neuse. A belated reconnaissance had convinced Barton that those defenses were impregnable; thus, he withheld his attack, contenting himself with dosing the defenders with artillery-fire. He would later contend that he had been "entirely misinformed as to the strength of the place," which would have inflicted exorbitant losses on his column.[22]

Not till the morning of the second did Pickett learn the grim details of Barton's failure. The news infuriated him, for now the element of surprise—which General Lee had identified as the key feature of the operation—had been lost. In his report Pickett noted that "the whole plan by which the place was to be reduced having failed, I deemed it prudent, after consultation with my officers, to withdraw, which we did at our leisure." Reunited with Barton at Kinston, he reprimanded his subordinate for failure to obey orders; once back at Petersburg, he demanded the brigadier be court-martialed. A disappointed Lee agreed that a court should be convened, but it never was, and Barton, to Pickett's dismay, retained command of Armistead's old brigade.[23]

Despite Barton's culpability, official blame for the failure attached itself to Pickett, as senior commander. Historians generally uphold this judgment, believing that had Hoke headed the operation somehow (they do not say how) the operation would have succeeded. Such a verdict seems too harsh: Pickett was, after all, carrying out a plan framed by Lee and based on suggestions by Hoke. If the plan failed, its creators should be held accountable to the same degree as the officer who supervised its execution. The same notion appears to have troubled Lee, who a week after the expedition returned had the poor grace to suggest that Pickett was guilty of adhering too faithfully to the plan: he should "have changed the mode of attack if circumstances prompted it."[24]

In the aftermath of defeat Pickett took out his anger and frustration on a band of enemy captives, but the measure of his satisfaction was small and the repercussions would haunt him for years to come. After turning away from the approaches to New Bern, Pickett's men captured the most extended of New Bern's outposts, situated at Beach Grove, several miles from the main garrison; their prisoners included numerous members of the Second North Carolina (Union) Volunteers. When marched to the rear, several captives were identified by former comrades in Hoke's command as deserters from local defense units taken into Confederate service. All told, twenty-two turncoats were unmasked and separated from the other prisoners.[25]

The deserters were brought before Pickett, who according to one eyewitness cursed and threatened them, at one point exclaiming, "I'll have you shot, and all other damned rascals who desert!" It appears that the evils of desertion had been on Pickett's mind throughout the operation; during the march to New Bern, someone had heard him mutter that "every God-damned man who didn't do his duty, or deserted, ought to be shot or hung." While still gagging on the bitter taste of defeat, he acted on his conviction. At Kinston he set up a court composed of Virginia, North Carolina, and Georgia officers, hauled the deserters-in-arms before it, and approved the death sentences it quickly handed down. The twenty-two men would be hanged in a field behind the city jail where they had been held since being brought to the city.[26]

When the Yankees learned of the fate awaiting the Beach Grove captives, the local commander, General Peck, sought assurances that Pickett would accord them "the same treatment in all respects as you will mete out to other prisoners of war." Pickett replied in an angry and sarcastic tone that launched a nasty debate over the rights of POWs. When Peck innocently furnished Pickett with a lengthy list of captives from the Second North Carolina, Pickett used it to try to determine if he held any traitors other than those previously identified. Rather sadistically, he informed Peck that the list would "prevent any mercy being shown any of the remaining number, should proper and just proof be brought of their having deserted the Confederate colors. . . ."[27]

The bitter, vituperative correspondence did Pickett no credit, especially when Peck brought to his attention a newspaper report that some of Pickett's troops had hanged a captured African-American soldier who had killed a Confederate colonel in battle. Pickett branded the report "ridiculous" but added that "had I caught any negro who had killed officer, soldier, or citizen of the Confederate States I should have caused him to be immediately executed." Noting that Peck had threatened to hang a Confederate prisoner should the report be verified, Pickett boasted that "I have in my hands and subject to my orders, captured in the recent operations in this department, some 450 officers and men of the U.S. Army, and for every man you hang I will hang 10 of the U.S. Army."[28]

By the time Pickett harangued General Peck, the issue of the captured deserters was moot, for the sentence of Pickett's court-martial had already been carried out. The public executions had taken place within three weeks of the return from New Bern, two of the convicted men dying on February 5, five more a week later, thirteen others on February 15, and the remaining two on the twenty-second. Reportedly, the victims included a soldier with severe physical deformities and a fourteen-year-old drummer boy.[29]

Pickett considered the executions—which, as he later claimed, had been approved by the Confederate government—to have been carried out in accordance with the conventions of war. Traditionally, capital punishment had been the fate of deserters captured in arms against their former comrades. In Pickett's mind the hangings were no less justified than those of the San Patricio captives, whose death his heroics at Chapultepec had triggered.

Whatever precedents the department commander might cite, however, there was no justifying Pickett's descent to the level of those, like Butler and Wild, he professed to despise as the vilest of military criminals. By early 1864 the war was turning into a grim, hate-filled struggle that knew few rules and no niceties, and Pickett was changing to fit the pattern.[30]

ELEVEN — Return to Glory

The approach of spring found Pickett still fretting about the promiscuous detaching of his field units and his inability to interest the War Department in strengthening the defenses of Petersburg. By early March 1864, the government had dispatched Terry's brigade to assist Major General William H. C. Whiting, Pickett's counterpart at Wilmington, in blocking an anticipated Union advance; meanwhile, Corse's brigade was in Kinston on a similar mission. Oblivious to Pickett's weakened condition, the authorities in Richmond, the focal point of a Union cavalry raid, petitioned him to send "if possible" two brigades to augment Hunton's command, still stationed below the capital. In fact it was not possible to comply with this request, but Pickett sent all the troops he had, two regiments from Clingman's brigade. Clingman's departure left Petersburg virtually unguarded.[1]

Unable to take time away from his hectic schedule to come home, Pickett sent Sallie a note of apology for his continued absence, explaining that "I have been hard at work my pet trying in every way with my limited force to strengthen my front" while filling requests to support every garrison commander in Virginia and North Carolina. It was, he confessed, a mind-numbing task.

By mid-March, with warm weather returning to Virginia and a resumption of active campaigning in the offing, he was feeling more harassed than usual. Only days earlier, his old friend Ulysses Grant, the North's most successful field commander, had been appointed general-in-chief of the Union armies with the announced intention of accompanying Meade's Army of the Potomac on its renewed push

Library of Congress
Ulysses S. Grant

toward the seat of the Confederacy. "Grant says he intends taking his 4th of July dinner in Richmond," he told Sallie, a boast that suggested a massive effort in Virginia, one to dwarf all that preceded it. Pickett's fervent hope was that Lee would remember his promise to recall him, at the head of his reinvigorated division, before the fighting began.[2]

Thoughts about the coming campaign prompted concern that Richmond would not be Grant's only objective. If the Yankees were finally serious about taking the capital, they might try to cut its supply lines to the south, which meant neutralizing Petersburg. Then, too, Grant might strike Richmond from below rather than above; in that event he would have to seize Petersburg to protect his own line of operations. In either case, lacking an adequate garrison, Pickett might wind up in a Yankee prison camp.

Rather than heed Pickett's repeated requests for reinforcements, the authorities continued to find reasons to haul his meager force to remote corners of his department. Late in March Braxton Bragg, recently installed as Jefferson Davis's chief military advisor, asked Pickett to provide a plan of operations against some of the larger outposts in North Carolina. Pickett's response, submitted on April 6, was a detailed proposal for an attack on the garrison at Plymouth, using Kemper's, Ransom's, and an unspecified third brigade of infantry plus a sizable cavalry force under James Dearing and four light batteries, Pickett to command the whole.[3]

Both Bragg and General Lee, who saw a copy of Pickett's plan, considered it well-researched and workable. Before mid-April the War Department determined to implement the plan pretty much as Pickett had devised, but without him. Bragg, who was still upset over the failure of the New Bern expedition, for which he blamed Pickett, decreed that the Plymouth project be entrusted to young General Hoke, whose brigade would again be detached from Lee to augment the forces to be withdrawn from Pickett's department. The expedition got under way in April.[4]

Understandably upset at being left out, Pickett probably felt a jolt of envy when he learned of Hoke's smashing success outside Plymouth, which fell to the Confederates after a two-day siege ending on the twentieth. He was likewise unhappy over his latest manpower loss. As Hoke's force had consisted largely of Pickett's troops—Ransom's and Terry's brigades plus small detachments from Corse's and Clingman's—Pickett hoped those commands would be returned to him upon Plymouth's surrender. Instead, they accompanied Hoke to Washington, preparatory to a new strike at New Bern. Here was a vexing development for the commander of the Department of North Carolina. It was hard enough to accept the fact that Hoke, using Pickett's own troops, was attempting to succeed where Pickett had failed; but no one could say how soon those troops would be returned to their ordained leader.[5]

The situation around Petersburg may have been undesirable but at least after April 23 Pickett could share the responsibilities it entailed and the headaches it caused. On that date General Pierre G. T. Beauregard, the Louisiana Creole who had been among the South's earliest heroes—victor at Fort Sumter and First Manassas—was appointed to command Confederate forces in North Carolina and Southside Virginia. In organizing his department Beauregard, who most recently had directed the defense of Charleston, created three districts, one of which—embracing the territory between the James and Roanoke Rivers—he assigned to Pickett.[6]

Beauregard's assumption of command suggested that Pickett would breathe more easily. It was common knowledge that the new commander—a grandiose planner, a humorless martinet, and a shameless self-promoter—had never been on intimate terms with Jefferson Davis. Still, Pickett now had an immediate superior who presumably would be as concerned as he was about inadequate defenses and defenders.

As it turned out, Beauregard's appointment came a little too late for Pickett's peace of mind. Before the Creole could reach Virginia at the head of many of the troops he had led in South Carolina, signs of enemy activity south of the James, which had been accumulating for several weeks, suddenly told Pickett that his worst fears were about to be realized.

* * *

From Petersburg Pickett oversaw a wide-ranging network of scouts and spies that helped him keep abreast of events in his department. Since early in the year his people in Hampton Roads had been warning of a Yankee buildup on and adjacent to the Peninsula. Although its objectives would not be apparent for some time, the troop increase appeared to signal an offensive from Fort Monroe by General Butler, doubtless in cooperation with Grant's operations farther north. Throughout the winter and into the spring Pickett had relayed the intelligence to Richmond, although his superiors did not always appear receptive to it. On April 16, for instance, General Bragg criticized him for passing along contradictory reports of enemy movements and exaggerated estimates of troop strengths. Stung by the implication that he was responsible for refining the raw intelligence before relaying it to Richmond, Pickett complained that Bragg's "tone is as harsh as the inferences to be drawn are unmerited."[7]

The capital continued to appear as disinclined to heed Pickett's scouting reports—which became more focused and accurate as time went on—as it had been to address his pleas for strengthened defenses. Hopeful that he would fare better with his new superior, on April 28 Pickett informed Beauregard (supposedly en route to Petersburg but as yet in North Carolina) that 50,000 Federals including 10,000 Colored Troops had been added to Butler's department while dozens of newly arrived men-of-war, gunboats, and troopships were clogging Hampton Roads. Pickett gave credence to reports that "the enemy will either advance up the Peninsula or will move by transports down river and up the James." The information was accurate and his conclusions were valid, but when passing the intelligence on to General Bragg Beauregard had only one comment: Pickett's troop estimates were "much exaggerated."[8]

Happily, Pickett would not have to deal with obtuse superiors much longer. On May 4, as warm breezes teased the Southside with an early hint of summer, Lee ordered Pickett to report for duty with the Army of Northern Virginia; he would return to the command of his division, which was being recalled from its far-flung posts of duty. Lee's correspondent could not remember feeling so elated at any point in his military career. The thought of quitting a desk job beset by problems great and small for an important command in the field was akin to leaving a cell for a romp in the wide outdoors. His only regret was that he would have to leave Sallie, an especially unhappy prospect given the fact that she had been unwell of late, apparently the result of a difficult pregnancy. Having lost two wives to natal complications, Pickett would have preferred to remain at her side, ensuring that she received the closest medical attention.[9]

At the last minute, he found he did not have to leave; in fact, he could not leave. On the morning of the fifth, before he could kiss his bride farewell and board a train for Hanover Junction, Pickett learned that a Union fleet was ascending the James, carrying an indeterminate number of troops. Later he heard that hundreds if not thousands of Yankees were debarking at City Point, a landing on the Appomattox opposite that river's confluence with the James, nine miles northeast of Petersburg. Later still came word that many more troops under Ben Butler—parts of two army corps, in fact—had disembarked across and upriver from City Point and had begun to construct works astride a peninsula known as Bermuda Hundred, twelve miles from Richmond. Surely the Confederate capital was the invader's target;

Battles and Leaders

Map of the Bermuda Hundred Campaign

quite possibly, the Cockade City was a secondary objective. For George Pickett, an early reunion with the Army of Northern Virginia was out of the question.[10]

An ashen-faced Pickett returned to his headquarters to find himself immersed in a crisis that quickly threatened to sweep him under. Reports flooded in to describe fortifications going up on both sides of the Appomattox, supply vessels unloading everything from crackers to cannon, Yankee cavalry raiding south and west of the capital, and fiends with crowbars and axes heading for Lee's lifeline, the railroad between Richmond and Petersburg. Pickett frantically wired the War Department for assistance—and found himself ignored yet again. Not even a plea to "please answer this" evoked a response. In desperation he sent a messenger to Richmond by train but never learned whether the man made it through.

By the morning of the sixth, having sent "eight or ten" telegrams to the War Office, he asked in exasperation whether the government planned to hold the railroad line. He did not bother to ask whether Petersburg would be defended for fear of receiving an answer he did not wish to hear.[11]

No longer surprised by the silence that greeted his most recent communique, he took it upon himself to defend Petersburg with his tiny force on hand: one infantry regiment, the Fifty-first North Carolina of Clingman's brigade, and twenty-one artillery pieces, augmented by a few militia units and the city's civilian defense battalion. To these would-be defenders he hoped to add the vanguard of Beauregard's force out of Charleston, slowly moving up the railroad along with their leader. But Pickett's hopes of strengthening his garrison were dashed when Beauregard relayed to him War Department demands that the first troops to reach Petersburg—Brigadier General Johnson Hagood's South Carolina brigade—be sent on to Richmond without delay. Pickett did so, against his better judgment, on the morning of May 6.[12]

Thanks to Pickett's prompt and selfless obedience, the advance detachment of Hagood's command reached a strategic rail depot, Port Walthall Junction, just in time to thwart a much larger but less resolute force that Butler had dispatched to cut the railroad. When more of Hagood's troops reached Petersburg later that day and early on the seventh, Pickett hastened them north to join their comrades. On the afternoon of the seventh, reinforced by a Tennessee brigade under Brigadier General Bushrod Rust Johnson, which had reached Richmond from western Virginia three days before, Hagood repulsed a poorly coordinated effort by two wings of Butler's expeditionary force to converge on their opponents. Under Johnson's overall command, the little force then withdrew to Swift Creek, an Appomattox tributary that flowed a few miles above Petersburg. At Pickett's order, Johnson dug in along the creek to oppose an apparent Yankee advance on Petersburg.[13]

The movement north of the city was the greatest threat so far to Pickett's emotional health, which was beginning to give way under the strain of overwork. By the ninth he had been trying for four days to counter threats against many sectors of his realm including a probing movement from City Point by a brigade of African-American troops; a combined land-sea advance against Fort Clifton, an earthwork on the Appomattox two miles from the city; and cavalry strikes against railroad track and bridges between Petersburg and the North Carolina border. When not apprising Richmond of the enemy's movements, communicating orders and intelligence to Johnson and Hagood, sending scouts galloping in all directions, and trying to hasten the progress of Beauregard's forces, Pickett had been shuttling noisy but empty trains in and out of town to give any Yankee within earshot the impression that Petersburg was being regularly reinforced. As time permitted, he had ridden out to the city works to encourage their defenders. Meanwhile, La Salle Pickett was doing her part to ease the crisis atmosphere, rising from a sickbed to open her house to the distressed families of militiamen and home guards, while furnishing biscuits, other baked goods, and hot coffee to husbands, sons, and fathers.[14]

By rights, Petersburg should have fallen to Butler's forces, who began to sweep across Swift Creek early on the ninth. At least partly through the long-distance direction of Pickett, however, the troops under Johnson and Hagood blocked the move so stoutly as to persuade Butler to head northward and strike Richmond instead. By nine A.M. on the tenth, the emergency began to abate as Beauregard finally reached Petersburg along with more of his troops from Charleston. While their leader lingered in the city to hear Pickett's situation report and congratulate him for keeping his wits and holding onto the city against great pressure, Beauregard's regiments rushed north to bar the door to Richmond against Butler's hordes.[15]

As befit his style, once at Petersburg Beauregard announced plans to strike Butler from the rear as well as from the Richmond side, utterly routing him. On paper he created an army corps composed of divisions assigned to Pickett and Robert Hoke, recently arrived in the city after aborting his expedition to New Bern. Pickett never got to serve under Beauregard, however; his health would not permit it. For nearly a week he had labored under great strain, seemingly abandoned by his superiors as he cobbled together a defense force to save one of the most important cities in the Confederacy. Over that period he had slept a few hours at most and had eaten sparingly if at all. On the evening of the tenth he suddenly gave way, suffering something akin to a nervous breakdown. He took to his room, cared for by Sallie and the family servants.[16]

Without him Beauregard went ahead with plans to save Richmond, complementing Pickett's rescue of Petersburg. First, however, he wired the news of Pickett's debility to the capital. Instead of thanking him for his critical services, Richmond began to resound with rumors that Pickett had collapsed in a drunken stupor.[17]

* * *

Under Sallie's devoted care, it took only ten days for her husband to regain his emotional and physical strength. By the afternoon of the twentieth, Pickett and his wife finally had their sad parting. Then, although still shaky from his ordeal, he entrained for Richmond and points north.

He passed up the tracks without fear of molestation by Butler's Federals. While Pickett lay abed at Petersburg, General Beauregard had effectively dealt with the politician-general, curtailing his clumsy foray through Southside Virginia. On the sixteenth, near Drewry's Bluff, Beauregard attacked Butler's large command with a hastily formed army composed of the troops sent up from Charleston and the defense forces of the capital including Corse's, Terry's, and Barton's brigades. The surprise assault made the flabbergasted Federals relinquish their hold on the James River and withdraw to the fortifications at Bermuda Hundred. Only the failure of General Whiting—assigned to command at Petersburg during Pickett's illness—to strike the enemy's rear in concert with Beauregard's attack in front had permitted Butler's army to return intact to its base of operations between the James and Appomattox. Drewry's Bluff had demonstrated that there was more to Beauregard than bluster and braggadocio. But the victory had been made possible by Pickett's staunch defense of Petersburg in the dark days of early May.[18]

Some of Pickett's regiments engaged at Drewry's Bluff had run up a long casualty list for the first time since Gettysburg. On the whole, however, the reunited command—enlarged by recruits and draftees—made an impressive appearance as it marched from Drewry's Bluff to rejoin Lee via the Richmond, Fredericksburg & Potomac. According to Colonel Flowerree of the Seventh Virginia, Secretary of War Seddon, who reviewed part of the brigade as it trooped through the capital, sans Pickett, remarked that it "presented the handsomest appearance in drill, discipline, and numbers ever . . . as a division in the Army of Northern Virginia."[19]

Because of its heavy contingent of green troops and its commander's post-recuperative weakness, it was well that Pickett's division was not heavily committed during its first engagement after rejoining Lee. Its major participation came in the preliminary stages of the North Anna Campaign. Early on the twenty-first, while still en route to the army, a portion of Terry's brigade, leading Pickett's advance, tangled with Union horsemen near the R, F & P depot at Milford. The troopers, members of a raiding expedition under the newly installed commander of cavalry, Army of the Potomac, the feisty and hard-driving Major General Philip Sheridan, had struck at Richmond two weeks ago and were now returning to Grant and Meade. Wielding repeating carbines and fighting aggressively on foot, the more numerous cavalry forced some of Terry's regiments to retreat across the Mattapony River. Thereafter the Confederates proceeded to join Lee, followed on the twenty-second by the balance of the troops under Pickett.[20]

Making contact with the army along the upper bank of the North Anna River, Pickett found his command temporarily assigned to A. P. Hill's corps. After the Army of the Potomac came down to the river on the twenty-second to precipitate four days of combat, Pickett's men—though never heavily engaged—provided support to Hill's main body along the Confederate left. Pickett's first fight since rejoining the army was a draw. When the shooting died out on the twenty-sixth Grant was forced to admit stalemate on the road to Richmond, as he had at numerous points since accompanying Meade's army across the Rapidan River on May 4.[21]

Not until early on the twenty-seventh, when Grant and Meade pulled out from Lee's front and swung south toward the Pamunkey River, did Pickett's troops link up with their old command, the First Army Corps. Not surprisingly, many changes had taken place during the eight months the division had been away. There were noticeable gaps in the ranks, among both officers and men, the result of the fighting the corps had seen in Tennessee and Georgia and later in Virginia against Grant. New faces led the other divisions of the corps: Major General Charles W. Field of Kentucky, who had replaced John Bell Hood (now a lieutenant general commanding a corps in the Army of Tennessee), and Brigadier General (soon to be Major General) Joseph B. Kershaw of South Carolina, who had taken Lafayette McLaws's command after McLaws was transferred to a desk job at Savannah.[22]

For Pickett the most distressing change had taken place at the very top: his friend and mentor Longstreet was gone, felled by a severe wound three weeks ago in the Virginia Wilderness during the first clash between Lee and Grant; he would not return to active duty for another five months. Richard H. Anderson had taken Longstreet's place; thus far his record in corps command had been solid if unspectacular. From what Pickett could learn, Anderson appeared to have Lee's confidence and trust, although the army commander would never rely on him for advice and moral support as he had on his predecessor.

Pickett, who was junior to Anderson and whose occasional service under him dated to Williamsburg, had no grounds for disputing the man's promotion. Even so, he may have been troubled that a general officer had been brought over from another corps (Hill's) to take Longstreet's place. Certainly he must have resented the fact— common knowledge throughout the corps—that he himself had not received serious consideration as Old Pete's successor. He never learned why Lee had chosen to overlook him, a Virginian in an army of Virginians, to assign a South Carolinian with a rather lackluster record. Even so, Pickett probably lodged another black mark against the army commander for dealing him such a slight.[23]

There are a number of possible explanations for Pickett's non-selection. The most obvious reason is that at the time of Longstreet's wounding Pickett was in the midst of an important operation at Petersburg, where, temporarily at least, he was irreplaceable. Another explanation is that Lee would have wanted a more senior officer in the position; each of the three finalists for Longstreet's job—Anderson, Major General Jubal A. Early, and Major General Edward Johnson— had more experience in division command than Pickett.

Another, perhaps less likely, explanation suggests itself. By mid-1864 Lee may have formed an opinion of Pickett that was as unfavorable, in its own way, as Pickett's of Lee. Although he had heaped praise on the gallantry of Pickett's division at Gettysburg, Lee had bestowed no such praise on Pickett himself, whose emergence unscathed from the carnage may have suggested that on July 3 he failed to exercise the kind of close, personal leadership Lee admired. Lee may also have come to believe that Pickett held him responsible for imaginary offenses such as the gutting of his division before Gettysburg. Lee may even have suspected that Pickett blamed him for the devastation of his command in front of Cemetery Ridge (a statement Pickett voiced after the war and quite possibly during its last year as well). If so, the army commander quite rightly would have resented his attitude.

Finally, Lee may have considered Pickett ineligible for higher command on the basis of his life-style. Although he had toned down his drinking since marrying Sallie, the division leader continued to enjoy liquor. Lee also may have remembered earlier times when Pickett lived by the credo "to fight like a gentleman a man must eat and drink like a gentleman." Lee, who did not drink, disapproved of the practice among his subordinates. According to his military secretary and biographer, Brigadier General A. Lindsay Long, "the intemperate habits of many of the persons under his command were always a source of pain to him, and . . . on more than one occasion he refused to promote officers addicted to intoxication, saying 'I cannot consent to place in the control of others one who cannot control himself'."[24]

* * *

Late on May 28, conforming to Meade's renewed advance toward Richmond, Anderson's corps started for the Chickahominy River, Pickett's command bringing up the rear on a march that carried the army across familiar ground. That night the corps bivouacked near Hanover Junction, where Pickett's men, who had not had a hot meal since rejoining the army, rejoiced at the long-delayed appearance of the divisional commissariat.

Well-fed at last, Pickett's troops moved eastward, then turned to the southeast along a country road leading to another familiar landmark—Gaines's Mill—and, just below the mill, the hamlet of New Cold Harbor, about ten miles above Richmond. Early on the thirtieth, the army settled into position along a skirt of woods northwest of Cold Harbor. Pickett's men went to work at once, digging rifle pits and throwing up breastworks—hard work made harder by severe heat and high humidity. The division hoped the weather would not deter Grant and Meade from attacking in an effort to remove this latest roadblock to Richmond—and from losing enough men to pare their numerical superiority.[25]

On the last day of the month, as Yankee infantry began to congregate to the east, Pickett's men, abutting Anderson's right flank just east of Gaines's Mill pond, extended their works to the south to connect with Jubal Early's Second Army Corps. After dark Pickett sent reconnaissance teams across the grassy field in his front; they returned with word that the Yankees opposite consisted of regiments in Butler's XVIII Corps, temporarily attached to the Army of the Potomac. Thus Pickett, who had missed an opportunity to engage the Army of the James at Petersburg, except at long range through the forces of Hagood and Johnson, would soon enjoy a chance to meet its men close up.

Late on June 1, Grant ordered a limited offensive, which struck just north of Pickett's place in the line, hitting Kershaw's division. A few units, including the majority of Clingman's brigade—short weeks ago part of Pickett's departmental force, now serving under Kershaw—gave way. Kershaw brought up his reserves for a counterattack; at General Anderson's order Pickett added his old brigade, under Hunton, to the retaliatory force. The counter-punch was successful, Kershaw regaining his lost ground, inflicting numerous casualties, and taking a number of prisoners.[26]

Pickett doubted that Grant, although once again stymied, was done attacking at Cold Harbor. He surmise was correct, although it took two days to prove. Early on June 3 the Federals advanced again, this time all along the line. Well-positioned behind their breastworks, surrounded by banks of field guns, the Confederates obliterated the Union line almost before it got moving. For those defenders whose memories dated back to December 1862, it was Fredericksburg all over again. "Column after column was hurled back from our works," recalled Lieutenant William Wood of the Nineteenth Virginia, "leaving the ground blue with the dead and dying."

Only on a few sectors of the field did the Yankees penetrate close enough to make things deadly for the defenders. That was not the case along the majority of Pickett's line, where, as Lieutenant Wood noted, "the fight was much of a bushwhacking affair on both sides." However, General Hunton, whose brigade had remained within supporting distance of Clingman, took an enfilading fire; for a time the brigadier reported that "my men were falling all around me." Finally he got up a strong skirmish force, augmented it with troops from Hoke's brigade on his left, and drove off the sharpshooters.[27]

At day's close, the carnage was so great that it appeared unlikely Grant and Meade would resume the offensive. As the infantry's battle became an artillery duel at long range, Pickett counted heads and nodded in satisfaction: very few losses. Although the odds had been with his well-entrenched army throughout the fight, he was pleased that his command—especially in its recruit- and conscript-heavy condition—had acquitted itself well throughout. Its first engagement as a division after nearly a year's separation from the Army of Northern Virginia seemed to indicate that although it had left many good men on Yankee soil, the casualties of Gettysburg did not include tenacity, fighting spirit, or marksmanship.

TWELVE – Approaching the End

The armies remained at Cold Harbor, glaring at each other across a grisly, stinking field, for days after the carnage on the third. Artillery exchanges and light skirmishing consumed most of that period, until a belated truce permitted burial teams to inter the many Yankees and the few Rebels who had fallen between the lines. When the truce expired, bluecoats and butternuts returned to the business of killing each other at long range. The stalemate threatened to last forever.

With Grant and Meade hopelessly bogged down, unable to move except to the rear, Lee wondered when they were going to return to countermarching in a futile effort to turn his flank. By the evening of the eighth, Lee suspected his enemy was moving at last; at his order, Anderson readied Pickett's division to strike in mid-withdrawal. The next morning Pickett sent his men forward, only to absorb a stout skirmish-fire. Evidently, the Yankees were not going anywhere just yet.[1]

Continuous skirmishing lulled some Confederates into the belief that Grant would sit out the rest of the war in this ordinarily pleasant corner of Hanover County. Thus they were stunned to disbelief when the morning of the thirteenth revealed their opponents to have evacuated their position. A few artillery units and sharpshooters remained to make it appear their army held the field in force, but reconnaissance established that Grant and Meade were gone.

For too long, Pickett and his superiors remained baffled by the pullout. How had they slipped away with such stealth? More importantly, where had they gone? The logical suspicion was that Richmond was under threat, so on the thirteenth Lee ordered the army south. That afternoon Pickett's division crossed the Chickahominy, trooping over McClellan's Bridge in rear of Kershaw's men and in front of Field's. On the far side the corps moved toward the capital via fields that made old wounds throb. Passing Seven Pines, they crossed over to the Charles City Road, approached the James River, and bivouacked near Frayser's Farm, where, two years ago, Major Charles Pickett had nearly lost a leg.[2]

For two days, the Army of Northern Virginia lay in wait along a line between Malvern Hill and White Oak Swamp, blocking a path that Grant was not taking. Finally, in the early hours of the sixteenth P. G. T. Beauregard, commanding at Petersburg, cabled Lee, reporting himself under attack and asking for help. Although Lee was not told the identity of the force pressing his colleague—perhaps it was not Grant's but Butler's—he immediately sent most of the five to six thousand troops Beauregard had requested. At his order, Pickett detached his 4,500-man division from its corps and left Frayser's Farm for Bermuda Hundred. Along the neck of that peninsula Beauregard had capped his May 16 victory at Drewry's Bluff by building a line of works parallel to Butler's fortifications, effectively bottling up the politician-general. Now, however, Beauregard had been forced to denude that line to bolster the defenses of Petersburg. Pickett was to reoccupy Beauregard's works and if he found Butler making mischief above the Appomattox he was to chastise him severely. Old grievances firmly in mind, Pickett looked forward to that prospect.[3]

Although Pickett was alert to a possible clash with Butler, his men seem to have been less vigilant. Crossing the James on a pontoon bridge at eight A.M. on the sixteenth, the lead brigade, Hunton's, reached Drewry's Bluff shortly before ten, struck the turnpike to Petersburg, and passed down it at a pace neither leisurely nor breakneck. An artilleryman attached to Hunton's column recalled that despite Pickett's instructions the men doubted they would see a fight short of Petersburg: "There was no more expectation of encountering the enemy than we should have of finding him in the streets of Charleston."[4]

When the head of the line came abreast of the upper stretch of Beauregard's abandoned works, the conventional wisdom changed. A barrage of rifle-fire suddenly ripped into Hunton's left flank. Turning in that direction, the brigade saw bands of blue infantry—Butler's troops, who had occupied some of Beauregard's defenses—coming at it on the run. Hunton's forward regiments tried to withdraw as the enemy swarmed over the turnpike, pushing them back on their main body.

As soon as he learned of the encounter, Pickett hastened down with the balance of his force, reinforced by the vanguard of Field's division. Under Pickett's leadership the men surged forward, over-whelming the Yankees and driving them from one outwork to another. It was an all-day job; the defenses were too many and too strong to clear in a single movement. They extended from the south bank of the James, where Beauregard had erected a strong battery at a plantation home, the Howlett house, southward for about seven miles, ending at Swift Creek close to where it met the Appomattox.[5]

By midafternoon of the seventeenth all but a portion of the lower flank, near a landmark known as the Clay house, had been recaptured. Pickett meant to regain that sector too, although Lee's engineers warned him that its capture would be quite costly and perhaps unnecessary. Lee came to agree but before he could call off the assault Pickett attacked in conjunction with Brigadier General John Gregg's Texas brigade of Field's division.

The attack was swift and decisive. Leaping over the entrenchments in front of the Clay house, Virginians and Texans pried their occupants loose at bayonet-point and put them to flight—without suffering heavily in return. As Butler's men hustled inside their own line farther east, there occurred the only recorded instance of Lee injecting quiet humor into an official dispatch. After congratulating Anderson on his success Lee noted that "we tried very hard to stop Pickett's men from capturing the breast-works of the enemy, but could not do it. . . ."[6]

Perusing a copy of this message, Thomas Goree of the corps staff exclaimed, "are these not compliments to be esteemed?" They were indeed, and Pickett and his men would savor them for weeks to come.[7]

★ ★ ★

Their early occupation of the so-called Howlett Line made Pickett's people the logical choice to hold that critical defensive position against Butler's Army of the James, keeping several thousand Yankees trapped between the rivers. Thus, while the rest of the army shuffled down the turnpike to thwart Grant's surprise assault on Petersburg, thereby setting the stage for a several-month siege, Pickett's soldiers remained astride Bermuda Hundred. They improved Beauregard's works, stocking them with heavy and light artillery, then settled back to wage a war of stasis and attrition.

It was a wearying kind of operation, one bound to produce boredom and discontent. Almost from the moment Pickett's men occupied the breastworks and rifle pits opposite Butler, they grumbled about the general inactivity, the tedious yet deadly exchanges of artillery- and sharpshooter-fire, the seas of mud and clouds of dust that changeable weather produced, the poor water and slim rations furnished them, the rats and the other vermin that infested their lines—the full spectrum of discomforts that trench warfare can breed. Within two weeks of taking his position between the rivers, a member of the Eighteenth Virginia was observing that "the long, dry, hot spell of weather, together with the want of exercise, causes a great deal of sickness in the army. Nearly all are complaining some, but very few are sick enough to leave." A couple of days later a comrade in the Fifty-sixth Regiment complained in a letter home that "we are seeing a very hard time out here lying in fortifications and on picket every other day and night and on guard at our fortifications . . . when off picket." Life in the trenches made him feel as though "confined and bound like a highway robber in custody and treated like a pointer dog. . . ."[8]

In some ways their commander fared more pleasantly than the majority of his men; he also suffered greater pain. Pickett turned an old house into a comfortable field headquarters at Port Walthall, a coaling depot along the Appomattox near his right flank. At the opposite end of the line, between the Howlett house and Chester Station on the Richmond & Petersburg Railroad, he made a home for himself and his expectant wife: a large tent, followed by a one-room cabin built by some of his men in a grove well behind the lines. While their habitation was nothing like the five-story house they had enjoyed at Petersburg, at least they were together in the field.

Life at the front had its dangers but its pleasures too. Sallie was not the only army wife in residence, especially after cold weather came on and the army went into winter quarters. She fondly recalled that "my brother-in-law and his little family were in a log cabin within a stone's throw from our own, and many of the officers had brought their wives to cheer their winter hours. So there was no lack of social diversion. In a small way we had our dances, our conversations and musicales, quite like the gay world that had never known anything about war except from the pages of books and the columns of newspapers. . . ."[9]

After a brief stay in June, Sallie left her husband to be with her family in Richmond for the last critical weeks of her pregnancy. Pickett's fears for her health proved groundless; on July 17 she gave birth to a son they named George, Jr., and nicknamed the "Little General." The new father was ecstatic; when not taking leave to visit mother and child, he wrote Sallie letters exalting her in madonna-like terms ("God bless you, little Mother . . . Heaven in all its glory shine upon you. . . .").[10]

In the days following the birth of the Little General, the camps of Pickett's regiments were lighted by bonfires in honor of the blessed event. In her postwar writings, La Salle Corbell Pickett relates that a couple of her husband's higher-ranking friends in blue—Ulysses S. Grant and his chief quartermaster, Rufus Ingalls—adopted the gesture, directing the Army of the Potomac to "strike a light for the young Pickett." According to her account, Grant and Ingalls joined with a third friend of her husband's, George Suckley (now chief surgeon to one of Ben Butler's army corps) to send through the lines the gift of a baby's silver service. While it makes a charming story—one retold many times over the years—the incident is a fabrication. From Bermuda Hundred Pickett could not have seen an illumination along the front of Meade's army; more significantly, extant correspondence makes it clear that Pickett did not inform Major Suckley of his son's birth until several months after the event. The same letter suggests that the "old friends" had not been in contact for years.[11]

Pickett's letter to Suckley mentions one of the saddest experiences along the Howlett line. On several occasions that summer, Butler sent scouting parties into the country between the Chickahominy and the James to forage off local secessionists and burn a few houses and barns. He was especially drawn to the homes of prominent Confederate officials such as Secretary of War Seddon, which he torched in supposed retaliation for the destruction of Unionists' homes in Virginia and Maryland. One of these pillaging expeditions swept down on Turkey Island; before it returned to Butler the Pickett ancestral home had been reduced to ashes. "If it had been burned in line of battle," Pickett bitterly informed Sallie in Richmond, "it would have been all right; but it was not. It was burned by Butler at a great expense to the Government and in revenge for having been outgeneraled by a little handful of my men at Petersburg." The vandalism left Pickett feeling rootless, as though he had no place to go should the war suddenly end.[12]

His melancholy was relieved when in mid-August Sallie returned to the army with George Jr., and his nurse, a young slave woman named Lucinda. Accordingly to the young mother, they were greeted with music from the band of the Seventh Virginia, after which "cheer after cheer went up for 'the General's baby'." A crowd gathered around the child, grimy veterans jostling one another for a look. Initially to Sallie's horror, a soldier seized the child and passed him from one pair of anxious hands to another. One young Confederate recalled: "Nor was his linen as spotless or his humor as sweet when handed back to his mother or nurse as when the boys received him."[13]

* * *

Only occasionally did events opposite Bermuda Hundred spawn large-scale activity along the Howlett Line. The consequential fighting occurred south of the line, at Petersburg, or, after mid-June—when Butler bridged the James to Deep Bottom and Lee sent a force to contain him—on the Northside. In early August, Butler's troops at Bermuda Hundred began to dig a canal across Dutch Gap, a strip of land that separated two loops of the James a few miles northeast of Pickett's left flank. From that time onward, the big guns on Pickett's line—especially the heavy Columbiads of Battery Dantzler, at the Howlett house—pounded away daily at the hundreds of laborers at work on the largest military excavation project of its time. When the Yankees emplaced long-range guns to defend the diggers, the confrontation resulted in daily barrages that only added to the discomforts of siege life.[14]

When not shelling the canal, Pickett's artillery cooperated with the Confederate navy to prevent wooden vessels and ironclad gunboats from advancing along strategic reaches of the James, thus menacing both the Howlett Line and Richmond. On numerous occasions Pickett worked closely with a kinsman, Flag Officer John K. Mitchell, C. S. N., to plant torpedoes and erect pilings in the James; he even devised a system of signal rockets with which to communicate with Mitchell and his seamen. In midwinter the two officers combined to support a bold but ill-starred effort to send a fleet of gunboats and rams downriver from Drewry's Bluff to attack bridges, headquarters, and supply bases at Bermuda Hundred and City Point.[15]

The Rebels were no match for their enemy in trying to break the deadlock of the siege. Late in July, Meade's army detonated a gunpowder-filled shaft it had dug under a Confederate salient northeast of Petersburg. Although a subsequent attack failed to capture the city, the Rebels brooded over the effectiveness of the Yankee trick and the casualties it had inflicted. They immediately set to work on a mine of their own, primed and set to explode under the Federal lines outside Petersburg on August 25. When something went wrong and the mine failed to go up, Pickett's men nevertheless attacked as ordered. They were repulsed with heavy loss, especially in captured, and suffered greater damage when the Yankees counterattacked. After that, Pickett mounted no large-scale offensives on his front, contenting himself with limited, probing attacks on selected portions of Butler's line and an occasional sortie to capture outposts manned by troops wanting in vigilance.[16]

Events along the Howlett Line heated up again in the last days of September, when Butler attacked out of his bridgehead on the James and captured Fort Harrison, a key position along the outer defense line of Richmond. As Lee rushed north to oversee a counterattack, Pickett dispatched a provisional brigade to assist him; the force remained on the Northside for three days after the effort failed to retake the work.[17]

At irregular intervals over the winter and well into 1865, Pickett sent portions of his troops north of the James as needed to counter movements by Butler and Grant. In time Pickett's role became that of an all-purpose mobile reserve. Given its centralized location, its interior lines of movement, and the inherent strength of its works, Pickett's command could be more easily shifted about than any other force available to Lee.

For the first several months of the siege, Pickett's mobile reserve operated under the direct control of Lee; after mid-October, however, it came under the authority of James Longstreet. Upon his return to the army following recuperation from his Wilderness wound, Pickett's favorite superior was given overall command of Confederate forces north of the Appomattox, including not only Pickett's force but the infantry divisions of Charles Field and Robert Hoke, a cavalry brigade, and the troops in the Department of Richmond. When not confined to his chores opposite Bermuda Hundred, Pickett spent as much time as possible at his old friend's command post on the Northside, seeking to regain that happy, convivial spirit of two years ago when Longstreet's headquarters was also an officer's club where friends and associates discussed topics both important and trivial over good whiskey and fine cigars.[18]

Trying to recapture old times and past glories was becoming a Herculean task by the winter of 1864-65. Lee's army was suffering from a wide range of ailments, and Pickett's division fared as poorly as any other command. Lack of rations, medicines, clothing, and equipment wore down the men's stamina, and their weakened condition was only aggravated by the rigors of life in the trenches. Sickness and disease wafted through the army like swamp gas. "Chills & Fevers are prevalent," wrote a member of the Thirtieth Virginia, adding that so many of his comrades showed symptoms of palsy that the Thirtieth was "a Regt of 'Shakies'." Pickett's inspector-general, Major Harrison, confirmed the poor health of the division, describing it as racked by ague and fever in summer, fall, and winter, most likely from the unhealthy influence of the river bottoms that flanked the siege line.[19]

Through summer and fall, Pickett was sick for extended periods, and when winter came his health further deteriorated. At several intervals he was unable to exercise command, confined to a sickbed by recurrences of the intestinal ills he had suffered since childhood. He was also beset by new maladies including a severe case of hemorrhoids that occasionally incapacitated him. The poor state of his general health, aggravated by the unusually stressful conditions of the past year, aged him beyond his years. By late in the year his face had become fleshy to the point of bloatedness, his hair no longer had a youthful sheen, his eyes had lost the luminous sparkle that not so long ago had arrested the attention of a young girl who thought him a paragon of masculine beauty.

Like their commander, Pickett's division had lost much of its youth and vigor. Still feeling the effects of old battles, its fighting strength diluted by recruits and draftees, the division experienced a dramatic decline in morale. Throughout the winter Pickett's soldiers complained of their static existence and the utter impossibility of escaping it through furlough. A member of the Eleventh Virginia wrote to his wife of his struggle against loneliness, which "will suddenly come upon me with tremendous & almost crushing power, away down here, tied fast, bound hand & foot as it were." Christmas was a bleak event, according to an enlisted man in the Thirtieth Virginia, because the men "had very little to drink—very little to eat—nothing like pleasure. . . . Am glad it can't come but once a year."[20]

As the war spirit waned, desertions became a major problem in Pickett's division, as in the rest of the army. Early in the new year, worsening living conditions and reports of Union victories at Franklin, Nashville, and Savannah combined to raise the desertion rate. On some nights, upwards of fifty men, including officers, would walk across the lines to Bermuda Hundred and give themselves up. In one week in February 1865, almost 1,100 men quit the army; inspectors-general identified Pickett's command as a major source of defections. Many of Pickett's regiments held morale-

Eleanor S. Brockenbrough Library
The Museum of the Confederacy
George E. Pickett, ca. 1864

building sessions throughout the winter, passing resolutions of continued support for the war effort. From interviewing deserters, however, the Yankees opposite the Howlett Line concluded that the patriotic outpourings at these gatherings was mainly "done for effect."[21]

The contrast between the plight of Pickett's men and the healthy, well-supplied Federals with whom they occasionally swapped newspapers and traded tobacco and coffee added to the miasma of discontent that fostered desertion. The Confederates knew that while their strength was fading, their enemy remained in peak health—and on the go. Rumors constantly spoke of Yankee movements north or south of the Howlett Line—movements that stretched Lee's flanks farther and farther toward Richmond and below Petersburg. Somewhere, both sides realized, those lines must be running very thin. A youngster in the Seventh Virginia, looking back years later, remarked that when the new year, 1865, came in, everyone in gray and butternut knew that "final overthrow must come, for our foe was growing stronger, we weaker. Our star was surely on the wane." Writing home in February, a semi-literate member of the Third Virginia put it concisely: the "Confederacy is gone. . . ."[22]

* * *

As the Federals continued to batter at Lee's lines, including his lines of supply, the role of Pickett's force as a maneuverable reserve began to increase. In December 1864 and again in March 1865 elements of the division left the Bermuda Hundred front to pursue large forces of Yankee cavalry—Brevet Major General Alfred T. A. Torbert's raiding column near Gordonsville, Virginia, and Phil Sheridan's corps on its march from the Shenandoah Valley to the Petersburg front. Both efforts—the first led by General Corse, the second commanded personally by James Longstreet—involved long marches in adverse weather, only to end short of bagging the quarry.[23]

When spring came in, the division departed the Howlett Line twice more—the second time, never to return. Late in March, when Lee launched a forlorn-hope assault against Fort Stedman, along the Union right flank at Petersburg, Pickett's men—temporarily led by his newest subordinate, Brigadier General George ("Maryland") Steuart, Pickett having been disabled by one of his periodic illnesses—tried to hasten to the scene of action. But logistical foul-ups and broken-down troop trains so hobbled them that they failed to reach their destination in time to participate in Lee's final offensive of the war.[24]

On March 27, two days after the assault on Fort Stedman, the command was again on the move. After rejoining Meade's army, Sheridan and his cavalry, some 13,000 strong, had moved south and west of Petersburg as though heading for Lee's far right flank. Confederate lookouts brought word of the movement but could not discern Sheridan's intentions. "Little Phil" might be planning a strike in hopes of breaking through to the Southside Railroad, the last intact supply line of the Army of Northern Virginia and the key to continued Confederate occupation of the Petersburg-Richmond front. On the other hand, Sheridan might be planning to slip across the border into North Carolina to augment the armies of William T. Sherman, which, having captured Atlanta and Savannah, were sweeping through the Carolinas toward, it was supposed, a link-up with Grant and Meade.

To counter either eventuality, Robert E. Lee contemplated sending his cavalry, including the divisions of his son, "Rooney", and his nephew, Fitzhugh Lee, to shadow Sheridan. Longstreet, from his headquarters on the Northside—near which much of Pickett's command was lingering after its return from Fort Stedman—suggested, instead, that Pickett and his mobile force, as well as horsemen and field guns, be sent to the far right against Sheridan. Although Longstreet doubted that he could spare Pickett's division from his front, he proposed that should the Union troopers be aiming for North Carolina Pickett move in that direction as well to bolster Sherman's opposition, the small army of Joe Johnston. Impressed by the power and flexibility inherent in his subordinate's strategy, Lee adopted it.

And so Pickett moved out on the morning of the twenty-ninth toward a fateful rendezvous with Sheridan in the vicinity of Dinwiddie Court House and a road junction known as Five Forks. As his men broke camp, their general returned to his cabin, where he embraced Sallie, kissed George, Jr., and told them: "Now, remember, I shall surely come back." Then he was off, pounding south aboard his favorite mare, Lucy.[25]

As per his orders, Pickett marched his command into Petersburg and put it once again aboard an aged train on the Southside Railroad. Throughout the day his division passed west of the city. When they reached Sutherland's Station, ten miles outside Petersburg, the men detrained. While they started south toward Dinwiddie Court House, Pickett lingered to confer with General Lee, who gave him his instructions and informed him of the composition of his expeditionary force.

On the morning of the thirtieth, Pickett advanced toward the assumed position of the enemy. As per his instructions, he had left Hunton's brigade in the trenches along that section of the White Oak

Road held by Bushrod Johnson's division. In addition to the brigades of Generals Corse, Steuart, and Terry, Pickett took two of Johnson's brigades—Matt Ransom's and Brigadier General William H. Wallace's—plus six artillery pieces under Colonel William J. Pegram. Arriving at Five Forks late that afternoon, he found Fitz Lee; next morning the rest of the cavalry—under Rooney Lee and Thomas L. Rosser—joined him at the crossroads, which lay five miles north of Dinwiddie and about a mile and a quarter below Hatcher's Run. As ranking officer on the scene, Pickett commanded 19,000 troops of all arms—more than enough, he reckoned, to deal with Sheridan.[26]

Late on the rainy morning of the last day of March Pickett started south after Sheridan, whose three divisions of cavalry had congregated north of the courthouse. The fighting got off to a promising start. Pickett's numerical superiority and his advantage in firepower—rifles versus short-range carbines and pistols—enabled him to shove the dismounted cavalry rearward on many parts of the field throughout the day, threatening Sheridan's left flank and rear. Though suffering numerous casualties, Pickett's men inflicted even more; by day's end they had thrust a weary, battered Sheridan well south of the courthouse, where he was calling on Grant for infantry support. Soon Major General Gouverneur K. Warren's V Corps was making a slow, deliberate advance to his side from the Petersburg lines.[27]

Shortly before midnight, learning of Warren's approach along a diagonal road toward his left flank, Pickett decided to withdraw before he could be cut off. By two A.M. on April 1 he was back at the crossroads. He would have preferred putting Hatcher's Run between his force and the enemy's, but Lee had supposedly sent him a telegram enjoining him to hold Five Forks "at all hazards." Lee's concern was that if the position were lost nothing would bar Sheridan's path to the railroad, whose capture would doom the army.[28]

No copy of Lee's telegram has come to light, although La Salle Corbell Pickett cited it in her postwar writings. Historians generally concede its existence, which appears to provide Pickett with grounds for asserting that he was forced to fight at Five Forks against his will. Pickett is usually criticized for his selection of a position, but if Lee ordered him to hold unfavorable ground, much of the blame for what happened at the crossroads should go to the army commander, not to his expeditionary leader.[29]

That night Pickett's men dug in along the White Oak Road, the east-west-running thoroughfare that provided two of the five forks of the road junction. The fruits of their labor appear to have been slim. Major Harrison asserts that the defenses consisted of a shallow ditch, and a "loose fence of pine logs, hastily thrown up, in about three

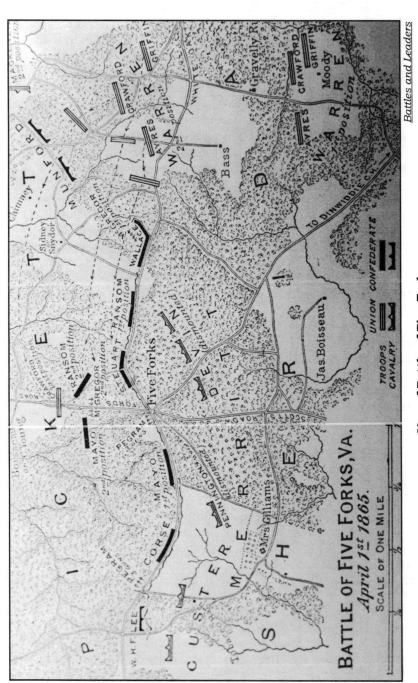

Map of Battle of Five Forks

hours' time." Lest this be taken as an implied criticism of his commander, Harrison adds that "Five Forks was not a point to be protected, except by a very large force. . . ." In a confrontation with two army corps, 34,000 strong, Pickett was going to lose no matter how strong his works.[30]

As though conceding defeat, Pickett made a hasty set of dispositions, without determining if certain strategic points should be held by the most numerous or the freshest units. He placed his own brigades on the right, covered by Rooney Lee's cavalry. Johnson's two brigades went into position on the left, protected by Fitz Lee's division under the direct command of Brigadier General Thomas T. Munford. He divided Pegram's artillery, placing half of it on the far right, the rest astride Five Forks. Rosser's division he stationed in the rear, below Hatcher's Run. Pickett did not seem to mind that the thinnest of cavalry cordons—a skirmish line from the understrength brigade of Brigadier General William P. Roberts—connected his position with the right flank of Lee's main line five miles closer to Petersburg. Apparently he suspected, like Fitz Lee, that Warren's corps had suspended its movement to Sheridan's side; certainly he was not ready to meet it.[31]

Upon falling back to Five Forks, Pickett appears to have sent to Lee for reinforcements, which he never received. From this point, he acted as though the responsibility for holding Five Forks was Lee's alone, perhaps reasoning that the position itself was not his but Lee's. Such a cavalier attitude toward a defense line that he had built and occupied is difficult to understand, unless it can be seen as a symptom of defeatism. At this point, like so many of the men under him, Pickett may have recognized the impossibility of the task confronting him—and the futility of prolonging the war against such lopsided odds. Some observers believed that on other fields he had acted "in a most half-hearted way, he being thoroughly tired of the war."[32]

Perhaps, too, he resented Lee's having placed him in such a wretched situation, where defeat would adhere to George Pickett but success would probably go to Robert E. Lee. By this point, Pickett may not have felt like trying to salvage a victory for Marse Robert. Through his petty, punitive actions over the past two years Lee had forfeited his claim to George Pickett's goodwill. Now, if Lee wished Five Forks to be held, he should see to it himself.

Whatever the reasons behind it, Pickett's lackadaisical effort at holding Five Forks is indefensible. So too is his incredibly derelict behavior late on the morning of April 1 when he slipped away from his command to cross Hatcher's Run in company with Fitz Lee and partake of a shad dinner provided by Tom Rosser. Quite possibly, Pickett, who had never stopped drinking, also consumed some liquor, although errors other than tippling would spell defeat this day. He completed his execrable performance by failing to designate a representative to take command in his absence. Apparently Rooney Lee, the senior officer on the field when Sheridan and Warren attacked late that afternoon, did not even know Pickett was gone.[33]

Not until about four-thirty did Pickett, Lee, and Rosser learn from frantic couriers that the Yankees had attacked, breaking the left flank and threatening to smash in the center as well. Although Lee was cut off and failed to make it back to his troops in time to join the fight, Pickett hastily mounted, recrossed the run, threw his body to the far side of his horse to shield himself from the enemy, and ran a gauntlet of infantry fire all the way to Five Forks. It was at once a brave act and a foolish stunt—or perhaps it was simply the pathetic reaction of one about to be overtaken by total disaster. The tempo of the firing and the steady flow of refugees from the front should have shown him the futility of his errand before he reached his lines.

Arriving on the scene breathless from exertion and fear, he found his left unhinged and swung back a mile or more from its original position and his center crumbling under combined infantry and cavalry attacks. Everywhere on the field men were throwing up their hands or raising their rifles bayonet-down in sign of surrender. Only on the far right, where Rooney Lee's cavalry and Montgomery Corse's infantry were holding firm under building pressure, did a semblance of defense remain. Pickett made a feeble attempt to shore up the line, then gave up the effort, turned, and fled north with those men who by some miracle had escaped entrapment. By hard riding he managed to cross Hatcher's Run to safety. On the north bank he paused to look back and to contemplate the ruins of the largest, and the last, combat force he would ever command.[34]

THIRTEEN — An Enemy Too Strong

When her husband marched off to Five Forks, La Salle Pickett left the army for home. She and her baby were at the old house at Sixth and Leigh when, two days after the disaster along Lee's right, the local garrison evacuated Richmond to join in the long, sad journey toward Appomattox Court House. Before Union troops arrived to receive the city's surrender, a wave of rioting and looting swept through Richmond, terrorizing the inhabitants even more than the thought of Yankee occupation. This was bad enough but when the last Confederates to leave put the torch to war goods to keep them out of enemy hands, winds and explosions spread the flames, transforming much of the city into an inferno.

Even as Richmond burned around her, Mrs. Pickett refused to panic. When the Yankees arrived to secure the streets and douse the flames, she went about her life as though nothing had changed, confident that the future meant improved conditions for her family, her city, and the reunited nation. Not even predictions of personal tragedy could unnerve her. When the normal flow of life resumed, newsboys passed the house shouting out the headlines, proclaiming, among other things, the death of General George Pickett at Five Forks. Refusing to credit the reports, La Salle awaited her husband's return with a sense of certitude that overrode her anxiety. Her composure was rewarded when, one morning in mid-April she heard "the familiar clatter of the hoofs of his little thoroughbred chestnut which he always rode when he came home." As he appeared in the doorway in his grimy uniform, looking haggard and weary but glad to be home,

Library of Congress

Richmond in Ruins, 1865

she slid down the banister from the second floor to embrace him. She could not describe "the peace, the bliss of that moment."[1]

Over the next few days he told her of his ordeal on the road to Appomattox, how he had kept the remnants of Five Forks moving across the Appomattox, then westward in unison with the troops streaming out of Richmond and Petersburg. Over the next week his survivors fended off Sheridan's cavalry pursuit until brought to bay by infantry as well as horsemen at Sayler's Creek. Along that turgid little stream on April 6 what remained of his division, perhaps 800 men, was surrounded and cut to pieces, a phalanx of high-ranking officers including Generals Hunton and Corse being captured. Through some miracle Pickett and his staff escaped the trap, but their freedom lasted only three days. At Appomattox Court House on the ninth Lee and Grant worked out surrender terms. When his men formally laid down their arms on the twelfth, perhaps 80 members of Pickett's division—less than a full-sized company—were on hand to sign parole papers. After the surrender ceremony Pickett bade these men a tearful farewell and thanked them for the loyalty and devotion they had shown him and their cause through four soul-trying years of conflict.[2]

In recounting his travail over the past fortnight, Pickett doubtless withheld from Sallie some of the more painful incidents of the retreat. One episode in particular humiliated and haunted him. The day following Sayler's Creek Lee had sent him and two other generals whose commands had disintegrated during the fighting on the sixth, Richard Anderson and Bushrod Johnson, an order relieving them of command as supernumerary officers, releasing them from the army, and sending them home. Although Pickett ignored the directive, remaining with the army until after Appomattox, he would never forget the injustice of Lee's action, which he ascribed to personal animus— punishment, perhaps, for the disaster at Five Forks. Later, a rumor would circulate that the only reason Pickett remained with the army after Five Forks was that Lee had placed him under arrest for his criminal negligence on April 1. After the war, however, the officer who supposedly penned this order, Major Taylor, categorically refuted the story.[3]

With their Turkey Island estate in ashes, his profession gone, their slaves liberated, and their funds tied up in Confederate bonds, a long, rough road separated the Picketts from financial stability, while prosperity seemed destined to remain beyond their reach. Their concerns were universal ones: hundreds of once-wealthy Confederates were facing, for the first times in their lives, financial uncertainty. Ten days after Appomattox, Major General Edward O. C. Ord, commander of the occupation forces in Richmond, informed Secretary of War Edwin M. Stanton that "Generals W. H. F. Lee, Heth, Pickett, Alexander, and others, and many prominent and formerly wealthy citizens, are asking me what they shall do to make their bread. . . ." Ord, a conservative Democrat with family ties to the South, sympathized with the plight of these fallen stars, but he could offer no quick remedy.[4]

One of the first postwar decisions the Picketts made was to relocate in a less crowded and more healthful venue. Doubting their ability to keep up the house in Richmond, they turned it over to Virginia Pickett Burwell and her husband. In mid-June they loaded their belongings in wagons, passed through the rubble-filled, fire-gutted streets, and headed for the Corbell estate in Chuckatuck. Doubtless in violation of George's pride, they moved in with Sallie's family until able to get back on their feet.[5]

Looking for work in the countryside, already overrun by jobless and displaced persons, was a monumental task for someone who had never tilled the soil. Before he could address questions of employment, however, he had responsibilities of a more pressing nature. Before leaving Richmond he had bowed to the inevitable by repairing to the provost marshal's office and taking the oath of allegiance to the federal government, his uncle Andrew serving as witness. Probably at General Ord's recommendation, he had also written to President Andrew Johnson to seek a pardon for having taken up arms against the United States. In this letter he described himself as "ready to renew my allegiance as a loyal citizen of the United States government, and [I] have advised and counseled all men belonging to my division to return to their homes and the peaceful pursuits of life."[6]

Despite doing all that was required of him, nothing came of his application. His brother took the oath of allegiance only a few days before he did, and Charlie's pardon came through in early August; months later, however, George was awaiting action on his case. As the year wound down he was still out of work and living on his in-laws' estate, and Sallie was pregnant again. But his greatest concern was that he had heard nothing about his pardon. He began to worry that there was something in his background—a special aspect of his Confederate service, perhaps—that was holding up action on his case.[7]

His fears were not groundless. Within weeks of Lee's surrender and Abraham Lincoln's assassination, Republicans in Congress began to investigate the wartime services of high Confederate officials with a view to official sanctions. By the summer of 1865 Jefferson Davis was in irons at Fort Monroe and the government was looking into the possibility of trying Robert E. Lee and other ranking military leaders for treason. Given his name recognition and the controversy he had stirred up during the war, Pickett could hardly have escaped the government's attention.

The most notorious aspect of his wartime service, of course, was his role in executing the North Carolina militiamen captured in blue uniforms outside New Bern. This was one *cause celebre* that ex-Union generals in Congress such as Robert C. Schenck of Ohio and Pickett's old enemy, Benjamin Butler of Massachusetts, would not permit the government to ignore. The interest these politicians expressed in investigating the hangings at Kinston, supported by a similar desire among local Unionists—some of them relatives of the twenty-two who had been hanged—eventually produced action.

In mid-September 1865 a U.S. officer at New Bern, acting in behalf of local citizens including the widows of the slain men, submitted a memorial to Brevet Major General Thomas H. Ruger, the occupation commander in North Carolina. Ruger was called on to help "bring to justice certain wicked and cruel men who have deliberately murdered, by public hanging, a number of loyal citizens and soldiers of the United States, when prisoners, during the late rebellion. . . ." Unable to ignore such a request, General Ruger impanelled a three-officer board of inquiry, which met at New Bern from late October till mid-November, taking testimony from numerous witnesses, Unionists and secessionists alike, and participants in the execution. A number of those who testified reported having heard that Pickett was the driving force behind the court-martial that condemned the North Carolinians, though none had personal knowledge of his actions. General Hoke, commanding at Kinston in February 1864, was singled out as officer in charge of the executions. The principal recommendation of the board, submitted on December 12 to Joseph Holt, Judge Advocate General of the Army, was "the immediate appointment of a military commission for the trial of the parties implicated, especially General Pickett, who ordered the execution; [and] General Hoke, who was in charge of it. . . ."

The board's findings failed to spur Holt into immediate action. Upon thorough review of the evidence he concluded that while "every sentiment of patriotism and public justice forbids that the blood of these murdered men should cry in vain from their dishonored graves for vengeance," he found no grounds to sustain personal charges against either of the "guilty parties." Lacking was evidence "showing conclusively by whom or by whose order these sufferers were arrested and prosecuted; by whom tried, condemned, or executed." Rather than dismissing the case, however, Holt returned the inquiry documents to Ruger and directed him "to cause further and minute investigations to be made into the circumstances of the case, with the view of tracing and fixing the guilt" of those responsible.[8]

Had Pickett been aware of this turn in the investigation, he would have breathed easier for little more than two weeks. A few days before Christmas Holt got in touch with John Peck, recently retired from the army and living in Syracuse, New York. Peck supplied the Judge Advocate General with details of his wartime encounters with Pickett; he even provided a copy of a letter dated February 17, 1864, in which Pickett acknowledged responsibility for those executions that had taken place up to that time. Here was the incriminating evidence that Ruger's board had failed to locate. Two days before year's end Holt informed Secretary Stanton of his recent discovery and his intention to share it with the Attorney General to "assist in determining the question of the writer's pardon, which is said to be pending before the President." Furthermore, Holt had decided to recommend Pickett's arrest and trial as a war criminal.[9]

Although probably unaware of Holt's recommendation, Pickett would have learned about the investigation at New Bern, which, being a matter of public record, would have received newspaper coverage. He may even have learned of the board's existence before it began taking testimony. The convening of the panel, added to the continuing uncertainty over his pardon, made him fear the worst. He and Sallie discussed the situation at great length, pondered their options, and made the painful decision to flee the country—separately, to avoid detection.

At a date unknown—before October 10, if not much earlier—he kissed his wife and child good-bye, left Chuckatuck in disguise (going so far as to shear his trademark ringlets), took a train at Norfolk, travelled up the East coast, crossed into Canada without difficulty, and under the name "Edwards" took a room at the Garreau Hotel in Montreal. A few weeks later Sallie and George, Jr., went to Montreal via the same route. After many alleged trials and tribulations, they were reunited with the husband and father and with him began a life of exile.[10]

How long they remained in Canada is something of a mystery. La Salle Pickett maintains that they had been there nearly a year before a summons from General Grant, through Rufus Ingalls, assured them that all was well and they could return without fear of molestation. She portrays their early months in the country as a life of elegance and ease. Her reminiscences include details of a several-month stay in a palatial mansion as guests of English-born friends vacationing in London. She also portrays her husband and herself as guests of wealthy and prominent benefactors. One of her better-known anecdotes depicts a breakfast party given by the governor-general of Canada at which her husband answered his host's question about the causes of Confederate defeat at Gettysburg with a sage observation: "I think the Yankees had a little something to do with it."

La Salle admits that life in Canada was not a sustained pleasure-spree. When their hosts returned from England the Picketts took up residence in a boarding-house until the snooping of their nosy proprietor forced them to flee to smaller, rented lodgings along the Champs de Mars. La Salle also maintains that when her husband fell ill and could no longer work (she never identifies the job he was forced to give up), she pawned her jewels, then took a position as a Latin teacher, to pay the rent and the doctor's bills. Despite their financial straits these were, she claims, "the happiest days of my whole life" in that she had been able to parlay her classical education into a paying job.[11]

The historical record fails to support such an extensive Canadian tour as Sallie alleges. If the Picketts did not arrive in Montreal until early October, their stay could have lasted no longer than six weeks. On November 24 one of their principal contacts in the city, former Brigadier General Edwin Gray Lee—cousin of Robert E. Lee and in the last months of the war the director of a Confederate espionage ring operating out of Montreal—stopped by their lodgings and found they had left Canada for home. Six weeks before—probably upon Pickett's arrival in the city—Lee had loaned him $100 to support him in exile; the record does not indicate whether he was repaid.[12]

Pickett was back in Richmond by the first week in December, although, as he wrote a friend, he feared the necessity of leaving— probably to return to Canada—on a moment's notice. He seems to have returned prematurely, perhaps believing that with the New Bern inquiry ended, the controversy regarding his pardon had blown over— only to learn of his impending indictment at the recommendation of the Judge Advocate General. He may have received some assurance from within military or political circles that despite Holt's actions he would not be prosecuted, for he remained in Richmond long after Holt filed his recommendation.[13]

In March 1866 Pickett travelled to Washington, perhaps to discuss the status of his pardon with lower-level government officials. While there he appealed to his old friend, Ulysses S. Grant, Commanding General of the Army, to protect him from "the assaults of those persons desirous of keeping up the War which has ended in my humble opinion *forever*." All he sought was "a guarantee that I may be permitted to live unmolested in my native State, where I am now trying to make a subsistence for my family, (much impoverished by the War,) by tilling the land."

Recalling their past association, Grant responded in a spirit of friendship and from a desire to lay aside the political and military controversies arising from the war. Four days after Pickett wrote, Grant forwarded the letter to President Johnson with a lengthy endorsement. He asked that clemency be granted Pickett or assurances given him that he would not be tried for war crimes. He based his request on the fact that during the conflict the United States government had granted the Confederacy belligerency rights, "and it is clear to me that the parole given by the Armies laying down their arms protects them against punishment for acts lawful for any other belligerent."

Grant admitted that the punishment meted out to the twenty-two North Carolinians "was a harsh one but it was in time of war and when the enemy no doubt felt it necessary to retain, by some power, the services of every man within their reach. Gen. Pickett I know personally to be an honorable man but in this case his judgement [*sic*] prompted him to do what can not well be sustained though I do not see how good, either to the friends of the deceased or by fixing an example for the future, can be secured by his trial now. It would only open up the question whether or not the Government did not disregard its contract . . . under the surrender of an armed enemy."[14]

Grant's rank and prominence, and the strong influence he enjoyed with the President, ensured that Pickett would no longer have to fear prosecution. Holt's recommendation failed to produce a trial. The following July Representative Schenck attempted to reopen the issue by pushing through a House resolution inquiring into the status of Pickett's pardon. When Schenck sought to learn if Pickett had been punished for his alleged role in the Kinston hangings, the White House threw up a wall of silence. Five months later, when Schenck stubbornly petitioned Johnson for a copy of the Judge Advocate's report on the Pickett investigation, Johnson's secretary replied that the President recalled seeing no such report; apparently it had failed to reach his hands. At that point Congressional efforts to bring Pickett to account for the hangings reached an end, although his case was not officially closed until Christmas Day 1868 when he was included in Johnson's blanket proclamation of "amnesty for the offense of treason."[15]

His prosecutorial problems finally behind him, General Pickett could attempt to rebuild his life and provide for his family, which

Eleanor S. Brockenbrough Library
The Museum of the Confederacy
George Pickett, Jr., and Corbell Pickett, ca. 1869

expanded in 1866 with the birth of his second son, Corbell. His spiritual renewal began with a symbolic act of reconstruction. His wife relates that "we went back to our dear old place, Turkey Island, on the James River, and built a little cottage in the place of the magnificent mansion which had been sacked and burned by order of General Butler." They lived there, reasonably happy, for some years, before giving the cottage up for a Richmond hotel suite close to her husband's place of business.

Pickett found it extremely difficult to find a profession in which he felt comfortable. The life of a gentleman farmer did not prove sufficiently remunerative. "He tried to turn his sword into a plowshare," La Salle recalled, "but he was not expert with plowshares; and, worse, he constantly received applications for employment from old comrades no more skilled than he. All were made welcome, though they might not be able to distinguish a rake from a rail fence or tell whether potatoes grew on trees or trellised vines." Many of his old officers and men, now destitute, sought employment, and, despite being only a step or two from poverty himself, he turned none away, gradually forming what his wife called "the agricultural army at Turkey Island." She adds, however, that "the inevitable came; resources were in time exhausted, and proprietor and assistants were forced to seek other fields."[16]

Pickett used to say that by education, training, and experience he was fitted only for soldiering. Still, when the Khedive of Egypt, seeking to impart a western influence for his armed forces, recruited Civil War veterans for his armies, Pickett turned him down twice. Friends who knew of his financial situation believed he was making a mistake; distinguished Confederates including Beauregard, Johnston, and Porter Alexander were rumored to be giving serious thought to the venture. According to Sallie, he rejected the proposition because he considered her love "worth all the gold and glory" any potentate could promise.[17]

He declined other opportunities for employment as well. Sallie recounts a several-day visit to the White House soon after Grant's election to the presidency in 1868, during which the President offered him "the marshalship of the State of Virginia." Because she provides somewhat contradictory versions of this story, its validity is suspect, and the way she phrases her husband's declination reads like an invented quote ("you cannot afford to do this for me, and I cannot afford to let you do it"). Her contention that he also declined the governorship of Virginia is not borne out by evidence, although it is probably true, as Sallie asserts, that after his old subordinate, James Kemper, was elected governor in 1873, they assisted the bachelor politician during his official receptions.[18]

Pickett found steady work only after he accepted an offer to become a general agent of the Washington Life Insurance Company of New York. Working out of an office at Eleventh and Main Streets, Richmond, he sold insurance policies himself, while supervising the work of other agents. The job provided him with an adequate income but the hours were long, the work required him to travel throughout the eastern part of the state, and the process of trying to sell a product that his impoverished customers could not afford and, in most cases, did not want, was a demeaning experience for a former major general in the Confederate army. Aspects of the job reminded him of another professional offer he had rejected, to involve himself with the famous Louisiana Lottery, in which General Beauregard was a high official. "There was a large salary attached to it," La Salle wrote of the lottery offer, "but he said there was not money enough in the world to induce him to lend his name to it."

The demands placed upon him by Washington Life wore Pickett down physically and robbed him of his spirit. Sallie characterized his professional life as "one of deep and tragic earnestness." He could not come to terms with a profession that made its profits through what one colleague called "gall, gall, old man, gall and grub." Pickett described for Sallie this man's tendency to lapse into the jargon of modern business to explain how one succeeded in the insurance trade: "I'd have to unbuckle a few notes and thaw out if I wanted to paint the monkey's tail sky-blue." He did not think himself capable of that: "I'm afraid your Soldier isn't much of an artist." Nor was he a much of a salesman. "I'd sooner face a cannon," he told her, "than ask a man to take out a policy with me."[19]

* * *

While trying to put the bitterness and disruptions of the war behind him, he could not disassociate himself from those with whom he had shared the hardships and glories of that four-year quest for the Lost Cause. He made himself accessible to veterans writing reminiscences of the war and professional and amateur historians seeking to confirm the details of events in which he played a part. He maintained an active interest in, and a connection with, a number of veterans' organizations. His deepest involvement was with the Virginia Division of the Association of the Army of Northern Virginia, whose second president he became (succeeding Fitzhugh Lee) in the early 1870s.[20]

He was also active in militia affairs, delivering addresses at banquets marking the election of officers and the dedication of flags. When in 1874 Virginia's adjutant general was disabled in an accident, Pickett took over some of his duties, without pay. In the main, he served as a special agent for the purchase and issuance of militia weapons and equipment, including ordnance, and for the sale or disposal of sur-plus supplies.[21]

In June 1872 he served as chief marshal at ceremonies honor-ing the reinterment in Richmond's Hollywood Cemetery of the first group of almost 3,000 Confederates who had fallen at Gettysburg. Reflecting on the huge crowds that gathered to pay their respects to the Southern dead, Pickett pronounced the event "a demonstration of devotion and sympathy . . . never before witnessed on earth."[22]

On at least one occasion his inability to break with the past caused him embarrassment and grief. In March 1870, while living with his family at the Ballard and Exchange Hotel, Richmond, he learned that General Lee was staying there while on a visit from Lex-ington, where he served as president of Washington College. Pickett wished to pay his respects but was unsure of his reception: his check-ered relationship with Lee was a source of lingering pain, and he had not spoken to his old commander in the years since Five Forks. Fi-nally he called on Lee in company with John Mosby, the "Gray Ghost of the Confederacy," now a Richmond attorney, who had just come from a pleasant interview with the army leader, though he had not brought up the subject of the war in Lee's presence.

Instead of following Mosby's lead, Pickett apparently brought his conversation with Lee around to Gettysburg. From that point on, as Mosby's relates, "the interview was cold and formal, and evidently embarrassing to both." Taking Lee's manner as an unmerited rebuff, Pickett rose and left the room. On the way out he complained to Mosby about "that old man" who had ruined Pickett's career and his com-mand: "He had my division massacred at Gettysburg." Pickett was not mollified by Mosby's rejoinder that "it made you immortal."[23]

* * *

But Pickett was not immortal. In the summer of 1875, borne down by the burdens of his profession and the recent death of his younger son, a sickly child who had succumbed to measles the previ-ous Easter, he cut short an overdue vacation at White Sulphur Springs to make a business trip to Norfolk. La Salle went with him; they took a room at a local hotel to which he returned, suffering from chills and fever, after two days of "anxious work." Moved to the Hospital of St. Vincent de Paul, the general lay in bed for several days, his illness worsening, as members of his family and Sallie's rushed to his side.

Though in obvious distress, he refused pain-killers that might impair his faculties. He spoke lovingly to his wife, recited with George, Jr., the Chinook prayers he had taught his son years before, and wrote letters of farewell to friends.

As his heart weakened, he turned to Sallie's uncle, with whom he had served in the Army of Northern Virginia, and remarked in a low voice: "Well, Colonel, the enemy is too strong for me again . . . my ammunition is all out." In truth, it had run out in a sun-baked valley in Pennsylvania a dozen years before. He closed his eyes, and settled back as if at peace for the first time in his life. Sallie never left his side; two hours after his death they gently pried her hands from his.[24]

ENDNOTES

ABBREVIATIONS USED IN NOTES

AAG	Assistant Adjutant General
B&L	*Battles and Leaders of the Civil War*
CV	*Confederate Veteran*
DU	Duke University (William R. Perkins Library)
F-SNMP	Fredericksburg-Spotsylvania National Military Park
LC	Library of Congress
M-, r-	Microcopy-, reel-
MR	Monthly Return
NA	National Archives
OR	*War of the Rebellion: A Compilation of the Official Records of the Union and Confederate Armies*
RG-, E-	Record Group-, Entry-
SHSP	*Southern Historical Society Papers*
UNC	University of North Carolina (Wilson Library)
USMA	United States Military Academy (Library/Archives)
UVA	University of Virginia (Alderman Library)
VHS	Virginia Historical Society
VMH&B	*Virginia Magazine of History and Biography*

PREFACE

1. Michael Shaara, *The Killer Angels* (New York, 1974), 58.

2. Ibid., 71.

3. Ibid., 64.

4. *The Heart of a Soldier, as Revealed in the Intimate Letters of Genl. George E. Pickett, C.S.A.*, ed. La Salle Corbell Pickett (New York, 1913); *Soldier of the South: General Pickett's War Letters to His Wife*, ed. Arthur Crew Inman (Boston, 1928).

5. Anyone who peruses La Salle Corbell Pickett's *Pickett's Men* (three editions, the first published in Atlanta, 1900) or any of her autobiographical works, then reads those compilations of letters purportedly written by her husband, will readily discover that the voice that speaks from *Heart of a Soldier* and *Soldier of the South* is not George Pickett's, but his widow's. There are other clues to authorship beyond empirical evidence. Both *Heart of a Soldier* and *Soldier of the South* include letters that detail certain events with which Pickett could not have been conversant at the time he supposedly wrote. Other passages bear an uncanny similarity to the published and unpublished writings of his contemporaries. Occasionally material is lifted whole from Walter Harrison's *Pickett's Men: A Fragment of War History* (New York, 1870); the wartime letters of Pickett's artillery chief, Major James Dearing; and other sources.

   Another indication of authorship is that many of the published letters contain long passages mimicking the African-American dialect of the mid-nineteenth century South. None of the extant Pickett letters contains such material—although stereotypical black dialect was a subject on which Mrs. Pickett wrote and lectured widely in her later years.

   Mrs. Pickett's involvement in rewriting her husband's letters was remarkably thorough. In *Soldier of the South*, she permitted the publication of three extant letters along with all but two of the letters originally published in *Heart of a Soldier*. It can be seen that she edited and embellished even the authentic missives, as if she could not bear to show the reading public material that did not contain her touch. For a more detailed study of her literary efforts, see Gary W. Gallagher, "A Widow and Her Soldier: La Salle Corbell Pickett as Author of the George E. Pickett Letters," *VMH&B* 94 (1986): 329-44. See also Appendix B ("The Pickett 'Letters'") in George R. Stewart, *Pickett's Charge: A Microhistory of the Final Attack at Gettysburg, July 3, 1863* (Greenwich, Conn., 1963), 259-60.

   Because portions of the published letters appear to contain authentic material, selected passages have been incorporated into the present work when they tally with known facts, when they present a reasonably accurate account of events, and when they offer a plausible interpretation of Pickett's frame of mind.

6. Letters and manuscripts in the *Century* Civil War Collection at the New York Public Library reveal that numerous contributions to the *B&L* series were heavily edited and in some cases rewritten without the knowledge or consent of their authors. The collection contains correspondence from contributors upset to find that the published version of their work bore little resemblance to their original submissions.

ONE

1. James Longstreet, "General James Longstreet's Account of the Campaign and Battle [of Gettysburg]," *SHSP* 5 (1877): 69-70; James Longstreet, "Lee's Right

Wing at Gettysburg," *B&L* 3: 344-45; James Longstreet, *From Manassas to Appomattox: Memoirs of the Civil War in America* (Philadelphia, 1896), 392; E. Porter Alexander, *Military Memoirs of a Confederate: A Critical Narrative* (New York, 1908), 423-24; E. Porter Alexander, *Fighting for the Confederacy: The Personal Recollections of General Edward Porter Alexander*, ed. Gary W. Gallagher (Chapel Hill, 1989), 260; "Causes of the Defeat of Gen. Lee's Army at the Battle of Gettysburg—Opinions of Leading Confederate Soldiers," *SHSP* 4 (1877): 107; James F. Crocker, *Gettysburg—Pickett's Charge and Other War Addresses* (Portsmouth, Va., 1915), 41; Randolph A. Shotwell, *The Papers of Randolph Abbott Shotwell*, ed. J. G. D. Hamilton and Rebecca Cameron, 3 vols. (Raleigh, 1929-31), 2: 8; John Purifoy, "Longstreet's Attack at Gettysburg," *CV* 32 (1924): 56; Douglas Southall Freeman, *Lee's Lieutenants: A Study in Command*, 3 vols. (New York, 1942-44), 3: 155; George R. Stewart, *Pickett's Charge: A Microhistory of the Final Attack at Gettysburg, July 3, 1863* (Greenwich, Conn., 1963), 150, 152; Edwin B. Coddington, *The Gettysburg Campaign: A Study in Command* (New York, 1968), 500.

2. Crocker, *Gettysburg—Pickett's Charge*, 41; Joseph C. Mayo, "Pickett's Charge at Gettysburg . . . .," *SHSP* 34 (1906): 331; Kathleen R. Georg and John W. Busey, *Nothing But Glory: Pickett's Division at Gettysburg* (Hightstown, N.J., 1987), 64; Glenn Tucker, *High Tide at Gettysburg: The Campaign in Pennsylvania* (Indianapolis, 1958), 357.

3. For sources covering Pickett's whereabouts during the charge that bears his name, see Chapter Nine, notes 23-27.

4. Stella Pickett Hardy, "Genealogy: The Pickett Family," *Bulletin [of the] Fauquier Historical Society* 1 (1921-24): 214; Walter Harrison, *Pickett's Men: A Fragment of War History* (New York, 1870), 64.

5. "Pickett Family of Virginia," *VMH&B* 49 (1941): 80-86, 186-90; Stella Pickett Hardy, *Colonial Families of the Southern States of America. . . .* (Baltimore, 1958), 414-28; *Richmond Times-Dispatch*, Apr. 11, 1909.

6. Richard L. Maury, Address on George E. Pickett, 8, Maury Papers, DU; La Salle Corbell Pickett, *What Happened to Me* (New York, 1917), 355.

7. Richard Selcer, "George Pickett: Another Look," *Civil War Times Illustrated* 33 (July-Aug. 1994): 46.

8. Ibid., 46; Leslie Jill Gordon, "Before the Storm: The Early Life of George E. Pickett," 7-8, Typescript in Earl Gregg Swem Library, College of William and Mary, Williamsburg, Va.

9. Hardy, "Genealogy: The Pickett Family," 214; Oliver Otis Howard, *Autobiography of Oliver Otis Howard, Major General United States Army*, 2 vols. (New York, 1907), 1: 62-63.

10. Gordon, "Before the Storm," 8-9; Abraham Lincoln, *Poetry and Prose by A. Lincoln*, ed. Paul M. Angle and Earl Schenck Miers (Kingsport, Tenn., 1956), 11.

11. Andrew Johnston to John T. Stuart, Aug. 19, 1841, Abraham Lincoln Association, Springfield, Ill.; George E. Pickett to John Canfield Spencer, Apr. 26, 1842, Cadet Application File, USMA.

12. La Salle Corbell Pickett, "General George E. Pickett: His Appointment to West Point . . . .", *SHSP* 24 (1896): 151-54; La Salle Corbell Pickett, *Pickett and His Men* (Atlanta, 1900), 126-28; George E. Pickett, *The Heart of a Soldier, as Revealed in the Intimate Letters of Genl. George E. Pickett, C.S.A.*, ed. La Salle Corbell Pickett (New York, 1913), 15-17.

13. George A. Bruce to Benjamin P. Owen, Dec. 27, 1927; to Margaret Heth Vaden, Apr. 22, 1928; both, VHS.

14. James L. Morrison, Jr., *"The Best School in the World": West Point, the Pre-Civil War Years, 1833-1866* (Kent, Ohio, 1986), 1-4; Edward C. Boynton, *History of West Point . . . and the Origin and Progress of the United States Military Academy* (New York, 1863), 238.

15. Ibid., 324; Morrison, *"Best School in the World"*, 61-63; *Report of the Chief of Engineers* (Senate Exec. Doc. no. 2, 29th Cong., 1st sess., 1845), 270-71.

16. *Report of the Chief of Engineers* (Senate Exec. Doc. no. 1, 28th Cong., 2nd sess., 1844), 204-05, 213.

17. Ibid., 211-12.

18. *Official Register of the Officers and Cadets of the U.S. Military Academy, West Point, N.Y.* (West Point, N.Y., 1843), 13, 21.

19. Morrison, *"Best School in the World,"* 73-74.

20. Dabney H. Maury, "Dabney Maury on Stonewall Jackson," *CV* 6 (1898): 53; James I. Robertson, Jr., *General A. P. Hill: The Story of a Confederate Warrior* (New York, 1987), 9; John C. Waugh, *The Class of 1846, from West Point to Appomattox: Stonewall Jackson, George McClellan and Their Brothers* (New York, 1994), 39; Cadet Delinquency Register, USMA, 268, 313, 332, 348; P. T. Turnley, *Reminiscences of Parmenas Taylor Turnley . . . .* (Chicago, 1892), 10.

21. Cadet Delinquency Register, 268; Pickett, *Heart of a Soldier*, 3.

22. Cadet Delinquency Register, 268, 313.

23. Pickett, *Heart of a Soldier*, 3.

24. Gordon, "Before the Storm," 11-14; Selcer, "George Pickett: Another Look," 47.

25. Cadet Delinquency Register, 268, 313, 332, 348; *Official Register of the Officers and Cadets of the U.S. Military Academy, West Point, N.Y.* (West Point, N.Y., 1844), 11, 21; *Official Register of the Officers and Cadets of the U.S. Military Academy, West Point, N.Y.* (West Point, N.Y., 1845), 10, 21.

26. Hardy, *Colonial Families of the Southern States*, 426; Henry Heth, *The Memoirs of Henry Heth*, ed. James L. Morrison, Jr. (Westport, Conn., 1974), 14, 18-19, 65.

27. *Official Register of the U.S. Military Academy [for 1845]*, 10; *Official Register of the Officers and Cadets of the U.S. Military Academy, West Point, N.Y.* (West Point, N.Y., 1846), 8.

28. Ibid., 19; Waugh, *Class of 1846*, 38-39; Robertson, *General A. P. Hill*, 14; Gordon, "Before the Storm," 15-16.

29. *Official Register of the U.S. Military Academy [for 1846]*, 7-8.

TWO

1. John C. Waugh, *The Class of 1846, from West Point to Appomattox: Stonewall Jackson, George McClellan and Their Brothers* (New York, 1994), 73-75; James I. Robertson, Jr., *General A. P. Hill: The Story of a Confederate Warrior* (New York, 1987), 13-15; James L. Morrison, Jr., *"The Best School in the World": West Point, the Pre-Civil War Years, 1833-1866* (Kent, Ohio, 1986), 129-31.

2. P. T. Turnley, *Reminiscences of Parmenas Taylor Turnley. . . .* (Chicago, 1892), 60, 62; "Minge Family Register," *William and Mary Quarterly* 1st ser., 21 (1912): 31; Stella Pickett Hardy, *Colonial Families of the Southern States of America. . . .* (Baltimore, 1958), 156; Military History of Officers, Eighth U.S. Infantry, 1838-69, RG-391, E-1285, NA.

3. Leslie Jill Gordon, "Before the Storm: The Early Life of George E. Pickett," 18-19, Typescript in Earl Gregg Swem Library, College of William and Mary, Williamsburg, Va.

4. Ibid., 20-21; Military History of Officers, Eighth U.S. Infantry, 1838-69, RG-391, E-1285; MR, Eighth U.S. Infantry, Aug. 1846, M-665, r-90; both, NA.

5. MR, Dec. 1846, M-665, r-90, NA; *Seventh Annual Reunion of the Association of the Graduates of the United States Military Academy. . . .* (New York, 1876), 11; G. Moxley Sorrel, *Recollections of a Confederate Staff Officer* (New York, 1905), 54; Jeffry D. Wert, *General James Longstreet, the Confederacy's Most Controversial Soldier: A Biography* (New York, 1993), 48-49.

6. MR, Eighth U.S. Infantry, Jan. 1847, M-665, r-90, NA; Richard Selcer, "George Pickett: Another Look," *Civil War Times Illustrated* 33 (July-Aug. 1994): 47.

7. K. Jack Bauer, *The Mexican War, 1846-1848* (New York, 1974), 232-41; John S. D. Eisenhower, *So Far from God: The U.S. War with Mexico, 1846-1848* (New York, 1989), 253-56; *Seventh Annual Reunion,* 11-12; Theophilus F. Rodenbough and William L. Haskin, eds., *The Army of the United States: Historical Sketches of Staff and Line. . . .* (New York, 1896), 516.

8. La Salle Corbell Pickett, *Pickett and His Men* (Atlanta, 1900), 90-91; Bauer, *Mexican War,* 239-46.

9. Rodenbough and Haskin, *Army of the United States,* 516; History of Officers, Eighth U.S. Infantry, 1838-69, RG-391, E-1285; MRs, Second U.S. Infantry, Mar.-July 1847, M-665, r-17; both, NA.

10. Rodenbough and Haskin, *Army of the United States,* 516; Bauer, *Mexican War,* 259-68.

11. Rodenbough and Haskin, *Army of the United States,* 516-17; MR, Seventh U.S. Infantry, July 1847, M-665, r-79; Military History of Officers, Seventh U.S. Infantry, 1808-1908, RG-391, E-1237; both, NA; *Seventh Annual Reunion,* 12.

12. MR, Eighth U.S. Infantry, July 1847, M-665, r-90, NA.

13. Bauer, *Mexican War,* 289-99; Eisenhower, *So Far from God,* 317-24; Winfield Scott, *Memoirs of Lieut.-General Scott . . . .,* 2 vols. (New York, 1864), 2: 484-86.

14. Bauer, *Mexican War,* 296-300; *Message from the President of the United States, to the Two Houses of Congress, at the Commencement of the First Session of the Thirtieth Congress* (Washington, D.C., 1847), 52-53, 56, 64; Wert, *General James Longstreet,* 44; Scott, *Memoirs,* 2: 486-88.

15. *Message from the President,* 54-56, 65-66; Pickett, *Pickett and His Men,* 94; Richard L. Maury, Address on George E. Pickett, 8, Maury Papers, DU; Rodenbough and Haskin, *Army of the United States,* 517; Military History of Officers, Eighth U.S. Infantry, 1838-69, RG-391, E-1285, NA.

16. Bauer, *Mexican War,* 301-08; Scott, *Memoirs,* 2: 503-05; Horace Haldeman to his brother, Aug. 28, 1847, Haldeman Correspondence, U.S. Army Military History Institute, Carlisle Barracks, Pa.

17. *Message from the President,* 152; Military History of Officers, Eighth U.S. Infantry, 1838-69, RG-391, E-1285, NA.

18. *Message from the President,* 150-54; MR, Eighth U.S. Infantry, Sept. 1847, M-665, r-90, NA; Bauer, *Mexican War,* 307-11; Scott, *Memoirs,* 2: 505-07; Pickett, *Pickett and His Men,* 94.

19. Bauer, *Mexican War,* 312-17; *Message from the President,* 182.

20. Scott, *Memoirs*, 2: 517; Pickett, *Pickett and His Men*, 95.

21. Justin H. Smith, *The War with Mexico*, 2 vols. (New York, 1919), 2: 154-57; Wert, *General James Longstreet*, 45; George W. Gordon, "Battles of Molino del Rey and Chapultepec," *Civil and Mexican Wars, 1861, 1846: Papers of the Military Historical Society of Massachusetts* 13 (1913): 627-28; Pickett, *Pickett and His Men*, 95-96; Rodenbough and Haskin, *Army of the United States*, 518; Scott, *Memoirs*, 2: 512-18; Bauer, *Mexican War*, 317-18.

22. Henry Heth, *The Memoirs of Henry Heth*, ed. James L. Morrison, Jr. (Westport, Conn., 1974), 66; Robert Ryal Miller, *Shamrock and Sword: The Saint Patrick's Battalion in the U.S.-Mexican War* (Norman, 1989), 85-107.

23. Military History of Officers, Eighth U.S. Infantry, 1838-69, RG-391, E-1285, NA; Eppa Hunton, IV, "Battle Abbey Committee Report," *VMH&B* 66 (1958): 238.

24. MRs, Eighth U.S. Infantry, Sept., Dec. 1847, M-665, r-90; Mar., June 1848, M-665, r-91; all, NA; Horace Haldeman to his brother, Nov. 11, 1847, Haldeman Correspondence.

25. Heth, *Memoirs*, 68.

26. George E. Pickett to George W. Cullum, Feb. 19, 1860, Cullum File, USMA; Edward S. Wallace, *General William Jenkins Worth, Monterey's Forgotten Hero* (Dallas, 1953), 185; MR, Eighth U.S. Infantry, July 1848, M-665, r-91, NA.

THREE

1. MR, Eighth U.S. Infantry, Jan. 1849, M-665, r-91, NA; George E. Pickett to George W. Cullum, Feb. 19, 1860, Cullum File, USMA; Horace Haldeman to his brother, Dec. 28, 1848, July 20, 1849, Haldeman Correspondence, U.S. Army Military History Institute, Carlisle Barracks, Pa.; Robert M. Utley, *Frontiersmen in Blue: The United States Army and the Indian, 1848-1865* (New York, 1967), 60, 63-64, 70-72; Harold B. Simpson, *Cry Comanche: The 2nd U.S. Cavalry in Texas, 1855-1861* (Hillsboro, Tex., 1979), 51-53.

2. MRs, Eighth U.S. Infantry, Dec. 1848, Apr. 1849, M-665, r-91, NA.

3. Simpson, *Cry Comanche*, 56.

4. Military History of Officers, Eighth U.S. Infantry, 1838-69, RG-391, E-1285; MRs, Eighth U.S. Infantry, July, Oct., 1849, M-665, r-91; all, NA; George E. Pickett to George W. Cullum, Feb. 19, 1860, Cullum File; Horace Haldeman to his brother, Dec. 15, 1849, Haldeman Correspondence; Robert W. Frazer, *Forts of the West: Military Forts . . . West of the Mississippi River to 1898* (Norman, 1965), 150.

5. Horace Haldeman to his brother, Jan. 12, 1850, Haldeman Correspondence.

6. Military History of Officers, Eighth U.S. Infantry, 1838-69, RG-391, E-1285; MR, Eighth U.S. Infantry, Nov. 1851, M-665, r-91; both, NA; "Minge Family Register," *William and Mary Quarterly*, 1st ser., 21 (1912): 31.

7. Leslie Jill Gordon, "Before the Storm: The Early Life of George E. Pickett," 32-33, Typescript in Earl Gregg Swem Library, College of William and Mary, Williamsburg, Va.; "Minge Family Register," 31-32.

8. Gordon, "Before the Storm," 33; George E. Pickett to Elizabeth Heth Vaden, Dec. 4, 1852, Heth Family Papers, VHS.

9. Military History of Officers, Eighth U.S. Infantry, 1838-69, RG-391, E-1285; MRs, Eighth U.S. Infantry, Nov., Dec. 1851, Apr., May 1852, M-665, r-91; all,

NA; George E. Pickett, *The Heart of a Soldier, as Revealed in the Intimate Letters of Genl. George E. Pickett, C.S.A.*, ed. La Salle Corbell Pickett (New York, 1913), 1-3.

10. La Salle Corbell Pickett, *What Happened to Me* (New York, 1917), 34-38.

11. Pickett, *Heart of a Soldier*, 3-4.

12. George E. Pickett to La Salle Corbell, July 31, 1863, Arthur Crew Inman Papers, John Hay Library, Brown University, Providence, R.I.

13. MRs, Eighth U.S. Infantry, Apr., Oct., Nov., Dec. 1852, Jan., May, Sept., Oct. 1853, Feb., Aug. 1854, M-665, r-91; Headquarters Eighth U.S. Infantry to Headquarters Eighth Military Dept., Aug. 13, Oct. 11, 1853, Headquarters Letterbooks, Eighth U.S. Infantry, 1838-1900, RG-391, E-1279; all, NA; Frazer, *Forts of the West*, 143-46, 154-55, 158-59; George E. Pickett to George W. Cullum, Feb. 19, 1860, Cullum File; George E. Pickett to Elizabeth Heth Vaden, Dec. 4, 1852, Heth Family Papers; Jeffry D. Wert, *General James Longstreet, the Confederacy's Most Controversial Soldier: A Biography* (New York, 1993), 48-49.

14. Headquarters Eighth U.S. Infantry to AAG, Dept. of Texas, Oct. 11, 1852, Mar. 1, 1853, Dec. 3, 1854, Headquarters Letterbooks, Eighth U.S. Infantry, 1838-1900, RG-391, E-1279, NA; Simpson, *Cry Comanche*, 56-58; Utley, *Frontiersmen in Blue*, 72-77.

15. MR, Eighth U.S. Infantry, May 1855, M-665, r-91; MRs, Ninth U.S. Infantry, Mar., June 1855, M-665, r-102; all, NA; Theophilus F. Rodenbough and William L. Haskin, eds., *The Army of the United States: Historical Sketches of Staff and Line. . . .* (New York, 1896), 526.

16. MR, Ninth U.S. Infantry, Sept. 1855, M-665, r-102, NA; George E. Pickett to George W. Cullum, Feb. 19, 1860, Cullum File.

17. Pickett, *What Happened to Me*, 40-41; La Salle Corbell Pickett, *Pickett and His Men* (Atlanta, 1900), 96-97.

18. MRs, Ninth U.S. Infantry, Nov. 1855, Mar. 1856, M-665, r-102, NA.

19. Utley, *Frontiersmen in Blue*, 179-80, 187-88; Dorothy O. Johanson and Charles M. Gates, *Empire of the Columbia: A History of the Pacific Northwest* (New York, 1967), 254-55; Benjamin Franklin Manring, *Conquest of the Coeur D' Aienes, Spokanes & Palouses* (Spokane, Wash., 1912), 32; Kent D. Richards, *Isaac I. Stevens, Young Man in a Hurry* (Provo, Utah, 1979), 331-32; "Army Officer's Report of [the Puget Sound] Indian War and Treaties," *Washington Historical Quarterly* 19 (1928): 136-38; Norman H. Clark, *Washington: A Bicentennial History* (New York, 1976), 34-36; Michael P. Vouri, "George Pickett and the Frontier Army Experience," 2-3, Typescript in possession of the author, Bellingham, Wash.

20. Utley, *Frontiersmen in Blue*, 188-93; Bruce Grant, *American Forts Yesterday and Today* (New York, 1965), 262; Johanson and Gates, *Empire of the Columbia*, 255-57; Clark, *Washington*, 35-36; Vouri, "Pickett and Frontier Experience," 3-5.

21. MR, Ninth U.S. Infantry, June 1856, M-665, r-102, NA; *Washington: A Guide to the Evergreen State* (Portland, Ore., 1941), 273; Rodenbough and Haskin, *Army of the United States*, 527; Utley, *Frontiersmen in Blue*, 194; Francis B. Heitman, comp., *Historical Register and Dictionary of the United States Army. . . .*, 2 vols. (Washington, D.C., 1903), 2: 402.

22. *Washington: A Guide to the Evergreen State*, 178; Grant, *American Forts*, 262; Lelah Jackson Edson, *The Fourth Corner: Highlights from the Early North West* (Bellingham, Wash., 1968), 53, 57-58; Vouri, "Pickett and Frontier Experience," 5, 19-21.

23. *Washington: A Guide to the Evergreen State,* 183; Edson, *Fourth Corner,* 57, 60-61; Vouri, "Pickett and Frontier Experience," 24-27, 51.

24. Utley, *Frontiersmen in Blue,* 196-200; Pickett, *Pickett and His Men,* 97-98.

25. Edson, *Fourth Corner,* 115; Vouri, "Pickett and Frontier Experience," 50-51; Clark, *Washington,* 54; Caroline C. Leighton, *Life at Puget Sound . . . 1865-1881* (Boston, 1884), 110, 141.

26. Edson, *Fourth Corner,* 58-59, 116, 123; Vouri, "Pickett and Frontier Experience," 51.

FOUR

1. *Report of the Secretary of War* (Senate Exec. Doc. no. 2, 36th Cong., 1st sess., 1859), 57; Keith A. Murray, *The Pig War* (Tacoma, Wash., 1968), 7-13, 23-25; Alfred Tunem, "The Dispute Over the San Juan Island Water Boundary," *Washington Historical Quarterly* 23 (1932): 38-45; Caroline C. Leighton, *Life at Puget Sound . . . 1865-1881* (Boston, 1884), 140; Hazard Stevens, *The Life of Isaac Ingalls Stevens,* 2 vols. (Boston, 1900), 2: 12-13; La Salle Corbell Pickett, *Pickett and His Men* (Atlanta, 1900), 104-05.

2. *Report of Secretary of War,* 39-40, 46; William S. Harney to AAG, U.S. Army, Aug. 29, 1859, Headquarters Letterbooks, Dept. of Oregon, 1858-61, RG-393, E-3570, NA; Murray, *Pig War,* 25-29; *San Juan Island National Historical Park, Washington* (Washington, D.C., 1991), 1; Thomas E. Pickett, *A Soldier of the Civil War, by a Member of the Virginia Historical Society* (Cleveland, 1900), 13-15.

3. William S. Harney to AAG, U.S. Army, Aug. 7, 1859, Headquarters Letterbooks, Dept. of Oregon, 1858-61, RG-393, E-3570, NA; Murray, *Pig War,* 32-34; *Report of Secretary of War,* 81-84.

4. Charles McKay, "History of San Juan Island," *Washington Historical Quarterly* 2 (1907): 290-93; *Report of Secretary of War,* 44-47, 84, 87; Stevens, *Life of Isaac Ingalls Stevens,* 2: 290; Lelah Jackson Edson, *The Fourth Corner: Highlights from the Early North West* (Bellingham, Wash., 1968), 100-01.

5. *Report of Secretary of War,* 40-43; William S. Harney to AAG, U.S. Army, Aug. 7, 8, 1859; William S. Harney to Secretary of War, Oct. 10, 1859, Headquarters Letterbooks, Dept. of Oregon, 1858-61, RG-393, E-3570; MR, Ninth U.S. Infantry, July 1859, M-665, r-102; all, NA; George E. Pickett to George W. Cullum, Feb. 19, 1860, Cullum File, USMA; Pickett, *Pickett and His Men,* 111.

6. *Report of Secretary of War,* 49, 56, 83-84; Murray, *Pig War,* 36-39; William S. Harney to AAG, U.S. Army, Aug. 8, 1859, Headquarters Letterbooks, Dept. of Oregon, 1858-61, RG-393, E-3570, NA; Stevens, *Isaac Ingalls Stevens,* 2: 290-91.

7. *Report of Secretary of War,* 72-73, 87; Alfred Pleasonton to George E. Pickett, Aug. 6, 1859, Headquarters Letterbooks, Dept. of Oregon, 1858-61, RG-393, E-3570, NA; Murray, *Pig War,* 39-42.

8. *Report of Secretary of War,* 48-53; *OR,* I, 50, pt. 2: 973.

9. *Report of Secretary of War,* 54, 59; Alfred Pleasonton to George E. Pickett, Aug. 6, 1859; William S. Harney to AAG, U.S. Army, Aug. 18, 1859; both, Headquarters Letterbooks, Dept. of Oregon, RG-393, E-3570, NA.

10. *Report of Secretary of War,* 47, 55-56; William S. Harney to Senior Officer U.S. Navy, Commanding Squadron on Pacific Coast, Aug. 7, 1859, Headquarters

Letterbooks, Dept. of Oregon, 1858-61, RG-393, E-3570, NA; Murray, *Pig War*, 40-43; Granville O. Haller, *San Juan and Secession: Possible Relation to the War of the Rebellion. . . .* (Seattle, 1967), 13.

11. Stevens, *Isaac Ingalls Stevens*, 2: 295n.; *Report of Secretary of War*, 59-63, 69, 79; William S. Harney to R. D. Gholson, Aug. 7, 1859; Alfred Pleasonton to Silas Casey, Aug. 16, 1859; William S. Harney to AAG, U.S. Army, Aug. 18, 30, 1859; William S. Harney to Newman S. Clarke, Sept. 1, 1859; all, Headquarters Letterbooks, Dept. of Oregon, 1858-61, RG-393, E-3570, NA; George E. Pickett to George W. Cullum, Feb. 19, 1860, Cullum File.

12. *Report of Secretary of War*, 62; Murray, *Pig War*, 44-45.

13. *Report of Secretary of War*, 43-44; Charles Winslow Elliott, *Winfield Scott, the Soldier and the Man* (New York, 1937), 665-66.

14. *Report of Secretary of War*, 57-59; Elliott, *Winfield Scott*, 666-71; Murray, *Pig War*, 53-61.

15. George E. Pickett to anon., Feb. 21, 1860, Simon Gratz Collection, Historical Society of Pennsylvania, Philadelphia, Pa.; Alfred Pleasonton to George E. Pickett, Sept. 28, 1859, Headquarters Letterbooks, Dept. of Oregon, 1858-61, RG-393, E-3570; MRs, Ninth U.S. Infantry, Oct., Dec. 1859, M-665, r-102; all, NA; George E. Pickett to George W. Cullum, Feb. 19, 1860; Copy of "House Joint Resolution, No. 15," Washington Territorial Legislature, Jan. 11, 1860; both, Cullum File; "Pickett Grateful for Recognition," *Washington Historical Quarterly* 1 (1906): 74.

16. Stevens, *Isaac Ingalls Stevens*, 2: 294; Edson, *Fourth Corner*, 104; Murray, *Pig War*, 60-63; Alfred Pleasonton to George E. Pickett, Apr. 10, 1860, Headquarters Letterbooks, Dept. of Oregon, 1858-61, RG-393, E-3570; MR, Ninth U.S. Infantry, May 1860, M-665, r-102; both, NA; Pickett, *Pickett and His Men*, 121-23.

17. Murray, *Pig War*, 64-65, 68; Elliott, *Winfield Scott*, 670; *OR*, I, 50, pt. 1: 435, 445; McKay, "History of San Juan Island," 292; Alfred Pleasonton to George E. Pickett, July 3, 1859, Headquarters Letterbooks, Dept. of Oregon, 1858-61, RG-393, E-3570, NA.

18. Pickett, *Pickett and His Men*, 123-25, 426-27; Haller, *San Juan and Secession*, 12; Edson, *Fourth Corner*, 105; Robin W. Winks, *Canada and the United States: The Civil War Years* (Baltimore, 1960), 35.

19. George E. Pickett, *The Heart of a Soldier, as Revealed in the Intimate Letters of Genl. George E. Pickett, C.S.A.*, ed. La Salle Corbell Pickett (New York, 1913), 34-36.

20. MRs, Ninth U.S. Infantry, July, Sept. 1861, M-665, r-102, NA; Edson, *Fourth Corner*, 111-12; Pickett, *Pickett and His Men*, 123; Leslie Jill Gordon, "Before the Storm: The Early Life of George E. Pickett," 47-50, Typescript in Earl Gregg Swem Library, College of William and Mary, Williamsburg, Va.; Richard L. Maury, Address on George E. Pickett, 10, Maury Papers, DU.

21. *OR*, I, 50, pt. 1: 512, 519-20; Murray, *Pig War*, 69.

22. Edson, *Fourth Quarter*, 116-19.

23. MR, Ninth U.S. Infantry, Sept. 1861, M-665, r-102, NA; *OR*, I, 50, pt. 1: 533, 544-45.

24. Edson, *Fourth Corner*, 117-18; Gordon, "Before the Storm," 51.

25. Pickett, *Heart of a Soldier*, 36; "Letters from Old Trunks: Letter from James Barron Hope to Commodore Samuel Barron," *VMH&B* 47 (1939): 349n.-50n., 352n., 355n.; Gideon Welles, *Diary of Gideon Welles, Secretary of the Navy*

190	ENDNOTES FOR — Pages 53 to 64

Under Lincoln and Johnson, ed. Howard K. Beale and Alan W. Brownsword, 3 vols. (New York., 1960), 1: 18-21.

26. Pickett, *Heart of a Soldier*, 36; Welles, *Diary*, 1: 36-37.

27. Gordon, "Before the Storm," 51-52 and n.; Pickett, *Heart of a Soldier*, 36; George E. Pickett to Imogen Wright Barron, Nov. 4, 1864, Barron Family Papers, VHS.

28. Minutes of Pickett-Buchanan Camp, Sons of Confederate Veterans, May 23, 1899, Charles Pickett Papers, VHS; Pickett, *Heart of a Soldier*, 36-37.

29. Register of Appointments, CSA, Army of Northern Virginia General and Staff Officers' File, M-331, r-197, NA.

30. Jeffry D. Wert, *General James Longstreet, the Confederacy's Most Controversial Soldier: A Biography* (New York, 1993), 53-77.

31. Pickett, *Heart of a Soldier*, 33-37; La Salle Corbell Pickett, *What Happened to Me* (New York, 1917), 79-81, 87.

32. *OR*, I, 5: 877.

FIVE

1. Ezra J. Warner, *Generals in Gray: Lives of the Confederate Commanders* (Baton Rouge, 1959), 141; Albert Castel, "Theophilus Holmes—Pallbearer of the Confederacy," *Civil War Times Illustrated* 16 (July 1977): 11-12.

2. *OR*, I, 5: 910-11; Leslie Jill Gordon, "Before the Storm: The Early Life of George E. Pickett," 55-56, Typescript in Earl Gregg Swem Library, College of William and Mary, Williamsburg, Va.

3. *OR*, I, 5: 913, 923, 927; I, 51, pt. 2: 359, 366.

4. *OR*, I, 5: 991-92; Gordon, "Before the Storm," 58-59.

5. *OR*, I, 5: 994; I, 51, pt. 2: 466-67.

6. *OR*, I, 5: 1006; I, 51, pt. 2: 427-28.

7. Jeffry D. Wert, *General James Longstreet, the Confederacy's Most Controversial Soldier: A Biography* (New York, 1993), 97, 440n.

8. *OR*, I, 5: 1085-86; Register of Appointments, CSA, Army of Northern Virginia General and Staff Officers' File, M-331, r-197, NA.

9. E. Porter Alexander, "Sketch of Longstreet's Division," *SHSP* 9 (1881): 515.

10. Walter Harrison, *Pickett's Men: A Fragment of War History* (New York, 1870), 23; G. Moxley Sorrel, *Recollections of a Confederate Staff Officer* (New York, 1905), 136; Robert K. Krick, *Lee's Colonels: A Biographical Register of the Field Officers of the Army of Northern Virginia* (Dayton, 1979), 28, 336, 377; Warner, *Generals in Gray*, 69, 146.

11. James I. Robertson, Jr., *18th Virginia Infantry* (Lynchburg, Va., 1984), 9; Sorrel, *Recollections*, 54; Gordon, "Before the Storm," 5n.

12. Eppa Hunton, *Autobiography of Eppa Hunton* (Richmond, 1933), 65; Sorrel, *Recollections*, 54; Douglas Southall Freeman, *Lee's Lieutenants: A Study in Command*, 3 vols. (New York, 1942-44), 1: 158-59.

13. Randolph A. Shotwell, *The Papers of Randolph Abbott Shotwell*, ed. J. G. D. Hamilton and Rebecca Cameron, 3 vols. (Raleigh, 1929-31), 1: 170-71.

14. *OR*, I, 51, pt. 2: 466; Minutes of Pickett-Buchanan Camp, Sons of Confederate Veterans, May 23, 1899, Charles Pickett Papers, VHS; Harrison, *Pickett's Men*, 70; *List of Staff Officers of the Confederate States Army, 1861-1865* (Washington, D.C., 1891), 6, 8, 20, 38, 129, 160.

15. Edward R. Baird to Willy Baird, Mar. 25, 1862, Baird Family Papers, Earl Gregg Swem Library, College of William and Mary; Shotwell, *Papers*, 1: 170-75.

16. Stephen W. Sears, *To the Gates of Richmond: The Peninsula Campaign* (New York, 1992), 47-48; Gordon, "Before the Storm," 71-72; George E. Pickett, *The Heart of a Soldier, as Revealed in the Intimate Letters of Genl. George E. Pickett, C.S.A.*, ed. La Salle Corbell Pickett (New York, 1913), 39-40.

17. Sears, *To the Gates of Richmond*, 26; Robert H. Moore, II, *The Richmond, Fayette, Hampden, Thomas, and Blount's Lynchburg Artillery* (Lynchburg, Va., 1991), 56-57; William L. Parker, *General James Dearing, C.S.A.* (Lynchburg, Va., 1990), 24-25.

18. Thomas J. Goree, *The Thomas Jewett Goree Letters*, ed. Langston J. Goree, V (Bryan, Tex., 1981), 146; Joseph E. Johnston, "Manassas to Seven Pines," *B&L* 2: 203-04.

19. Sears, *To the Gates of Richmond*, 67-69; *OR*, I, 11, pt. 1: 564, 580, 589-90.

20. Ibid., I, 11, pt. 1: 584; William Nathaniel Wood, *Reminiscences of Big I*, ed. Bell Irvin Wiley (Jackson, Tenn., 1956), 11-12; Shotwell, *Papers*, 1: 193.

21. *OR*, I, 11, pt. 1: 584-85; Hunton, *Autobiography*, 66; Moore, *Richmond, Fayette Artillery*, 59; Shotwell, *Papers*, 1: 195.

22. Wood, *Big I*, 12.

23. *OR*, I, 11, pt. 1: 580-81, 585, 591; Wert, *General James Longstreet*, 105; Joseph E. Johnston, *Narrative of Military Operations. . . .* (New York, 1874), 120-21; Sears, *To the Gates of Richmond*, 73-74.

24. *OR*, I, 11, pt. 1: 487, 586, 588; La Salle Corbell Pickett to anon., May 10, 1908, UVA.

25. Wood, *Big I*, 13.

26. *OR*, I, 11, pt. 1: 567, 569, 586.

SIX

1. *OR*, I, 11, pt. 1: 23-25, 276; Stephen W. Sears, *To the Gates of Richmond: The Peninsula Campaign* (New York, 1992), 85-89, 94-97; Gustavus W. Smith, "Two Days of Battle at Seven Pines (Fair Oaks)," *B&L* 2: 221-23.

2. George E. Pickett, *The Heart of a Soldier, as Revealed in the Intimate Letters of Genl. George E. Pickett, C.S.A.*, ed. La Salle Corbell Pickett (New York, 1913), 41-42.

3. William Nathaniel Wood, *Reminiscences of Big I*, ed. Bell Irvin Wiley (Jackson, Tenn., 1956), 16.

4. *OR*, I, 11, pt. 1: 27-28, 37-38, 933; Sears, *To the Gates of Richmond*, 117-18; Smith, "Seven Pines (Fair Oaks)," 223-24.

5. *OR*, I, 11, pt. 1: 933-34, 939-41, 982; Smith, "Seven Pines (Fair Oaks)," 237, 250, 262-63; Jeffry D. Wert, *General James Longstreet, the Confederacy's Most Controversial Soldier: A Biography* (New York, 1993), 114-17; Wood, *Big I*, 17.

6. Sears, *To the Gates of Richmond*, 128-29, 135-36.

7. Wood, *Big I*, 17.

8. *OR*, I, 11, pt. 1: 944-45, 982.

9. Ibid., 982; Randolph A. Shotwell, *The Papers of Randolph Abbott Shotwell*, ed. J. G. D. Hamilton and Rebecca Cameron, 3 vols. (Raleigh, 1929-31), 1: 219.

10. *OR*, I, 11, pt. 1: 982; Pickett, *Heart of a Soldier*, 47; Richard Selcer, "George Pickett: Another Look," *Civil War Times Illustrated* 33 (July-Aug. 1994): 60; Hal Bridges, *Lee's Maverick General: Daniel Harvey Hill* (New York, 1961), 49.

11. *OR*, I, 11, pt. 1: 982; Shotwell, *Papers*, 1: 219-20; Wood, *Big I*, 18; Gustavus W. Smith, *The Battle of Seven Pines* (New York, 1891), 124.

12. Wood, *Big I*, 18; *OR*, I, 11, pt. 1: 945, 982-83, 985, 989; Pickett, *Heart of a Soldier*, 47-48; Richard L. Maury, Address on George E. Pickett, 11-12, Maury Papers, DU.

13. *OR*, I, 11, pt. 1: 983-84; Smith, "Seven Pines (Fair Oaks)," 259; James Longstreet, *From Manassas to Appomattox: Memoirs of the Civil War in America* (Philadelphia, 1896), 108.

14. *OR*, I, 11, pt. 1: 935, 941, 945, 984; Joseph E. Johnston, *Narrative of Military Operations. . . .* (New York, 1874), 139.

15. *OR*, I, 11, pt. 1: 984; Walter Harrison, *Pickett's Men: A Fragment of War History* (New York, 1870), 52-53.

16. Sears, *To the Gates of Richmond*, 145-48; Smith, "Seven Pines (Fair Oaks)," 261; Ezra J. Warner, *Generals in Gray: Lives of the Confederate Commanders* (Baton Rouge, 1959), 180-81; Pickett, *Heart of a Soldier*, 42.

17. Harrison, *Pickett's Men*, 25; William A. Young, Jr., and Patricia C. Young, *56th Virginia Infantry* (Lynchburg, Va., 1990), 33-37, 42-43.

18. La Salle Corbell Pickett, *Pickett and His Men* (Atlanta, 1900), 170; Pickett, *Heart of a Soldier*, 46, 48.

19. Ervin L. Jordan, Jr., and Herbert A. Thomas, Jr., *19th Virginia Infantry* (Lynchburg, Va., 1987), 17; Wood, *Big I*, 21.

20. Pickett, *Heart of a Soldier*, 50; Eppa Hunton, "Gaines's Mill," *CV* 7 (1899): 223; Wood, *Big I*, 21-22.

21. Sears, *To the Gates of Richmond*, 151-56, 174-77.

22. *OR*, I, 11, pt. 2: 767; Joseph P. Cullen, "Gaines's Mill," *Civil War Times Illustrated* 3 (Apr. 1964): 11-16; Eppa Hunton, *Autobiography of Eppa Hunton* (Richmond, 1933), 69.

23. *OR*, I, 11, pt. 2: 756-57; Longstreet, *Manassas to Appomattox*, 127; Pickett, *Pickett and His Men*, 179; C. Irvine Walker, *The Life of Lieutenant General Richard Heron Anderson of the Confederate States Army* (Charleston, S.C., 1917), 84.

24. Selcer, "George Pickett: Another Look," 60; *OR*, I, 11, pt. 2: 767; Longstreet, *Manassas to Appomattox*, 127.

25. *OR*, I, 11, pt. 2: 563-64; Hunton, "Gaines's Mill," 223; J. Cooper, "Pickett's Brigade at Gaines's Mill," *CV* 6 (1898): 472; George Wise, ["Pickett's Brigade at Gaines's Mill"], *CV* 6 (1898): 568; Jordan and Thomas, *19th Virginia*, 18; Cullen, "Gaines's Mill," 16; Wood, *Big I*, 23-24; Oliver Otis Howard, *Autobiography of Oliver Otis Howard, Major General United States Army*, 2 vols. (New York, 1907), 1: 244-45; Alexander Hunter, *Johnny Reb and Billy Yank* (New York, 1905), 174-75; Pickett, *Pickett and His Men*, 180-81; Sears, *To the Gates of Richmond*, 232-33.

26. *OR*, I, 11, pt. 2: 758, 767; Pickett, *Pickett and His Men*, 181-82; Hunton, "Gaines's Mill," 224; Fitz John Porter, "Hanover Court House and Gaines's Mill," *B&L* 2: 335n.; Hunton, *Autobiography*, 70, 70n.-71n.; Shotwell, *Papers*, 1: 245-46; Thomas J. Goree, *The Thomas Jewett Goree Letters*, ed. Langston J. Goree, V (Bryan, Tex., 1981), 160.

27. John Cheves Haskell, *The Haskell Memoirs*, ed. Gilbert E. Govan and James W. Livingood (New York, 1960), 32; La Salle Corbell Pickett, *What Happened to Me* (New York, 1917), 110; Pickett, *Heart of a Soldier*, 8.

SEVEN

1. George E. Pickett, *The Heart of a Soldier, as Revealed in the Intimate Letters of Genl. George E. Pickett, C.S.A.*, ed. La Salle Corbell Pickett (New York, 1913), 52, 131; Stella Pickett Hardy, *Colonial Families of the Southern States of America. . . .* (Baltimore, 1958), 427; La Salle Corbell Pickett, *What Happened to Me* (New York, 1917), 110-12.

2. Stephen W. Sears, *To the Gates of Richmond: The Peninsula Campaign* (New York, 1992), 233-52, 335-41; Richard Selcer, "George Pickett: Another Look," *Civil War Times Illustrated* 33 (July-Aug. 1994): 60-61.

3. *OR*, I, 11, pt. 2: 503, 508, 768-70.

4. "The Last Roll: Lieut. Benjamin H. Hutchison," *CV* 24 (1916): 80; Minutes of Pickett-Buchanan Camp, Sons of Confederate Veterans, May 23, 1899, Charles Pickett Papers, VHS.

5. Pickett, *Heart of a Soldier*, 131-32; Pickett, *What Happened to Me*, 112-14, 277-78.

6. *OR*, I, 12, pt. 2: 560; 19, pt. 1: 147, 810, 895-96; Eppa Hunton, *Autobiography of Eppa Hunton* (Richmond, 1933), 74-81; Douglas Southall Freeman, *Lee's Lieutenants: A Study in Command*, 3 vols. (New York, 1942-44), 1: 588.

7. Pickett, *Heart of a Soldier*, 8, 58-59.

8. Ibid., 52, 61-62; Ezra J. Warner, *Generals in Gray: Lives of the Confederate Commanders* (Baton Rouge, 1959), 99; Walter Harrison, *Pickett's Men: A Fragment of War History* (New York, 1870), 18-22.

9. Register of Appointments, CSA, Army of Northern Virginia General and Staff Officers' File, M-331, r-197, NA; Pickett, *Heart of a Soldier*, 59-61; Jeffry D. Wert, *General James Longstreet, the Confederacy's Most Controversial Soldier: A Biography* (New York, 1993), 210; *OR*, I, 19, pt. 2: 683, 699.

10. Selcer, "George Pickett: Another Look," 61-62; Leslie Jill Gordon, "Before the Storm: The Early Life of George E. Pickett," 89, Typescript in Earl Gregg Swem Library, College of William and Mary, Williamsburg, Va.; Gerard A. Patterson, "George E. Pickett," *Civil War Times Illustrated* 5 (May 1966): 21; Warner, *Generals in Gray*, 155, 169; *OR*, I, 19, pt. 1: 804-05; 21: 539.

11. Ibid., 540 and n.; La Salle Corbell Pickett, *Pickett and His Men* (Atlanta, 1900), 206-09.

12. *OR*, I, 19, pt. 2: 660, 683; 21: 539 and n.

13. Harrison, *Pickett's Men*, 70; Pickett, *Pickett and His Men*, 206; Joseph V. Bidgood, "List of General Officers and Their Staffs. . . .," *SHSP* 38 (1910): 176; *List of Staff Officers of the Confederate States Army, 1861-1865* (Washington, D.C., 1891), 30, 71, 88, 146; Robert K. Krick, *Lee's Colonels: A Biographical Register of the Field Officers of the Army of Northern Virginia* (Dayton, 1979), 193-94.

14. *History of the Seventeenth Virginia Infantry, C.S.A.* (Baltimore, 1870), 121; John E. Dooley, *John Dooley, Confederate Soldier: His War Journal*, ed. Joseph T. Durkin (Washington, D.C., 1945), 67; *OR*, I, 19, pt. 2: 686-87.

15. Ibid., 721; William G. Cason to his wife, Dec. 11, 1862, F-SNMP; Robert W. Hall memoirs, 3, ibid.; John H. Lewis, *Recollections from 1860 to 1865. . . .*, ed. Jim D. Moody (Dayton, 1983), 61-62.

16. Hunton, *Autobiography*, 82; Lee A. Wallace, Jr., *1st Virginia Infantry* (Lynchburg, Va., 1985), 37; Benjamin W. Trask, *19th Virginia Infantry* (Lynchburg, Va., 1984), 20; Robert T. Bell, *11th Virginia Infantry* (Lynchburg, Va., 1985), 34; Michael J. Andrus, *The Brooke, Fauquier, Loudoun and Alexandria Artillery* (Lynchburg, Va., 1990), 73.

17. *OR*, I, 19, pt. 2: 677-78, 683; 21: 539-540, 540n., 1071; Harrison, *Pickett's Men*, 62-63; Hunton, *Autobiography*, 81; Freeman, *Lee's Lieutenants*, 2: 326; Lee A. Wallace, Jr., *17th Virginia Infantry* (Lynchburg, Va., 1990), 42; Richard B. Garnett to Edward A. Palfrey, Feb. 2, 1863, Simon Gratz Collection, Historical Society of Pennsylvania, Philadelphia, Pa.; Pickett, *Heart of a Soldier*, 61.

18. *OR*, I, 21: 552-53, 569, 622; 51, pt. 2: 660; Charles M. Blackford, Jr., *Annals of the Lynchburg Home Guard* (Lynchburg, Va., 1891), 95; James Longstreet, "The Battle of Fredericksburg," *B&L* 3: 72; E. Porter Alexander, "The Battle of Fredericksburg," *SHSP* 10 (1882): 383, 457; E. Porter Alexander, *Fighting for the Confederacy: The Personal Recollections of General Edward Porter Alexander*, ed. Gary W. Gallagher (Chapel Hill, 1989), 172; Oliver Otis Howard, *Autobiography of Oliver Otis Howard, Major General United States Army*, 2 vols. (New York, 1907), 1: 331.

19. J. Howard Gregory, *38th Virginia Infantry* (Lynchburg, Va., 1988), 30; John D. McConnell memoirs, 5, Winthrop College Archives and Special Collections, Rock Hill, S.C.

20. William H. Morgan, *Personal Reminiscences of the War of 1861-5* (Lynchburg, Va., 1911), 148; Charles W. Sublett, *57th Virginia Infantry* (Lynchburg, Va., 1985), 19.

21. *OR*, I, 21: 559, 562, 570, 573, 626-27; 51, pt. 1: 174-75; Blackford, *Lynchburg Home Guard*, 96-97; Nathan T. Bartley to Editor, *CV*, Mar. 5, 1929, DU.

22. John Bratton to his wife, Dec. 16, 1862, Bratton Correspondence, Southern Historical Collection, UNC.

23. Nathan T. Bartley to Editor, *CV*, Mar. 5, 1929, DU.

24. Pickett, *Heart of a Soldier*, 65-66; Selcer, "Pickett: Another Look," 62; James Longstreet, *From Manassas to Appomattox: Memoirs of the Civil War in America* (Philadelphia, 1896), 306-07, 309; Wert, *General James Longstreet*, 220.

25. Randolph A. Shotwell, *The Papers of Randolph Abbott Shotwell*, ed. J. G. D. Hamilton and Rebecca Cameron, 3 vols. (Raleigh, 1929-31), 1: 426.

26. Morgan, *Personal Reminiscences*, 153-54; Edgar Warfield, *A Confederate Soldier's Memoirs.* . . . (Richmond, 1936), 139.

27. George E. Pickett to La Salle Corbell, Feb. 23, 1863, Arthur Crew Inman Papers, John Hay Library, Brown University, Providence, R.I.

28. John Perry Alderman, *29th Virginia Infantry* (Lynchburg, Va., 1989), 23; Harrison, *Pickett's Men*, 63; John Bratton to his wife, Jan. 2, 1863, Bratton Correspondence.

29. *OR*, I, 51, pt. 2: 673-74; Gregory, *38th Virginia*, 32.

30. *OR*, I, 25, pt. 2: 623, 630; Wert, *General James Longstreet*, 228-29; Richard P. Weinert, "The Suffolk Campaign," *Civil War Times Illustrated* 7 (Jan. 1969): 31-32; Robert E. Lee, *The Wartime Papers of R. E. Lee*, ed. Clifford Dowdey and Louis H. Manarin (Boston, 1961), 376-77.

31. *OR*, I, 18: 876-78; 25, pt. 2: 624-25, 627, 630-31.

32. *OR*, I, 18: 882-84, 889; 25, pt. 2: 631-32, 672; Thomas J. Goree, *The Thomas Jewett Goree Letters*, ed. Langston J. Goree, V (Bryan, Tex., 1981), 179; Samuel Cooper to George E. Pickett, Feb. 18, 1863, Army of Northern Virginia General and Staff Officers' File, M-331, r-197, NA.

33. *OR*, I, 18: 889-90; Harrison, *Pickett's Men*, 73; Lewis, *Recollections*, 68 and n.; Andrus, *Brooke, Fauquier, Loudoun and Alexandria Artillery*, 74.; Pickett, *Heart of a Soldier*, 69-71.

34. Morgan, *Personal Reminiscences*, 156; David E. Johnston, *The Story of a Confederate Boy in the Civil War* (Portland, Ore., 1914), 179-80; *Seventeenth Virginia Infantry*, 135; George E. Pickett to La Salle Corbell, Feb. 21, 1863, Arthur Crew Inman Papers.

EIGHT

1. Robert E. Lee, *The Wartime Papers of R. E. Lee*, ed. Clifford Dowdey and Louis H. Manarin (Boston, 1961), 377-78; Douglas Southall Freeman, *Lee's Lieutenants: A Study in Command*, 3 vols. (New York, 1942-44), 2: 481; La Salle Corbell Pickett, *Pickett and His Men* (Atlanta, 1900), 236-37; James Longstreet, *From Manassas to Appomattox: Memoirs of the Civil War in America* (Philadelphia, 1896), 324; Jeffry D. Wert, *General James Longstreet, the Confederacy's Most Controversial Soldier: A Biography* (New York, 1993), 231; Richard P. Weinert, "The Suffolk Campaign," *Civil War Times Illustrated* 7 (Jan. 1969): 32-33.

2. Wert, *General James Longstreet*, 231-32; Walter Harrison, *Pickett's Men: A Fragment of War History* (New York, 1870), 76; *History of the Seventeenth Virginia Infantry, C.S.A.* (Baltimore, 1870), 136-37; Eppa Hunton, *Autobiography of Eppa Hunton* (Richmond, 1933), 84-85; Richard Irby, *The Captain Remembers: The Papers of Captain Richard Irby*, ed. Virginia Fitzgerald Jordan (Blackburn, Va., 1975), 82-83; *OR*, I, 18: 923-24, 932-33, 937-38, 941; David E. Johnston, *The Story of a Confederate Boy in the Civil War* (Portland, Ore., 1914), 181-82.

3. *OR*, I, 18: 909-10.

4. Ibid., 924-27; 25, pt. 2: 675; George E. Pickett to La Salle Corbell, ca. Mar. 19, 1863, Arthur Crew Inman Papers, John Hay Library, Brown University, Providence, R.I.

5. *OR*, I, 18: 942, 944, 954, 956-60, 963; *Seventeenth Virginia Infantry*, 137; William H. Morgan, *Personal Reminiscences of the War of 1861-5* (Lynchburg, Va., 1911), 159-60; Charles T. Loehr, *The History of the Old First Virginia Infantry Regiment, Army of Northern Virginia* (Richmond, 1884), 34; Wert, *General James Longstreet*, 233-35.

6. *OR*, I, 18: 275, 605; 25, pt. 2: 207; *Seventeenth Virginia Infantry*, 140-41; Steven A. Cormier, *The Siege of Suffolk: The Forgotten Campaign, April 11-May 4, 1863* (Lynchburg, Va., 1989), 95-99.

7. Ibid., 145-52; *OR*, I, 51, pt. 2: 691-92; Edward R. Baird to his father, May 7, 1863, Baird Family Papers, Earl Gregg Swem Library, College of William and Mary, Williamsburg, Va.; Osmun Latrobe diary, Apr. 19, 1863, VHS; Samuel G. French, *Two Wars: An Autobiography. . . .* (Nashville, 1901), 160-66; William L. Parker, *General James Dearing, C.S.A.* (Lynchburg, Va., 1990), 34; Frank Moore, ed., *The Rebellion Record: A Diary of American Events*, 12 vols. (New York, 1861-68), 7: 292.

8. Cormier, *Siege of Suffolk*, 230-36; *OR*, I, 18: 340-41, 1021; *Seventeenth Virginia Infantry*, 143-44; Osmun Latrobe diary, Apr. 24, 1863; Weinert, "Suffolk Campaign," 38-39.

9. La Salle Corbell Pickett, *What Happened to Me* (New York, 1917), 117-21.

10. G. Moxley Sorrel, *Recollections of a Confederate Staff Officer* (New York, 1905), 155-56.

11. William A. Young, Jr., and Patricia C. Young, *56th Virginia Infantry* (Lynchburg, Va., 1990), 74; George E. Pickett, *The Heart of a Soldier, as Revealed in the Intimate Letters of Genl. George E. Pickett, C.S.A.*, ed. La Salle Corbell Pickett (New York, 1913), 76n.; Pickett, *What Happened to Me*, 124.

12. *OR*, I, 25, pt. 2: 708-09, 720, 725-26, 752, 756-59; French, *Two Wars*, 166.

13. *OR*, I, 18: 1038, 1045; *Seventeenth Virginia Infantry*, 144-45; John H. Lewis, *Recollections from 1860 to 1865. . . .*, ed. Jim D. Moody (Dayton, 1983), 71n.; Osmun Latrobe diary, May 3, 1863.

14. Louis H. Manarin, *15th Virginia Infantry* (Lynchburg, Va., 1990), 42; Powhatan B. Whittle to his brother, May 19, 1863, Whittle Correspondence, F-SNMP.

15. *OR*, I, 18: 1046; 51, pt. 2: 705; Morgan, *Personal Reminiscences*, 162; Irby, *Captain Remembers*, 84; Loehr, *Old First Virginia*, 34; Young and Young, *56th Virginia*, 75; *Seventeenth Virginia Infantry*, 145-47; Thomas Jackson Arnold, *Early Life and Letters of General Thomas J. Jackson. . . .* (New York, 1916), 360-61.

16. *OR*, I, 18: 1059, 1062; 25, pt. 2: 801-02; 51, pt. 2: 711; Powhatan B. Whittle to his brother, May 19, 1863, Whittle Correspondence; William H. Cocke to his parents, May 18, 1863, Cocke Family Papers, VHS; *Seventeenth Virginia Infantry*, 147; Morgan, *Personal Reminiscences*, 162-63; George E. Pickett to La Salle Corbell, May 18, 1863, Arthur Crew Inman Papers.

17. *OR*, I, 18: 1066, 1071, 1075, 1077-78, 1088; 25, pt. 2: 811, 826-27, 831, 833, 848-49; 27, pt. 3: 880, 882.

18. Ibid., 18: 1089-91; 25, pt. 2: 850, 852-53; 27, pt. 2: 777-79, 782; pt. 3: 861; Powhatan B. Whittle to his brother, June 7, 1863, Whittle Correspondence; Edwin B. Coddington, *The Gettysburg Campaign: A Study in Command* (New York, 1968), 100; Dorothy Francis Atkinson, *King William County in the Civil War. . . .* (Lynchburg, Va., 1990), 84.

19. *OR*, I, 27, pt. 3: 869, 875-76.

20. Ibid., 874, 925-26; Manarin, *15th Virginia*, 43-44; Robert K. Krick, *30th Virginia Infantry* (Lynchburg, Va., 1983), 38.

21. *OR*, I, 27, pt. 2: 295; pt. 3: 910, 944-45.

22. Francis W. Dawson, *Reminiscences of Confederate Service, 1861-1865*, ed. Bell I. Wiley (Baton Rouge, 1980), 90-91.

23. Loehr, *Old First Virginia*, 34-35; George E. Pickett to La Salle Corbell, June 13, 1863, Arthur Crew Inman Papers.

24. *OR*, I, 27, pt. 2: 295, 306, 357, 371; pt. 3: 223, 888; Loehr, *Old First Virginia*, 35; Osmun Latrobe diary, June 15-23, 1863; William H. Cocke to his parents, July 11, 1863, Cocke Family Papers; Hunton, *Autobiography*, 86; Robert A. Bright, "Pickett's Charge at Gettysburg," *CV* 38 (1930): 264; Powhatan B. Whittle to his brother, June 23, 1863, Whittle Correspondence.

25. John E. Dooley, *John Dooley, Confederate Soldier: His War Journal*, ed. Joseph T. Durkin (Washington, D.C., 1945), 98; Robert H. Moore, II, *The Richmond, Fayette, Hampden, Thomas, and Blount's Lynchburg Artillery* (Lynchburg, Va., 1991), 76-77; Pickett, *Heart of a Soldier*, 81-83.

26. *OR*, I, 27, pt. 2: 317; pt. 3: 948; 51, pt. 2: 728-29, 732-33.

27. William Garrett Piston, ed., " 'The Rebs Are Yet Thick About Us': The Civil War Diary of Amos Stouffer of Chambersburg," *Civil War History* 38 (1992): 218-19; William Youngblood, "Personal Observations at Gettysburg," *CV* 19 (1911): 286.

NINE

1. William Nathaniel Wood, *Reminiscences of Big I*, ed. Bell Irvin Wiley (Jackson, Tenn., 1956), 43; William H. Cocke to his parents, July 11, 1863, Cocke Family Papers, VHS; Eppa Hunton, *Autobiography of Eppa Hunton* (Richmond, 1933), 88; Randolph A. Shotwell, *The Papers of Randolph Abbott Shotwell*, ed. J. G. D. Hamilton and Rebecca Cameron, 3 vols. (Raleigh, 1929-31), 1: 498-99; James Dearing to his mother, July 26, 1863, Dearing Family Papers, UVA; William Youngblood, "Personal Observations at Gettysburg," *CV* 19 (1911): 286.

2. Edwin B. Coddington, *The Gettysburg Campaign: A Study in Command* (New York, 1968), 260-322.

3. *Richmond Times-Dispatch*, Dec. 20, 1903; Walter Harrison, *Pickett's Men: A Fragment of War History* (New York, 1870), 88; Coddington, *Gettysburg Campaign*, 359-441, 458; J. B. Hood, *Advance and Retreat: Personal Experiences of the United States and Confederate States Armies* (New Orleans, 1880), 57; Douglas Southall Freeman, *R. E. Lee: A Biography*, 4 vols. (New York, 1934-35), 3: 89; James Longstreet, *From Manassas to Appomattox: Memoirs of the Civil War in America* (Philadelphia, 1896), 362-84.

4. *OR*, I, 27, pt. 2: 308; Harrison, *Pickett's Men*, 88.

5. *OR*, I, 27, pt. 2: 359; Coddington, *Gettysburg Campaign*, 456-59; Longstreet, *From Manassas to Appomattox*, 385-86; Freeman, *R. E. Lee*, 3: 107, 151; Douglas Southall Freeman, *Lee's Lieutenants: A Study in Command*, 3 vols. (New York, 1942-44), 3: 114-15; George R. Stewart, *Pickett's Charge: A Microhistory of the Final Attack at Gettysburg, July 3, 1863* (Greenwich, Conn., 1963), 21-22; Jeffry D. Wert, *General James Longstreet, the Confederacy's Most Controversial Soldier: A Biography* (New York, 1993), 282-83.

6. Coddington, *Gettysburg Campaign*, 459-60; Kathleen R. Georg and John W. Busey, *Nothing But Glory: Pickett's Division at Gettysburg* (Hightstown, N.J., 1987), 21-22.

7. *OR*, I, 27, pt. 2: 320; Longstreet, *Manassas to Appomattox*, 386-87; James Longstreet, "General James Longstreet's Account of the Campaign and Battle [of Gettysburg]," *SHSP* 5 (1877): 70-71; Lafayette McLaws, "Gettysburg," *SHSP* 7 (1879): 83; E. Porter Alexander, *Fighting for the Confederacy: The Personal Recollections of General Edward Porter Alexander*, ed. Gary W. Gallagher (Chapel Hill, 1989), 252, 280; Walter H. Taylor, *Four Years with General Lee. . . .* (New York, 1877), 103, 107-08; A. L. Long, *Memoirs of Robert E. Lee: His Military and Personal History. . . .* (New York, 1886), 294.

8. Ibid., 461-64, 490-91; Freeman, *Lee's Lieutenants*, 3: 146, 185; Stewart, *Pickett's Charge*, 48-51; Wert, *General James Longstreet*, 285; Harrison, *Pickett's Men*, 99-100.

9. *OR*, I, 27, pt. 2: 608, 619; Coddington, *Gettysburg Campaign*, 463; Freeman, *Lee's Lieutenants*, 3: 185.

10. Georg and Busey, *Nothing But Glory*, 22-26; Harrison, *Pickett's Men*, 91-92; James F. Crocker, *Gettysburg—Pickett's Charge and Other War Addresses* (Portsmouth, Va., 1915), 36-37; Glenn Tucker, *High Tide at Gettysburg: The Campaign in Pennsylvania* (Indianapolis, 1958), 331.

11. Georg and Busey, *Nothing But Glory*, 27; James I. Robertson, Jr., *18th Virginia Infantry* (Lynchburg, Va., 1984), 21.

12. Georg and Busey, *Nothing But Glory*, 28.

198 ENDNOTES FOR – Pages 119 to 125

13. Alexander, *Fighting for the Confederacy*, 255; E. Porter Alexander, *Military Memoirs of a Confederate: A Critical Narrative* (New York, 1908), 421-22; D. B. Fry, "Pettigrew's Charge at Gettysburg," *SHSP* 7 (1879): 92.

14. Robert A. Bright, "Pickett's Charge at Gettysburg," *CV* 38 (1930): 263; Shotwell, *Papers*, 2: 9-10.

15. Edmund Berkeley, "Rode with Pickett," *CV* 38 (1930): 175.

16. James Longstreet, "Lee's Right Wing at Gettysburg," *B&L* 3: 343.

17. *OR*, I, 27, pt. 2: 376; E. Porter Alexander, "The Great Charge and Artillery Fighting at Gettysburg," *B&L* 3: 363-64; Alexander, *Fighting for the Confederacy*, 257; John H. Lewis, *Recollections from 1860 to 1865. . . .*, ed. Jim D. Moody (Dayton, 1983), 81; Crocker, *Gettysburg—Pickett's Charge*, 40-41; Coddington, *Gettysburg Campaign*, 493-94.

18. Shotwell, *Papers*, 2: 8; David E. Johnston, *The Story of a Confederate Boy in the Civil War* (Portland, Ore., 1914), 207; Joseph Mayo, Jr., Report of Kemper's Brigade at Gettysburg, July 25, 1863, George E. Pickett Papers, DU; John E. Dooley, *John Dooley, Confederate Soldier: His War Journal*, ed. Joseph T. Durkin (Washington, D.C., 1945), 103; James L. Kemper to E. Porter Alexander, Sept. 20, 1869, Dearborn Collection, Houghton Library, Harvard University, Cambridge, Mass.

19. Bright, "Pickett's Charge," 263; Alexander, "Great Charge and Artillery Fighting," 362-64; John C. Haskell to John W. Daniel, May 19, 1906, Daniel Papers, DU; James Longstreet to E. Porter Alexander, July 3, 1863 [two letters]; E. Porter Alexander to James Longstreet, July 3, 1863 [two letters]; all, Alexander Papers, LC.

20. Alexander, *Fighting for the Confederacy*, 258-59; E. Porter Alexander to George E. Pickett, July 3, 1863 [two letters: 1:25 P.M., 1:40 P.M.], Alexander Papers, LC.

21. Shotwell, *Papers*, 2: 8-9; Alexander, "Great Charge and Artillery Fighting," 365; Longstreet, "Lee's Right Wing," 345.

22. Monroe F. Cockrell, "Where Was Pickett at Gettysburg?," 5-8, 11-12, Typescript in DU; "Committee's Report on General Pickett, and His Command and Participation in the Battle of Gettysburg, July 3, 1863," 1-3, Typescript in Gregory Family Papers, VHS; "Testimony About Battle of Gettysburg," *CV* 18 (1910): 524-25; Charles Pickett to Editor, *Richmond Times*, Nov. 11, 1894, Charles Pickett Papers, VHS; W. W. Wells to G. R. Harrison, Dec. 13, 1894, Gettysburg National Military Park, Gettysburg, Pa.; James L. Kemper to E. Porter Alexander, Sept. 20, 1869, Dearborn Collection; Dr. Clayton G. Coleman to John W. Daniel, July 1, 1904, Daniel Papers, UVA; John C. Haskell to John W. Daniel, May 19, 1906, Daniel Papers, DU; *Richmond Times*, Dec. 19, 1894; Rawley W. Martin, "The Battle of Gettysburg, and the Charge of Pickett's Division. . . .," *SHSP* 32 (1904): 187-88; Georg and Busey, *Nothing But Glory*, 202n.; Hunton, *Autobiography*, 98-99; John Cheves Haskell, *The Haskell Memoirs*, ed. Gilbert E. Govan and James M. Livingood (New York, 1960), 51-52.

23. Coddington, *Gettysburg Campaign*, 504-05, 794n.; Georg and Busey, *Nothing But Glory*, 194-205; Stewart, *Pickett's Charge*, 180; Bright, "Pickett's Charge at Gettysburg," 265.

24. Thomas R. Friend to Charles Pickett, Dec. 10, 1894, Charles Pickett Papers.

25. Ibid.; Georg and Busey, *Nothing But Glory*, 201-02.

26. Coddington, *Gettysburg Campaign*, 504; Louis G. Young to J. Bryan Grimes, Sept. 7, 1911, Grimes Papers, UNC; Charles F. Adams, Jr., to S. Weir Mitchell,

Dec. 18, 1913, Society Collection, Historical Society of Pennsylvania, Philadelphia, Pa.

27. Bright, "Pickett's Charge at Gettysburg," 263-65; Louis G. Young to J. Bryan Grimes, Sept. 7, 1911, Grimes Papers; Coddington, *Gettysburg Campaign*, 515-16; Georg and Busey, *Nothing But Glory*, 204; Stewart, *Pickett's Charge*, 168.

28. Bright, "Pickett's Charge at Gettysburg," 264; W. Stuart Symington to Francis W. Dawson, May 12, 1885, Dawson Papers, UVA; to Charles Pickett, Oct. 17, 1892, Charles Pickett Papers; to James Longstreet, Oct. 26, 1892, Longstreet Papers, DU; Rawley W. Martin to Robert A. Bright, Jan. 7, 1904, Southall Collection, Earl Gregg Swem Library, College of William and Mary, Williamsburg, Va.; Alexander, *Fighting for the Confederacy*, 264.

29. *OR*, I, 27, pt. 2: 619-20, 632; "Testimony about Gettysburg," 525; Coddington, *Gettysburg Campaign*, 519-20, 801n.; Martin W. Hazlewood, "Gettysburg Charge: Paper as to Pickett's Men," *SHSP* 23 (1895): 234-35; Francis P. Fleming, "Gettysburg: The Courageous Part Taken . . . by the Florida Brigade. . . .," *SHSP* 27 (1899): 196, 198-99; Robert A. Bright to Charles Pickett, Oct. 15, 1892; W. Stuart Symington to Charles Pickett, Oct. 17, 1892; Charles Pickett to Editor, *Richmond Times*, Nov. 11, 1894; all, Charles Pickett Papers.

30. Coddington, *Gettysburg Campaign*, 505, 803n.; Robert A. Bright to Charles Pickett, Oct. 15, 1892, Charles Pickett Papers; George E. Pickett Speech, 1865, 2, Henry E. Huntington Library, San Marino, Calif.; *OR*, I, 27, pt. 2: 329-30, 339; Crocker, *Gettysburg—Pickett's Charge*, 34, 46; Stewart, *Pickett's Charge*, 232-38; Hunton, *Autobiography*, 99; Freeman, *Lee's Lieutenants*, 3: 196; John E. Divine, *8th Virginia Infantry* (Lynchburg, Va., 1893), 24; Harrison, *Pickett's Men*, 102-04.

31. Francis W. Dawson, *Reminiscences of Confederate Service, 1861-1865*, ed. Bell I. Wiley (Baton Rouge, 1980), 97.

32. Youngblood, "Personal Observations," 317; Bright, "Pickett's Charge at Gettysburg," 266.

TEN

1. John D. Imboden, "The Confederate Retreat from Gettysburg," *B&L* 3: 421.

2. George E. Pickett, *The Heart of a Soldier, as Revealed in the Intimate Letters of Genl. George E. Pickett, C.S.A.*, ed. La Salle Corbell Pickett (New York, 1913), 212-15; *OR*, I, 27, pt. 3: 1075; James Longstreet to "My Dear Major Nash," Sept. 3, 1892; to Charles Pickett, Oct. 5, 1892; both, Charles Pickett Papers, VHS.

3. *OR*, I, 27, pt. 3: 983, 987-88; Randolph A. Shotwell, *The Papers of Randolph Abbott Shotwell*, ed. J. G. D. Hamilton and Rebecca Cameron, 3 vols. (Raleigh, 1929-31), 2: 35-36; John L. Collins, "A Prisoner's March from Gettysburg to Staunton," *B&L* 3: 431-32.

4. William N. Cocke to his parents, July 11, 1863, Cocke Family Papers, VHS.

5. *OR*, I, 27, pt. 3: 986-87.

6. Charles T. Loehr, *War History of the Old First Virginia Infantry Regiment, Army of Northern Virginia* (Richmond, 1884), 39-40; Louis H. Manarin, *15th Virginia Infantry* (Lynchburg, Va., 1990), 47.

7. Jedediah Hotchkiss, *"Make Me A Map of the Valley": The Civil War Journal of Stonewall Jackson's Topographer*, ed. Archie McDonald (Dallas, 1973), 162; Shotwell, *Papers*, 2: 37-38; *OR*, I, 27, pt. 1: 937, 945; pt. 2: 362; George E. Pickett to La Salle Corbell, July 23, 31, 1863, Arthur Crew Inman Papers, John Hay Library, Brown University, Providence, R.I.; George E. Pickett, *Soldier of the South: General Pickett's War Letters to His Wife*, ed. Arthur Crew Inman (Boston, 1928), 78-80.

8. George E. Pickett to La Salle Corbell, July 31, 1863, Arthur Crew Inman Papers; La Salle Corbell Pickett, *Pickett and His Men* (Atlanta, 1900), 318-19.

9. *OR*, I, 29, pt. 2: 706, 708, 710-11, 716-17, 728, 731, 738; *History of the Seventeenth Virginia Infantry, C.S.A.* (Baltimore, 1870), 164-65; Dorothy Francis Atkinson, *King William County in the Civil War.* . . . (Lynchburg, Va., 1990), 132; Loehr, *Old First Virginia*, 40; Douglas Southall Freeman, *Lee's Lieutenants: A Study in Command*, 3 vols. (New York, 1942-44), 3: 223-24; Walter Harrison, *Pickett's Men: A Fragment of War History* (New York, 1870), 108.

10. Pickett, *Pickett and His Men*, 319-23; Pickett, *Heart of a Soldier*, 10-12, 117-19; La Salle Corbell Pickett, *What Happened to Me* (New York, 1917), 128-31, 276.

11. *OR*, I, 29, pt. 2: 746; George E. Pickett to Samuel Cooper, Sept. 20, 1863, Army of Northern Virginia General and Staff Officers' File, M-331, r-197, NA; Pickett, *What Happened to Me*, 131; Pickett, *Pickett and His Men*, 343.

12. Harrison, *Pickett's Men*, 108-09; *Seventeenth Virginia*, 165-66; Eppa Hunton, *Autobiography of Eppa Hunton* (Richmond, 1933), 103-04; *OR*, I, 29, pt. 2: 716-17, 728, 731, 738, 741; 30, pt. 4: 668-69.

13. Ibid., 29, pt. 2: 906.

14. Charles C. Flowerree to Editor, *Vicksburg Herald*, n.d., Flowerree Family Papers, VHS; Loehr, *Old First Virginia*, 53.

15. *OR*, I, 29, pt. 2: 773-74, 777-78, 789, 828-30, 833-34, 847-48, 850; Charles W. Sublett, *57th Virginia Infantry* (Lynchburg, Va., 1985), 34.

16. *OR*, I, 29, pt. 2: 853; 33: 1068, 1072-74.

17. Ibid., 29, pt. 2: 778, 789-91, 793, 818, 827-29, 833-34, 872-73, 886-88, 892-93, 897; Pickett, *Pickett and His Men*, 325-26.

18. *OR*, I, 29, pt. 1: 911-17; pt. 2: 397, 447, 595-98; John G. Barrett, *The Civil War in North Carolina* (Chapel Hill, 1963), 177-80.

19. *OR*, I, 29, pt. 2: 872-73, 876-77, 881-83; 33: 543; II, 6: 845-47, 858.

20. Ibid., I, 33: 1061, 1099-1104; Barrett, *Civil War in North Carolina*, 202-03; Pickett, *Pickett and His Men*, 330-31; Robert G. H. Kean, *Inside the Confederate Government: The Diary of Robert Garlick Hill Kean, Head of the Bureau of War*, ed. Edward Younger (New York, 1957), 145.

21. Pickett, *Heart of a Soldier*, 120-21.

22. *OR*, I, 33: 82-103; Robert E. Lee, *The Wartime Papers of R. E. Lee*, ed. Clifford Dowdey and Louis H. Manarin (Boston, 1961), 638-39; Barrett, *Civil War in North Carolina*, 203-07; C. R. Fontaine, *A Complete Roster of the Field and Staff Officers of the 57th Virginia Regiment of Infantry.* . . . (N.p., n.d.), 18-19; Harrison, *Pickett's Men*, 110-14.

23. *OR*, I, 33: 94, 100, 1186-87.

24. Robert E. Lee, *Lee's Dispatches: Unpublished Letters of General Robert E. Lee, C.S.A., to Jefferson Davis and the War Department of the Confederate States of America*, ed. Douglas Southall Freeman and Grady C. McWhiney (New York, 1957), 136.

25. *Murder of Union Soldiers in North Carolina: Letter from the Secretary of War . . . May 3, 1866* (House Exec. Doc. no. 98, 39th Cong., 1st sess., 1866), 4-6, 12; *OR*, I, 33: 556, 867; Barrett, *Civil War in North Carolina*, 207n.-08n.; Harrison, *Pickett's Men*, 115-17; E. W. Gaines, "Fayette Artillery: The Movement on New Berne. . . .," *SHSP* 25 (1897): 296; Frank Moore, ed., *The Rebellion Record: A Diary of American Events*, 12 vols. (New York, 1861-68), 8: 379.

26. *Murder of Union Soldiers*, 25, 43, 69, 71, 77, 80-82.

27. Ibid., 6-10; *OR*, I, 33: 569, 580, 866-70; Richard N. Current, *Lincoln's Loyalists: Union Soldiers from the Confederacy* (Boston, 1992), 120-21.

28. *OR*, I, 33: 866-68; II, 6: 1006-07; Harrison, *Pickett's Men*, 120.

29. *Murder of Union Soldiers*, 6, 11-87; *OR*, II, 6: 993-95; W. Buck Yearns and John G. Barrett, eds., *North Carolina Civil War Documentary* (Chapel Hill, 1980), 58-59; Gaines, "Fayette Artillery," 296-97; Moore, *Rebellion Record*, 8: 379.

30. George E. Pickett to Ulysses S. Grant, Mar. 12, 1866, Pickett's Amnesty File, M-1003, r-67, NA.

ELEVEN

1. *OR*, I, 33: 1206-07, 1230, 1237-38; Charles T. Loehr, *War History of the Old First Virginia Infantry Regiment, Army of Northern Virginia* (Richmond, 1884), 42; Lee A. Wallace, Jr., *3rd Virginia Infantry* (Lynchburg, Va., 1986), 43; David F. Riggs, *7th Virginia Infantry* (Lynchburg, Va., 1982), 31; Ralph White Gunn, *24th Virginia Infantry* (Lynchburg, Va., 1987), 50.

2. George E. Pickett to La Salle Corbell Pickett, ca. Mar. 15, 1864, Arthur Crew Inman Papers, John Hay Library, Brown University, Providence, R.I.

3. George E. Pickett to Braxton Bragg, Apr. 6, 1864, Charles S. Venable Papers, Southern Historical Collection, UNC.

4. *OR*, I, 33: 1273-74; 51, pt. 2: 857-58; Herbert M. Schiller, *The Bermuda Hundred Campaign: "Operations on the South Side of the James River, Virginia"— May, 1864* (Dayton, 1988), 18.

5. La Salle Corbell Pickett, *Pickett and His Men* (Atlanta, 1900), 337-39; Loehr, *Old First Virginia*, 42-44; *OR*, I, 33: 281, 284-85, 295-301; 51, pt. 2: 869; Schiller, *Bermuda Hundred Campaign*, 53-54.

6. *OR*, I, 33: 1292, 1305, 1307-08; 36, pt. 2: 207n.; Schiller, *Bermuda Hundred Campaign*, 53-56; Robert E. Lee, *The Wartime Papers of R. E. Lee*, ed. Clifford Dowdey and Louis H. Manarin (Boston, 1961), 640.

7. *OR*, I, 51, pt. 2: 863-65.

8. William Glenn Robertson, *Back Door to Richmond: The Bermuda Hundred Campaign, April-June 1864* (Newark, 1987), 49; *OR*, I, 51, pt. 2: 877, 879.

9. Ibid., 886; 36, pt. 2: 950; Pickett, *Pickett and His Men*, 339; Lee, *Wartime Papers*, 718.

10. *OR*, I, 36, pt. 2: 951, 955-57; 51, pt. 2: 891-92; Robertson, *Back Door to Richmond*, 65-67.

11. *OR*, I, 36, pt. 2: 956-58; 51, pt. 2: 895-97; Robertson, *Back Door to Richmond*, 66-68, 73n.-74n.; Schiller, *Bermuda Hundred Campaign*, 70-71.

12. *OR*, I, 36, pt. 2: 957; 51, pt. 2: 891; Douglas Southall Freeman, *Lee's Lieutenants: A Study in Command*, 3 vols. (New York, 1942-44), 3: 455.

13. *OR*, I, 36, pt. 2: 255-56; 51, pt. 2: 898; Walter Harrison, *Pickett's Men: A Fragment of War History* (New York, 1870), 125; Johnson Hagood, *Memoirs of the War of Secession.* . . . (Columbia, S.C., 1910), 217-23; P. G. T. Beauregard, "The Defense of Drewry's Bluff," *B&L* 4: 196; T. Harry Williams, *P. G. T. Beauregard, Napoleon in Gray* (Baton Rouge, 1954), 210; Charles M. Cummings, *Yankee Quaker, Confederate General: The Curious Career of Bushrod Rust Johnson* (Rutherford, N.J., 1971), 282-83; Freeman, *Lee's Lieutenants*, 3: 458-60.

14. *OR*, I, 51, pt. 2: 906; Robertson, *Back Door to Richmond*, 71, 77-78; George E. Pickett, *The Heart of a Soldier, as Revealed in the Intimate Letters of Genl. George E. Pickett, C.S.A.*, ed. La Salle Corbell Pickett (New York, 1913), 123-24; La Salle Corbell Pickett, *What Happened to Me* (New York, 1917), 139-40.

15. *OR*, I, 36, pt. 2: 243-44, 975, 978-79; 51, pt. 2: 907; Hagood, *Memoirs*, 227-30; Freeman, *Lee's Lieutenants*, 3: 465-71; Cummings, *Yankee Quaker, Confederate General*, 283-84; Robertson, *Back Door to Richmond*, 107-16, 117n.

16. Ibid., 122, 128, 253; *OR*, I, 51, pt. 2: 915, 920; Pickett, *Pickett and His Men*, 344.

17. Josiah Gorgas, *The Civil War Diary of General Josiah Gorgas*, ed. Frank E. Vandiver (University, Ala., 1947), 100.

18. *OR*, I, 36, pt. 2: 1023; Robertson, *Back Door to Richmond*, 182-215; Schiller, *Bermuda Hundred Campaign*, 229-92.

19. *OR*, I, 51, pt. 2: 945, 951; Copy of Special Orders 117, Adjutant and Inspector General's Office, CSA, May 20, 1864, Pickett Papers, DU; Lee A. Wallace, Jr., *1st Virginia Infantry* (Lynchburg, Va., 1985), 50; Louis H. Manarin, *15th Virginia Infantry* (Lynchburg, Va., 1990), 60; Charles C. Flowerree to Editor, *Vicksburg Herald*, n.d., Flowerree Family Papers, VHS.

20. *OR*, I, 36, pt. 3: 48-49; Wallace, *1st Virginia*, 51; Riggs, *7th Virginia*, 35-36; J. Michael Miller, *The North Anna Campaign: "Even to Hell Itself," May 21-26, 1864* (Lynchburg, Va., 1989), 16-17, 21, 24; Joseph P. Cullen, "When Grant Faced Lee Across the North Anna," *Civil War Times Illustrated* 3 (Feb. 1965): 19-20; David M. Jordan, *Winfield Scott Hancock: A Soldier's Life* (Bloomington, 1988), 134.

21. *OR*, I, 36, pt. 1: 1058; Harrison, *Pickett's Men*, 127; William Nathaniel Wood, *Reminiscences of Big I*, ed. Bell Irvin Wiley (Jackson, Tenn., 1956), 58-59; Miller, *North Anna Campaign*, 90-91, 101.

22. *OR*, I, 36, pt. 3: 843-44; "Memoranda of [the] Thirty-eighth Virginia Infantry: From [the] Diary of Colonel George K. Griggs," *SHSP* 14 (1886): 255; G. Moxley Sorrel diary, May 27, 1864, Museum of the Confederacy, Richmond, Va.; Ezra J. Warner, *Generals in Gray: Lives of the Confederate Commanders* (Baton Rouge, 1959), 87-88, 171.

23. G. Moxley Sorrel, *Recollections of a Confederate Staff Officer* (New York, 1905), 248; Jeffry D. Wert, *General James Longstreet, the Confederacy's Most Controversial Soldier: A Biography* (New York, 1993), 387-90.

24. Sorrel, *Recollections*, 248-49; John S. Wise, *The End of an Era* (Boston, 1899), 338; A. L. Long, *Memoirs of Robert E. Lee: His Military and Personal History.* . . . (New York, 1886), 29.

25. *OR*, I, 36, pt. 1: 1058; pt. 3: 843-44; George E. Pickett to G. Moxley Sorrel, May 28, 1864, E. Porter Alexander Papers, Southern Historical Collection, UNC; Robert T. Bell, *11th Virginia Infantry* (Lynchburg, Va., 1985), 51.

26. E. M. Law, "From the Wilderness to Cold Harbor," *B&L* 4: 138; Wood, *Big I*, 59-60; Pickett, *Pickett and His Men*, 354; *OR*, I, 36, pt. 1: 1059; E. Porter Alexander,

Fighting for the Confederacy: The Personal Recollections of General Edward Porter Alexander, ed. Gary W. Gallagher (Chapel Hill, 1989), 400-01; Loehr, *Old First Virginia*, 51; Robert Stiles, *Four Years Under Marse Robert* (New York, 1903), 274-75.

27. *OR*, I, 36, pt. 1: 1059; Wood, *Big I*, 63-65; Loehr, *Old First Virginia*, 51; Eppa Hunton, *Autobiography of Eppa Hunton* (Richmond, 1933), 111-13.

TWELVE

1. *OR*, I, 36, pt. 1: 1059; pt. 3: 880, 883; 51, pt. 1: 247; George E. Pickett to G. Moxley Sorrel, June 6, 1864, E. Porter Alexander Papers, Southern Historical Collection, UNC; Charles T. Loehr, *War History of the Old First Virginia Infantry Regiment, Army of Northern Virginia* (Richmond, 1884), 51.

2. Ibid., 51-52; George E. Pickett to G. Moxley Sorrel, June 13, 1864, E. Porter Alexander Papers, Southern Historical Collection, UNC; Loehr, *Old First Virginia*, 51; *OR*, I, 36, pt. 1: 1059-60; G. Moxley Sorrel diary, June 13, 1864, Museum of the Confederacy, Richmond, Va.; Edgar Warfield, *A Confederate Soldier's Memoirs.* . . . (Richmond, 1936), 177.

3. Douglas Southall Freeman, *R. E. Lee: A Biography*, 4 vols. (New York, 1934-35), 3: 409-11; Loehr, *Old First Virginia*, 52; E. Porter Alexander, *Fighting for the Confederacy: The Personal Recollections of General Edward Porter Alexander*, ed. Gary W. Gallagher (Chapel Hill, 1989), 428.

4. *OR*, I, 51, pt. 2: 1078; Francis W. Dawson, *Reminiscences of Confederate Service, 1861-1865*, ed. Bell I. Wiley (Baton Rouge, 1980), 117.

5. *OR*, I, 40, pt. 1: 749, 760; pt. 2: 98-111, 130-32, 144-53, 661; Charles R. Francis to "Dear Cousin," July 9, 1864, Francis Correspondence, F-SNMP; William Nathaniel Wood, *Reminiscences of Big I*, ed. Bell Irvin Wiley (Jackson, Tenn., 1956), 65-66; Warfield, *Confederate Soldier's Memoirs*, 177-78; Richard L. Maury, Address on George E. Pickett, 19-20, Maury Papers, DU; W. Gordon McCabe, "Defence [sic] of Petersburg," *SHSP* 2 (1876): 268-69; Loehr, *Old First Virginia*, 52.

6. *OR*, I, 40, pt. 1: 760; 51, pt. 2: 1019-20; Charles S. Venable, "The Campaign from the Wilderness to Petersburg. . . .," *SHSP* 14 (1886): 538-39; Loehr, *Old First Virginia*, 52; G. Moxley Sorrel diary, June 17, 1864; Freeman, *R. E. Lee*, 3: 416; Eppa Hunton, *Autobiography of Eppa Hunton* (Richmond, 1933), 114-15.

7. Thomas J. Goree, *The Thomas Jewett Goree Letters*, ed. Langston J. Goree, V (Bryan, Tex., 1981), 211.

8. James I. Robertson, Jr., *18th Virginia Infantry* (Lynchburg, Va., 1984), 29; William A. Young, Jr., and Patricia C. Young, *56th Virginia Infantry* (Lynchburg, Va., 1990), 94-95.

9. *OR*, I, 40, pt. 1: 272-73; La Salle Corbell Pickett, *Pickett and His Men* (Atlanta, 1900), 357; La Salle Corbell Pickett, *What Happened to Me* (New York, 1917), 140-41.

10. George E. Pickett, *The Heart of a Soldier, as Revealed in the Intimate Letters of Genl. George E. Pickett, C.S.A.*, ed. La Salle Corbell Pickett (New York, 1913), 147-52; Pickett, *Pickett and His Men*, 362-63.

11. Pickett, *Heart of a Soldier*, 18-19, 151; George E. Pickett to Dr. George Suckley, Jan. 2, 1865, Ferdinand Dreer Collection, Historical Society of Pennsylvania, Philadelphia, Pa.

12. Pickett, *Heart of a Soldier*, 138-43; Robert S. Holzman, *Stormy Ben Butler* (New York, 1954), 128-29.

13. Pickett, *Pickett and His Men*, 362-64; David E. Johnston, *The Story of a Confederate Boy in the Civil War* (Portland, Ore., 1914), 235.

14. Pickett, *Heart of a Soldier*, 159-60; *OR*, I, 42, pt. 2: 1168, 1172-73, 1242, 1291-92; *Official Records of the Union and Confederate Navies in the War of the Rebellion*, 2 series, 30 vols. (Washington, D.C., 1894-1922), I, 10: 729-31.

15. *OR*, I, 42, pt. 2: 1168, 1242; 1297-98; *Official Records of Navies*, I, 10: 186-87, 705, 720, 744-45, 752-53, 778, 784; 11: 664, 666, 668, 672, 773-74, 777, 805-06, 808; George E. Pickett to John K. Mitchell, Sept. 25, 1864, Jan. 24, 1865, Mitchell Papers, VHS.

16. *OR*, I, 42, pt. 2: 468, 479, 498, 500, 518, 1202; John E. Divine, *8th Virginia Infantry* (Lynchburg, Va., 1983), 31-32.

17. *OR*, I, 42, pt. 1: 875-76; pt. 2: 1304; pt. 3: 17, 65, 119, 234; Alexander, *Fighting for the Confederacy*, 477; Richard J. Sommers, *Richmond Redeemed: The Siege at Petersburg* (Garden City, N.Y., 1981), 22, 50, 69, 120, 125, 582n.-83n.; Dorothy Francis Atkinson, *King William County in the Civil War. . . .* (Lynchburg, Va., 1990), 190-91.

18. *OR*, I, 42, pt. 1: 871; James Longstreet, *From Manassas to Appomattox: Memoirs of the Civil War in America* (Philadelphia, 1896), 574-75; Douglas Southall Freeman, *Lee's Lieutenants: A Study in Command*, 3 vols. (New York, 1942-44), 3: 627.

19. Robert K. Krick, *30th Virginia Infantry* (Lynchburg, Va., 1983), 58-59; *OR*, I, 42, pt. 2: 1271-72.

20. George E. Pickett to La Salle Corbell Pickett, Aug. —, 1864, Arthur Crew Inman Papers, John Hay Library, Brown University, Providence, R.I.; George E. Pickett, *Soldier of the South: General Pickett's War Letters to His Wife*, ed. Arthur Crew Inman (Boston, 1928), 114; William B. Randolph to anon., Nov. 6, 1864, LC; Robertson, *18th Virginia*, 29-30; Charles A. Douglas to Caroline M. S. Douglas, Dec. 19, 1864, Douglas Correspondence, VHS; Krick, *30th Virginia*, 60.

21. *OR*, I, 42, pt. 2: 299, 576; pt. 3: 1213; 46, pt. 2: 576; pt. 3: 1332, 1353; Robert E. Lee to James Longstreet, Jan. 19, 1865, Lee Papers, VHS; Loehr, *Old First Virginia*, 55; Lee A. Wallace, Jr., *1st Virginia Infantry* (Lynchburg, Va., 1985), 56; J. Howard Gregory, *38th Virginia Infantry* (Lynchburg, Va., 1988), 60-61.

22. Johnston, *Confederate Boy*, 283; Lee A. Wallace, Jr., *3rd Virginia Infantry* (Lynchburg, Va., 1986), 53.

23. *OR*, I, 42, pt. 3: 1289-90, 1292, 1295, 1301; 43, pt. 1: 91, 94, 678; pt. 2: 943-44; 46, pt. 1: 474-80, 503; pt. 2: 880, 993-94, 1281-82, 1290-91, 1308-13; pt. 3: 14-15, 38, 41, 43; Longstreet, *From Manassas to Appomattox*, 591; Loehr, *Old First Virginia*, 57-58; Benjamin J. Huddle diary, Mar. 9-18, 1865, F-SNMP.

24. *OR*, I, 46, pt. 3: 187-88, 237, 1341-43, 1345-46, 1349-51; Longstreet, *From Manassas to Appomattox*, 592-95.

25. Ibid., 595-96; *OR*, I, 46, pt. 3: 1357, 1360, 1363; Pickett, *What Happened to Me*, 175.

26. *OR*, I, 46, pt. 1: 1287; pt. 3: 291, 324, 1371; Harrison, *Pickett's Men*, 142-43; Loehr, *Old First Virginia*, 58; Wood, *Big I*, 71; *History of the Seventeenth Virginia Infantry, C.S.A.* (Baltimore, 1870), 218-19; Pickett, *Pickett and His Men*, 382-83; Christopher Calkins and Edwin C. Bearss, *The Battle of Five Forks* (Lynchburg, Va., 1985), 10-11; Freeman, *R. E. Lee*, 4: 27-28; Freeman, *Lee's Lieutenants*, 3: 656-57; Transcript of Testimony by Fitzhugh Lee at Warren Court of Inquiry,

June 1, 1880, Typescript in John W. Daniel Papers, UVA; Joshua L. Chamberlain, *The Passing of the Armies: An Account of the Final Campaign of the Army of the Potomac.* . . . (New York, 1915), 60-61.

27. *OR*, I, 46, pt. 1: 1102-03, 1116-17, 1123, 1128, 1144, 1298-99; pt. 3: 325, 338; Philip H. Sheridan, *Personal Memoirs of P. H. Sheridan*, 2 vols. (New York, 1888), 2: 148-52; *Seventeenth Virginia*, 220-22; Harrison, *Pickett's Men*, 143-45; Loehr, *Old First Virginia*, 58; Calkins and Bearss, *Five Forks*, 32-47; John Horn, *The Petersburg Campaign, June 1864-April 1865* (Conshohocken, Pa., 1993), 226-30.

28. *OR*, I, 46, pt. 3: 1371; *Seventeenth Virginia*, 226; Horn, *Petersburg Campaign*, 230-31; Harrison, *Pickett's Men*, 138.

29. Pickett, *Pickett and His Men*, 386; Freeman, *R. E. Lee*, 4: 36 and n.; Freeman, *Lee's Lieutenants*, 3: 661 and n.

30. Pickett, *Pickett and His Men*, 392; Longstreet, *From Manassas to Appomattox*, 600; Freeman, *R. E. Lee*, 4: 40n.; Harrison, *Pickett's Men*, 138-40.

31. Harrison, *Pickett's Men*, 139-40, 145-46; Calkins and Bearss, *Five Forks*, 77-78; Fitzhugh Lee Testimony, Warren Court of Inquiry, n.d., Daniel Papers, UVA; Fitzhugh Lee, *General Lee* (New York, 1894), 376; Alexander, *Fighting for the Confederacy*, 513.

32. Harrison, *Pickett's Men*, 145; Freeman, *Lee's Lieutenants*, 3: 662n.; Pickett, *Pickett and His Men*, 387; Charles F. Adams, Jr., to S. Weir Mitchell, Dec. 18, 1913, Society Collection, Historical Society of Pennsylvania.

33. A. S. Parham to Robert A. Bright, Feb. 11, 1904, Bright Correspondence, Southall Collection, Earl Gregg Swem Library, College of William and Mary, Williamsburg, Va.; Thomas T. Munford to John W. Daniel, Nov. 14, 1905, Nov. 29, 1907, Daniel Papers; to Robert E. Cowart, July 27, Nov. 11, 1908, Cowart Papers; all, DU; C. Irvine Walker, *The Life of Lieutenant General Richard Heron Anderson of the Confederate States Army* (Charleston, S.C., 1917), 225-27, 229-30; Freeman, *Lee's Lieutenants*, 3: 665-67.

34. *OR*, I, 46, pt. 1: 1100-01, 1263-64; pt. 3: 1371; Harrison, *Pickett's Men*, 145-48; Sheridan, *Memoirs*, 2: 157-65; *Seventeenth Virginia*, 226-29; Benjamin J. Huddle diary, Apr. 1, 1865; George K. Griggs, "The Thirty-eighth Virginia (Steuart's Brigade) at Battle of Five Forks," *SHSP* 16 (1888): 231; Loehr, *Old First Virginia*, 59; J. C. Goolsby, "Crenshaw['s] Battery, Pegram's Battalion, Confederate States Artillery. . . . ," *SHSP* 28 (1900): 372-73; Freeman, *Lee's Lieutenants*, 3: 669-71; Hunton, *Autobiography*, 119-20.

THIRTEEN

1. La Salle Corbell Pickett, *Pickett and His Men* (Atlanta, 1900), 376-77; La Salle Corbell Pickett, *What Happened to Me* (New York, 1917), 160-64, 179-82, 185; George E. Pickett, *The Heart of a Soldier, as Revealed in the Intimate Letters of Genl. George E. Pickett, C.S.A.*, ed. La Salle Corbell Pickett (New York, 1913), 14, 17-18.

2. *OR*, I, 46, pt. 1: 1120-21, 1277, 1289-91; pt. 3: 496, 1378, 1385, 1389; Walter Harrison, *Pickett's Men: A Fragment of War History* (New York, 1870), 149, 152-57; Eppa Hunton, *Autobiography of Eppa Hunton* (Richmond, 1933), 120-24; Christopher Calkins, *The Battles of Appomattox Station and Appomattox Court House, April 8-9, 1865* (Lynchburg, Va., 1987), 9, 51, 126; Christopher Calkins, *Thirty-six Hours Before Appomattox* (N.p., 1980), 16-17, 20, 22; John S. Wise,

206

The End of an Era (Boston, 1899), 428; *History of the Seventeenth Virginia Infantry, C.S.A.* (Baltimore, 1870), 234-38; C. F. James, "Battle of Sailor's Creek. . . .," *SHSP* 24 (1896): 84-88; David E. Johnston, *The Story of a Confederate Boy in the Civil War* (Portland, Ore., 1914), 325-29.

3. Douglas Southall Freeman, *Lee's Lieutenants: A Study In Command*, 3 vols. (New York, 1942-44), 3: 720-21; Henry A. Wise, "The Career of Wise's Brigade, 1861-5. . . .," *SHSP* 25 (1897): 17-19; Charles M. Cummings, *Yankee Quaker, Confederate General: The Curious Career of Bushrod Rust Johnson* (Rutherford, N.J., 1971), 326-29; John Singleton Mosby, *The Memoirs of Colonel John S. Mosby*, ed. Charles Wells Russell (Boston, 1917), 381-82; Unidentified newspaper clipping, "Gen. Pickett Not Arrested by Gen. Lee," George A. Martin Papers, Southern Historical Collection, UNC.

4. Pickett, *What Happened to Me*, 188-89; *OR*, I, 46, pt. 3: 835.

5. Pickett, *What Happened to Me*, 186, 191; Pickett, *Heart of a Soldier*, 18-19.

6. George E. Pickett to Andrew Johnson, June 1, 1865; Oath of Allegiance of George E. Pickett, Provost Marshal's Office, Richmond, Va., June 16, 1865; both, Pickett's Amnesty File, M-1003, r-67, NA.

7. Oath of Allegiance of Charles Pickett, Provost Marshal's Office, Richmond, Va., June 7, 1865; Charles Pickett to William H. Seward, June 20, 1865; both, George E. Pickett's Amnesty File, M-1003, r-67, NA.

8. *Murder of Union Soldiers in North Carolina: Letter from the Secretary of War . . . May 3, 1866* (House Exec. Doc. no. 98, 39th Cong., 1st sess., 1866), 14-53.

9. Ibid., 53-55.

10. Pickett, *What Happened to Me*, 206-39.

11. Ibid., 240-70, 271, 281; Pickett, *Heart of a Soldier*, 19-20.

12. Edwin Gray Lee diary, Oct. 10, Nov. 24, 1865, Edmund Jennings Lee Papers, Southern Historical Collection, UNC; Alexandra Lee Levin, "The Canada Contact: Edwin Gray Lee," *Civil War Times Illustrated* 18 (June 1979): 46.

13. George E. Pickett to Samuel Barron, Dec. 8, 1865, Barron Papers, UVA.

14. George E. Pickett to Ulysses S. Grant, Mar. 12, 1866, and Grant's endorsement of same, Pickett's Amnesty File, M-1003, r-67, NA.

15. Clerk of the House of Representatives to Andrew Johnson, Dec. 3, 1866; William G. Moore to "Dear Sir," Dec. 5, 1866; both, ibid.; Richard N. Current, *Lincoln's Loyalists: Union Soldiers from the Confederacy* (Boston, 1992), 123.

16. Pickett, *Heart of a Soldier*, 20-21; Pickett, *What Happened to Me*, 273, 278-79, 315.

17. Ibid., 278; Pickett, *Heart of a Soldier*, 21, 189; William B. Hesseltine and Hazel C. Wolf, *The Blue and the Gray on the Nile* (Chicago, 1961), 9, 19-22.

18. Pickett, *Heart of a Soldier*, 21-23, 186; Pickett, *What Happened to Me*, 280-81, 303-04.

19. Pickett, *Heart of a Soldier*, 22, 198-202; T. Harry Williams, *P. G. T. Beauregard, Napoleon in Gray* (Baton Rouge, 1954), 273.

20. George E. Pickett Speech, 1865, Henry E. Huntington Library, San Marino, Calif.; "Strength of General Lee's Army in the Seven Days Battles Around Richmond," *SHSP* 1 (1876): 415; "Editorial Paragraphs," *SHSP* 2 (1876): 159.

21. James L. Kemper to Benjamin J. Barbour, Feb. 5, 1880, Kemper Correspondence, VHS.

22. Thomas W. Howard, "Journey of the Dead," *America's Civil War* 7 (Sept. 1994): 64-65; Pickett, *Heart of a Soldier*, 203-07.

23. Mosby, *Memoirs*, 380-81; John S. Mosby to Eppa Hunton, Jr., Mar. 25, 28, 1911, Mosby Papers, VHS.

24. *New York Times*, July 31, 1875; Pickett, *Heart of a Soldier*, 24-25, 208-09; Pickett, *What Happened to Me*, 341-46, 352-63; Albin Trant Butt, "A Century of Service to the Sick: The 100 Year History of the Hospital of St. Vincent de Paul, Norfolk, Virginia, 1856-1956," 16, Typescript in Archives of St. Joseph Provincial House, Emmitsburg, Md.

BIBLIOGRAPHY

I. MANUSCRIPTS AND UNPUBLISHED STUDIES

Adams, Charles F., Jr. Letter of December 18, 1913. Society Collection. Historical Society of Pennsylvania, Philadelphia, Pa.

Alexander, E. Porter. Papers. Confederate Miscellany Collection. Robert W. Woodruff Library, Emory University, Atlanta, Ga.

_____. Papers. Library of Congress, Washington, D.C.

_____. Papers. Southern Historical Collection. Wilson Library, University of North Carolina, Chapel Hill, N.C.

Aylett, William R. Correspondence. Fredericksburg-Spotsylvania National Military Park, Fredericksburg, Va.

Baird, Edward R. Correspondence. Baird Family Papers. Earl Gregg Swem Library, College of William and Mary, Williamsburg, Va.

Bartley, Nathan T. Letter of March 5, 1929. William R. Perkins Library, Duke University, Durham. N.C.

Bratton, John. Correspondence. Southern Historical Collection. Wilson Library, University of North Carolina.

Bright, Robert A. Letter of September 28, 1894. Charles Pickett Papers. Virginia Historical Society, Richmond, Va.

_____. Correspondence. Southall Collection. Earl Gregg Swem Library, College of William and Mary.

Bruce, George A. Correspondence. Virginia Historical Society.

Burwell, Blair. Letter of May 26, 1864. Earl Gregg Swem Library, College of William and Mary.

Butt, Albin Trant. "A Century of Service to the Sick: The 100 Year History of the Hospital of St. Vincent de Paul, Norfolk, Virginia, 1856-1956." Typescript in Archives of St. Joseph Provincial House, Emmitsburg, Md.

Carrington, Alexander. Correspondence. Carrington Family Papers. Virginia Historical Society.

Cason, William G. Letter of December 11, 1862. Fredericksburg-Spotsylvania National Military Park.

Century Civil War Collection. New York Public Library, New York, N.Y.

Cocke, John N. Correspondence. Cocke Family Papers. Virginia Historical Society.

Cocke, William H. Correspondence. Cocke Family Papers. Virginia Historical Society.

Cockrell, Monroe F. "Where Was Pickett at Gettysburg?" Typescript in William R. Perkins Library, Duke University.

Cogbill, Marcus A. Letter of September 28, 1894. Charles Pickett Papers. Virginia Historical Society.

Coghill, Edwin R. Diaries, 1861-65. Fredericksburg-Spotsylvania National Military Park.

Coleman, Clayton G. Letter of July 1, 1904. John W. Daniel Papers. Alderman Library, University of Virginia, Charlottesville, Va.

"Committee's Report on General Pickett, and His Command and Participation in the Battle of Gettysburg, July 3, 1863." Typescript in Gregory Family Papers, Virginia Historical Society.

Daniel, John W. Papers. Alderman Library, University of Virginia.

_____. Papers. William R. Perkins Library, Duke University.

Dawson, Francis W. Correspondence. Alderman Library, University of Virginia.

Dearing, James. Correspondence. Dearing Family Papers. Alderman Library, University of Virginia.

Department of Oregon. Headquarters Letterbooks, 1858-61. Record Group 393, Entry 3570, National Archives, Washington, D.C.

Douglas, Charles A. Correspondence. Virginia Historical Society.

Eighth United States Infantry. Headquarters Letterbooks, 1838-1900. Record Group 391, Entry 1279, National Archives.

_____. Military History of Officers, 1838-69. Record Group 391, Entry 1285, National Archives.

_____. Regimental Returns, 1846-55. Microcopy 665, reels 90-91, National Archives.

Fitzhugh, E. C. Letter of April 5, 1857. Isaac I. Stevens Papers. University of Washington Library, Seattle, Wash.

Flowerree, Charles C. Undated letter. Flowerree Family Papers. Virginia Historical Society.

Francis, Charles R. Correspondence. Fredericksburg-Spotsylvania National Military Park.

Friend, Thomas R. Letter of December 10, 1894. Charles Pickett Papers. Virginia Historical Society.

Garnett, Richard B. Letter of February 2, 1863. Simon Gratz Collection. Historical Society of Pennsylvania.

Gayle, Levin C. Diary, 1863. Gettysburg National Military Park, Gettysburg, Pa.

Gordon, Leslie Jill. "Before the Storm: The Early Life of George E. Pickett." Typescript in Earl Gregg Swem Library, College of William and Mary.

Haldeman, Horace. Correspondence. U.S. Army Military History Institute, Carlisle Barracks, Pa.

Hall, Robert W. Memoirs. Fredericksburg-Spotsylvania National Military Park.

Haskell, John C. Letter of May 19, 1906. John W. Daniel Papers. William R. Perkins Library, Duke University.

Huddle, Benjamin J. Diaries, 1861-65. Fredericksburg-Spotsylvania National Military Park.

Hunton, Eppa. Correspondence. John W. Daniel Papers. William R. Perkins Library, Duke University.

Johnston, Andrew. Letter of August 19, 1841. Abraham Lincoln Association, Springfield, Ill.

Jones, William H. Correspondence. William R. Perkins Library, Duke University.

Kemper, James L. Correspondence. Alderman Library, University of Virginia.

_____. Correspondence. Confederate Miscellany Collection. Robert W. Woodruff Library, Emory University.

_____. Correspondence. Virginia Historical Society.

_____. Letter of September 20, 1869. Dearborn Collection. Houghton Library, Harvard University, Cambridge, Mass.

Latrobe, Osmun. Diaries, 1861-64. Virginia Historical Society.

Lee, Edwin Gray. Diary, 1865. Edmund Jennings Lee Papers. Southern Historical Collection. Wilson Library, University of North Carolina.

Lee, Robert E. Papers. Virginia Historical Society.

Longstreet, James. Correspondence. Charles Pickett Papers. Virginia Historical Society.

_____. Papers. Southern Historical Collection. Wilson Library, University of North Carolina.

_____. Papers. William R. Perkins Library, Duke University.

Martin, George A. Papers. Southern Historical Collection. Wilson Library, University of North Carolina.

Maury, Richard L. Papers. William R. Perkins Library, Duke University.

McCabe, James Dabney. Papers. Milton S. Eisenhower Library, The Johns Hopkins University, Baltimore, Md.

McConnell, John D. Memoirs. Winthrop College Archives and Special Collections, Rock Hill, S.C.

McKnight, William. Correspondence. Fredericksburg-Spotsylvania National Military Park.

Morton, William G. Correspondence. Fredericksburg-Spotsylvania National Military Park.

Mosby, John S. Papers. Virginia Historical Society.

Munford, Thomas T. Correspondence. John W. Daniel Papers. William R. Perkins Library, Duke University.

_____. Correspondence. Robert E. Cowart Papers. William R. Perkins Library, Duke University.

Ninth United States Infantry. Regimental Returns, 1855-61. Microcopy 665, reel 102, National Archives.

Petty, James T. Diaries, 1861-63. Museum of the Confederacy, Richmond, Va.

Pickett, Charles. Letter of March 5, 1894. Richard L. Maury Papers. William R. Perkins Library, Duke University.

_____. Letter of October 12, 1892. James Longstreet Papers. Southern Historical Collection. Wilson Library, University of North Carolina.

_____. Papers. Virginia Historical Society.

Pickett, George E. Amnesty File. Microcopy 1003, reel 67, National Archives.

_____. Army of Northern Virginia General and Staff Officers' File. Microcopy 331, reel 197, National Archives.

_____. Cadet Application File. United States Military Academy Archives, West Point, N.Y.

_____. Cadet Delinquency Register. United States Military Academy Archives.

_____. Correspondence. Arthur Crew Inman Papers. John Hay Library, Brown University, Providence, R.I.

_____. Correspondence. Charles S. Venable Papers. Southern Historical Collection. Wilson Library, University of North Carolina.

_____. Correspondence. Cullum File. United States Military Academy Library.

_____. Correspondence. E. P. Alexander Papers. Southern Historical Collection. Wilson Library, University of North Carolina.

_____. Correspondence. Ferdinand Dreer Collection. Historical Society of Pennsylvania.

_____. Correspondence. Howard E. Buswell Collection. Center for Pacific Northwest Studies. Western Washington University, Bellingham, Wash.

_____. Correspondence. I. H. Carrington Papers. William R. Perkins Library, Duke University.

_____. Correspondence. John K. Mitchell Papers. Virginia Historical Society.

_____. Correspondence. Simon Gratz Collection. Historical Society of Pennsylvania.

_____. Letter of April 17, 1864. James Dabney McCabe Papers. William R. Perkins Library, Duke University.

_____. Letter of December 4, 1852. Heth Family Papers. Virginia Historical Society.

_____. Letter of December 8, 1865. Samuel Barron Papers. Alderman Library, University of Virginia.

_____. Letter of January 14, 1867. Aylett Family Papers. Virginia Historical Society.

_____. Letter of July 9, 1864. Alderman Library, University of Virginia.

_____. Letter of May 18, 1875. Munford-Ellis Papers. William R. Perkins Library, Duke University.

_____. Letter of November 4, 1864. Barron Family Papers. Virginia Historical Society.

_____. Papers. William R. Perkins Library, Duke University.

_____. Speech, 1865. Henry E. Huntington Library, San Marino, Calif.

_____. Undated letter. Museum of the Confederacy.

Pickett, George E., Jr. Correspondence. Alderman Library, University of Virginia.

Pickett, La Salle Corbell. Letter of July 5, 1889. In possession of Mrs. Greta W. James, Arlington, Va.

_____. Letter of May 10, 1908. Alderman Library, University of Virginia.

_____. Letter of November 22, 1875. John A. Elder Papers. William R. Perkins Library, Duke University.

Randolph, William B. Letter of November 6, 1864. Library of Congress.

Richards, King D. Correspondence. Richmond National Battlefield Park, Richmond, Va.

Routt, William H. Correspondence. Museum of the Confederacy.

Sadlow, Jeanne Louise. "Life and Campaigns of General George Edward Pickett." M. A. thesis, St. John's University, 1959.

Second United States Infantry. Regimental Returns, 1847. Microcopy 665, reel 17, National Archives.

Seventh United States Infantry. Military History of Officers, 1808-1908. Record Group 391, Entry 1237, National Archives.

_____. Regimental Returns, 1847. Microcopy 665, reel 79, National Archives.

Smith, George W. Letter of May 20, 1863. Fredericksburg-Spotsylvania National Military Park.

Sorrel, J. Moxley. Diary, 1864. Museum of the Confederacy.

Swank, Luther L. Correspondence. Museum of the Confederacy.

Symington, W. Stuart. Correspondence. Charles Pickett Papers. Virginia Historical Society.

_____. Letter of May 12, 1885. Francis W. Dawson Papers. Alderman Library, University of Virginia.

Terrell, Charles. Correspondence. Fredericksburg-Spotsylvania National Military Park.

Trimble, Isaac R. Letter of November 24, 1875. John W. Daniel Papers. William R. Perkins Library, Duke University.

Vouri, Michael P. "George Pickett and the Frontier Army Experience." Typescript in possession of the author, Bellingham, Wash.

Wells, W. W. Letter of December 13, 1894. Gettysburg National Military Park.

Whittle, Powhatan B. Correspondence. Fredericksburg- Spotsylvania National Military Park.

Wise, George N. Diary, 1863. William R. Perkins Library, Duke University.

Young, Louis G. Letter of September 7, 1911. J. Bryan Grimes Papers. Southern Historical Collection. Wilson Library, University of North Carolina.

II. NEWSPAPERS

Daily Richmond Enquirer

New York Times

Petersburg Express

Petersburg Register

Philadelphia Weekly Times

Richmond Examiner

Richmond Times

Richmond Times-Dispatch

III. ARTICLES AND ESSAYS

"About the Death of General Garnett." Confederate Veteran 14 (1906): 81.

Alexander, E. Porter. "The Battle of Fredericksburg." Southern Historical Society Papers 10 (1882): 382-92, 445-64.

_____. "The Great Charge and Artillery Fighting at Gettysburg." Battles and Leaders of the Civil War 3 (1887-88): 357-68.

_____. "Sketch of Longstreet's Division." Southern Historical Society Papers 9 (1881): 512-18.

"Army Officer's Report of [the Puget Sound] Indian War and Treaties." Washington Historical Quarterly 19 (1928): 134-41.

Beauregard, P. G. T. "The Defense of Drewry's Bluff." Battles and Leaders of the Civil War 4 (1887-88): 195-205.

Berkeley, Edmund. "Rode with Pickett." Confederate Veteran 38 (1930): 175.

Bidgood, Joseph V. "List of General Officers and Their Staffs. . . ." Southern Historical Society Papers 38 (1910): 156-83.

Bright, Robert A. "Pickett's Charge at Gettysburg." Confederate Veteran 38 (1930): 263-66.

_____. "Pickett's Charge: The Story of It as Told by a Member of His Staff." Southern Historical Society Papers 31 (1903): 228-36.

Bruce, George A. "The Strategy of the Civil War." *Civil and Military Wars, 1861, 1846: Papers of the Military Historical Society of Massachusetts* 13 (1913): 487-542.

Castel, Albert. "Theophilus Holmes—Pallbearer of the Confederacy." *Civil War Times Illustrated* 16 (July 1977): 11-17.

"Causes of Lee's Defeat at Gettysburg: Letter from Gen. C. M. Wilcox." *Southern Historical Society Papers* 4 (1877): 11-17.

"Causes of Lee's Defeat at Gettysburg: Letter from General E. P. Alexander, Late Chief of Artillery, First Corps, A. N. V." *Southern Historical Society Papers* 4 (1877): 97-111.

"Causes of Lee's Defeat at Gettysburg: Letter from General John B. Hood." *Southern Historical Society Papers* 4 (1877): 145-50.

"Causes of the Defeat of Gen. Lee's Army at the Battle of Gettysburg—Opinions of Leading Confederate Soldiers." *Southern Historical Society Papers* 4 (1877): 49-160.

Collins, John L. "A Prisoner's March from Gettysburg to Staunton." *Battles and Leaders of the Civil War* 3 (1887-88): 429-33.

Cooper, J. "Pickett's Brigade at Gaines's Mill." *Confederate Veteran* 6 (1898): 565-67.

Cullen, Joseph P. "Gaines's Mill." *Civil War Times Illustrated* 3 (April 1964): 10-17, 24.

_____. "When Grant Faced Lee Across the North Anna." *Civil War Times Illustrated* 3 (February 1965): 16-23.

Daniel, W. Harrison, ed. "Chaplains of the Army of Northern Virginia: A List Compiled in 1864 and 1865 by Robert L. Dabney." *Virginia Magazine of History and Biography* 71 (1963): 327-40.

Devereux, Arthur F. "Some Account of Pickett's Charge at Gettysburg." *Magazine of American History* 18 (1887): 13-19.

Easley, D. B. "Saw Pickett 'Riding Grandly Down'." *Confederate Veteran* 38 (1930): 133.

"Editorial Paragraphs." *Southern Historical Society Papers* 2 (1876): 159-60.

"E. P. Alexander and Pickett's Charge." *Civil War Times Illustrated* 17 (April 1978): 22-24.

Fleming, Francis P. "Gettysburg: The Courageous Part Taken . . . by the Florida Brigade. . . ." *Southern Historical Society Papers* 27 (1899): 192-205.

Fry, D. B. "Pettigrew's Charge at Gettysburg." *Southern Historical Society Papers* 7 (1879): 91-93.

Gaines, E. W. "Fayette Artillery: The Movement on New Berne. . . ." *Southern Historical Society Papers* 25 (1897): 288-97.

Gallagher, Gary W. "The Army of Northern Virginia in May 1864: A Crisis of High Command." *Civil War History* 36 (1990): 102-18.

____. "A Widow and Her Soldier: La Salle Corbell Pickett as Author of the George E. Pickett Letters." *Virginia Magazine of History and Biography* 94 (1986): 329-44.

"General Lewis Addison Armistead." *Confederate Veteran* 22 (1914): 502-04.

"Generals in the Confederate States Army from Virginia." *Southern Historical Society Papers* 36 (1908): 105-20.

Goolsby, J. C. "Crenshaw['s] Battery, Pegram's Battalion, Confederate States Artillery. . . ." *Southern Historical Society Papers* 28 (1900): 336-77.

Gordon, George W. "Battles of Molino del Rey and Chapultepec." *Civil and Mexican Wars, 1861, 1846: Papers of the Military Historical Society of Massachusetts* 13 (1913): 601-39.

Griggs, George K. "The Thirty-eighth Virginia (Steuart's Brigade) at Battle of Five Forks." *Southern Historical Society Papers* 16 (1888): 230-31.

Hardy, Stella Pickett. "Genealogy: The Pickett Family." *Bulletin [of the] Fauquier Historical Society* 1 (1921-24): 207-15.

Hazlewood, Martin W. "Gettysburg Charge: Paper as to Pickett's Men." *Southern Historical Society Papers* 23 (1895): 229-37.

Hogan, N. B. ["Pickett's Brigade at Gaines's Mill."] *Confederate Veteran* 6 (1898): 567-68.

Howard, Thomas W. "Journey of the Dead." *America's Civil War* 7 (September 1994): 62-65.

Hunt, Henry J. "The Third Day at Gettysburg." *Battles and Leaders of the Civil War* 3 (1887-88): 369-85.

Hunton, Eppa. "Gaines's Mill." *Confederate Veteran* 7 (1899): 223-24.

Hunton, Eppa, IV. "Battle Abbey Committee Report." *Virginia Magazine of History and Biography* 66 (1958): 238.

Imboden, John D. "The Confederate Retreat from Gettysburg." *Battles and Leaders of the Civil War* 3 (1887-88): 420-29.

James, C. F. "Battle of Sailor's Creek. . . ." *Southern Historical Society Papers* 24 (1896): 83-88.

Johnston, Joseph E. "Manassas to Seven Pines." *Battles and Leaders of the Civil War* 2 (1887-88): 202-18.

Jones, J. William, comp. "The Treatment of Prisoners During the War Between the States." *Southern Historical Society Papers* 1 (1876): 113-221.

"The Last Roll: Lieut. Benjamin H. Hutchison." *Confederate Veteran* 24 (1916): 80.

Law, E. M. "From the Wilderness to Cold Harbor." *Battles and Leaders of the Civil War* 4 (1887-88): 118-44.

"Letters from Old Trunks: Letter from James Barron Hope to Commodore Samuel Barron." *Virginia Magazine of History and Biography* 47 (1939): 349-55.

Levin, Alexandra Lee. "The Canada Contact: Edwin Gray Lee." *Civil War Times Illustrated* 18 (June 1979): 4-8, 42-47.

Loehr, Charles T. "The 'Old First' Virginia at Gettysburg. . . ." *Southern Historical Society Papers* 32 (1904): 33-40.

Longstreet, James. "The Battle of Fredericksburg." *Battles and Leaders of the Civil War* 3 (1887-88): 70-85.

_____. "General James Longstreet's Account of the Campaign and Battle [of Gettysburg]." *Southern Historical Society Papers* 5 (1877): 54-85.

_____. "General Longstreet's Second Paper on Gettysburg." *Southern Historical Society Papers* 5 (1877): 257-70.

_____. "Lee's Right Wing at Gettysburg." *Battles and Leaders of the Civil War* 3 (1887-88): 339-54.

Mahone, William. "On the Road to Appomattox." *Civil War Times Illustrated* 9 (January 1971): 5-11, 42-47.

Martin, Rawley W. "The Battle of Gettysburg, and the Charge of Pickett's Division. . . ." *Southern Historical Society Papers* 32 (1904): 183-89.

Maury, Dabney H. "Dabney Maury on Stonewall Jackson." *Confederate Veteran* 6 (1898): 53-55.

Mayo, Joseph C. "Pickett's Charge at Gettysburg. . . ." *Southern Historical Society Papers* 34 (1906): 327-35.

McCabe, W. Gordon. "Defence [sic] of Petersburg." *Southern Historical Society Papers* 2 (1876): 257-306.

McCulloch, Robert. "The 'High Tide at Gettysburg'." *Confederate Veteran* 21 (1913): 473-76.

McKay, Charles. "History of San Juan Island." *Washington Historical Quarterly* 2 (1907): 290-93.

McLaws, Lafayette. "Gettysburg." *Southern Historical Society Papers* 7 (1879): 64-90.

"Memoranda of [the] Thirty-eighth Virginia Infantry: From [the] Diary of Colonel George K. Griggs." *Southern Historical Society Papers* 14 (1886): 250-57.

"Minge Family Register." *William and Mary Quarterly* 1st ser., 21 (1912): 31-33.

"The Monument to General Robert E. Lee: History of the Movement for its Erection." *Southern Historical Society Papers* 17 (1889): 187-335.

Moore, J. Staunton. "The Battle of Five Forks." *Confederate Veteran* 16 (1908): 403-04.

"Official Diary of First Corps, A. N. V., While Commanded by Lieutenant-General R. H. Anderson, from May 7th to 31st, 1864." *Southern Historical Society Papers* 7 (1879): 491-94.

"Official Diary of First Corps, A. N. V., While Commanded by Lt.-General R. H. Anderson, from June 1st to October 18, 1864." *Southern Historical Society Papers* 7 (1879): 503-12.

Owen, H. T. "Error in Hon. James W. Boyd's Speech [on General Richard B. Garnett]." *Confederate Veteran* 12 (1904): 7.

Patterson, Gerard A. "George E. Pickett." *Civil War Times Illustrated* 5 (May 1966): 19-24.

"Pickett Family of Virginia." *Virginia Magazine of History and Biography* 49 (1941): 80-86, 186-90.

"Pickett Grateful for Recognition." *Washington Historical Quarterly* 1 (1906): 74.

Pickett, La Salle Corbell. "General George E. Pickett: His Appointment to West Point. . . ." *Southern Historical Society Papers* 24 (1896): 151-54.

_____. "My Little Brother." *Confederate Veteran* 7 (1899): 201.

Piston, William Garrett, ed. "'The Rebs Are Yet Thick About Us': The Civil War Diary of Amos Stouffer of Chambersburg." *Civil War History* 38 (1992): 210-31.

Porter, Fitz John. "Hanover Court House and Gaines's Mill." *Battles and Leaders of the Civil War* 2 (1887-88): 319-43.

Porter, Horace. "Five Forks and the Pursuit of Lee." *Battles and Leaders of the Civil War* 4 (1887-88): 708-22.

_____. "The Surrender at Appomattox Court House." *Battles and Leaders of the Civil War* 4 (1887-88): 729-46.

Purifoy, John. "Longstreet's Attack at Gettysburg." *Confederate Veteran* 32 (1924): 54-56.

"Report of Brigadier-General Wilcox of the Battle of Gettysburg." *Southern Historical Society Papers* 7 (1879): 280-87.

Rice, Edmund. "Repelling Lee's Last Blow at Gettysburg." *Battles and Leaders of the Civil War* 3 (1887-88): 387-90.

Selcer, Richard. "George Pickett: Another Look." *Civil War Times Illustrated* 33 (July-August 1994): 44-49, 60-73.

Smith, Gustavus W. "Two Days of Battle at Seven Pines (Fair Oaks)." *Battles and Leaders of the Civil War* 2 (1887-88): 220-63.

Smith, J. B. "The Charge of Pickett, Pettigrew, and Trimble." *Battles and Leaders of the Civil War* 3 (1887-88): 354-55.

"Strength of General Lee's Army in the Seven Days Battles Around Richmond." *Southern Historical Society Papers* 1 (1876): 407-24.

Talcott, T. M. R. "The Third Day at Gettysburg." *Southern Historical Society Papers* 41 (1916): 37-48.

"Testimony About Battle of Gettysburg." *Confederate Veteran* 18 (1910): 524-25.

Todd, George T. "Gaines's Mill—Pickett and Hood." *Confederate Veteran* 6 (1898): 565-67.

Todd, Ronald, ed. "Letters of Governor Isaac I. Stevens, 1857-1858." *Pacific Northwest Quarterly* 31 (1940): 403-59.

"The Treatment of Prisoners During the War Between the States." *Southern Historical Society Papers* 1 (1876): 113-221, 225-327.

Tunem, Alfred. "The Dispute Over the San Juan Island Water Boundary." *Washington Historical Quarterly* 23 (1932): 38-46.

Venable, Charles S. "The Campaign from the Wilderness to Petersburg. . . ." *Southern Historical Society Papers* 14 (1886): 522-42.

Watson, Walter C. "The Fighting at Sailor's Creek." *Confederate Veteran* 25 (1917): 448-52.

_____. "Sailor's Creek." *Southern Historical Society Papers* 42 (1917): 136-51.

Weinert, Richard P. "The Suffolk Campaign." *Civil War Times Illustrated* 7 (January 1969): 31-39.

Wise, George. ["Pickett's Brigade at Gaines's Mill."] *Confederate Veteran* 6 (1898): 568-69.

Wise, Henry A. "The Career of Wise's Brigade, 1861-5. . . ." *Southern Historical Society Papers* 25 (1897): 1-22.

Youngblood, William. "Personal Observations at Gettysburg." *Confederate Veteran* 19 (1911): 286-87.

_____. "Unwritten History of the Gettysburg Campaign." *Southern Historical Society Papers* 38 (1910): 312-18.

IV. BOOKS AND PAMPHLETS

Alderman, John Perry. *29th Virginia Infantry.* Lynchburg, Va.: H. E. Howard, Inc., 1989.

Alexander, E. Porter. *Fighting for the Confederacy: The Personal Recollections of General Edward Porter Alexander.* Edited by Gary W. Gallagher. Chapel Hill: University of North Carolina Press, 1989.

_____. *Military Memoirs of a Confederate: A Critical Narrative.* New York: Charles Scribner's Sons, 1908.

Andrus, Michael J. *The Brooke, Fauquier, Loudoun and Alexandria Artillery.* Lynchburg, Va.: H. E. Howard, Inc., 1990.

The Annals of the War, Written by Leading Participants North and South. Philadelphia: Times Publishing Co., 1879.

Arnold, Thomas Jackson. *Early Life and Letters of General Thomas J. Jackson. . . .* New York: Fleming H. Revell Co., 1916.

Atkinson, Dorothy Francis. *King William County in the Civil War. . . .* Lynchburg, Va.: H. E. Howard, Inc., 1990.

Barrett, John G. *The Civil War in North Carolina.* Chapel Hill: University of North Carolina Press, 1963.

Bauer, K. Jack. *The Mexican War, 1846-1848.* New York: Macmillan Publishing Co., Inc., 1974.

Bell, Robert T. *11th Virginia Infantry.* Lynchburg, Va.: H. E. Howard, Inc., 1985.

Blackford, Charles M., Jr. *Annals of the Lynchburg Home Guard.* Lynchburg, Va.: John W. Rohr, 1891.

Bond, W. R. *Pickett or Pettigrew? An Historical Essay.* Weldon, N.C.: Hall & Sledge, 1888.

Boynton, Edward C. *History of West Point . . . and the Origin and Progress of the United States Military Academy.* New York: D. Van Nostrand, 1863.

Bridges, Hal. *Lee's Maverick General: Daniel Harvey Hill.* New York: McGraw-Hill Book Co., Inc., 1961.

Calkins, Christopher. *The Battles of Appomattox Station and Appomattox Court House, April 8-9, 1865.* Lynchburg, Va.: H. E. Howard, Inc., 1987.

_____. *Thirty-six Hours Before Appomattox.* N.p.: privately issued, 1980.

_____, and Edwin C. Bearss. *The Battle of Five Forks.* Lynchburg, Va.: H. E. Howard, Inc., 1985.

Catton, Bruce. *Glory Road: The Bloody Route from Fredericksburg to Gettysburg.* Garden City, N.Y.: Doubleday & Co., Inc., 1952.

_____. *A Stillness at Appomattox.* Garden City, N.Y.: Doubleday & Co., Inc., 1953.

Chamberlain, Joshua L. *The Passing of the Armies: An Account of the Final Campaign of the Army of the Potomac. . . .* New York: G. P. Putnam's Sons, 1915.

Clark, Norman H. *Washington: A Bicentennial History.* New York: W. W. Norton & Co., Inc., 1976.

Clark, Walter. *North Carolina at Gettysburg and Pickett's Charge a Misnomer.* N.p.: privately issued, 1921.

_____, ed. *Histories of the Several Regiments and Battalions from North Carolina in the Great War 1861-'65. . . .* 5 vols. Goldsboro: Nash Brothers; Raleigh: E. M. Uzzell, 1901.

Coddington, Edwin B. *The Gettysburg Campaign: A Study in Command.* New York: Charles Scribner's Sons, 1968.

Coffman, Edward M. *The Old Army: A Portrait of the American Army in Peacetime, 1784-1898.* New York: Oxford University Press, 1986.

Cooke, Joel. *The Siege of Richmond: A Narrative of the Military Operations of Major-General George B. McClellan During May and June, 1862.* Philadelphia: G. W. Childs, 1862.

Cormier, Steven A. *The Siege of Suffolk: The Forgotten Campaign, April 11-May 4, 1863.* Lynchburg, Va.: H. E. Howard, Inc., 1989.

Coward, Asbury. *The South Carolinians: Colonel Asbury Coward's Memoirs.* Edited by Natalie Jenkins Bond and Osmun Latrobe Coward. New York: Vantage Press, 1968.

Crocker, James F. *Gettysburg—Pickett's Charge and Other War Addresses.* Portsmouth, Va.: W. A. Fiske, 1915.

Cullum, George W., comp. *Biographical Register of the Officers and Graduates of the U.S. Military Academy. . . .* 2 vols. Boston: Houghton, Mifflin & Co., 1891.

Cummings, Charles M. *Yankee Quaker, Confederate General: The Curious Career of Bushrod Rust Johnson.* Rutherford, N.J.: Fairleigh Dickinson University Press, 1971.

Current, Richard N. *Lincoln's Loyalists: Union Soldiers from the Confederacy.* Boston: Northeastern University Press, 1992.

Davis, Burke. *To Appomattox: Nine April Days, 1865.* New York: Rinehart & Co., Inc., 1959.

Dawson, Francis W. *Reminiscences of Confederate Service, 1861-1865.* Edited by Bell I. Wiley. Baton Rouge: Louisiana State University Press, 1980.

DeLaney, Richard W., and Marie E. Bowery, eds. *The Seventeenth Virginia Volunteer Infantry Regiment, C.S.A.* Washington, D.C.: American Printing Co., 1961.

Divine, John E. *8th Virginia Infantry.* Lynchburg, Va.: H. E. Howard, Inc., 1983.

Dooley, John E. *John Dooley, Confederate Soldier: His War Journal.* Edited by Joseph T. Durkin. Washington, D.C.: Georgetown University Press, 1945.

Edson, Lelah Jackson. *The Fourth Corner: Highlights from the Early North West.* Bellingham, Wash.: Whatcom Museum of History and Art, 1968.

Eisenhower, John S. D. *So Far from God: The U.S. War with Mexico, 1846-1848.* New York: Random House, 1989.

Elliott, Charles Winslow. *Winfield Scott, the Soldier and the Man.* New York: Macmillan Co., 1937.

Elliott, Joseph C. *Lieutenant General Richard Heron Anderson, Lee's Noble Soldier.* Dayton: Morningside, 1985.

Evans, Clement A., ed. *Confederate Military History.* 13 vols. Atlanta: Confederate Publishing Co., 1899.

Fields, Frank E. *28th Virginia Infantry.* Lynchburg, Va.: H. E. Howard, Inc., 1985.

Figg, Royall W. *"Where Men Only Dare to Go!" or the Story of a Boy Company.* Richmond: Whittet & Shepperson, 1885.

Fontaine, C. R. *A Complete Roster of the Field and Staff Officers of the 57th Virginia Regiment of Infantry. . . .* N.p.: privately issued, n.d.

Frazer, Robert W. *Forts of the West: Military Forts . . . West of the Mississippi River to 1898.* Norman: University of Oklahoma Press, 1965.

Freeman, Douglas Southall. *Lee's Lieutenants: A Study in Command.* 3 vols. New York: Charles Scribner's Sons, 1942-44.

_____. *R. E. Lee: A Biography.* 4 vols. New York: Charles Scribner's Sons, 1934-35.

Fremantle, Arthur James Lyon. *Three Months in the Southern States, April-June, 1863.* New York: John Bradburn, 1864.

French, Samuel G. *Two Wars: An Autobiography.* . . . Nashville: Confederate Veteran, 1901.

Georg, Kathleen R., and John W. Busey. *Nothing But Glory: Pickett's Division at Gettysburg.* Hightstown, N.J.: Longstreet House, 1987.

Gordon, John B. *Reminiscences of the Civil War.* New York: Charles Scribner's Sons, 1903.

Goree, Thomas J. *The Thomas Jewett Goree Letters.* Edited by Langston J. Goree, V. Bryan, Tex.: Family History Foundation, 1981.

Gorgas, Josiah. *The Civil War Diary of General Josiah Gorgas.* Edited by Frank E. Vandiver. University, Ala.: University of Alabama Press, 1947.

Grant, Bruce. *American Forts Yesterday and Today.* New York: E. P. Dutton & Co., Inc., 1965.

Gregory, J. Howard. *38th Virginia Infantry.* Lynchburg, Va.: H. E. Howard, Inc., 1988.

Gunn, Ralph White. *24th Virginia Infantry.* Lynchburg, Va.: H. E. Howard, Inc., 1987.

Hagood, Johnson. *Memoirs of the War of Secession.* . . . Columbia, S.C.: State Co., 1910.

Haller, Granville O. *San Juan and Secession: Possible Relation to the War of the Rebellion.* . . . Seattle: Shorey Book Store, 1967.

Hardy, Stella Pickett. *Colonial Families of the Southern States of America.* . . . Baltimore: Southern Book Co., 1958.

Harrison, Walter. *Pickett's Men: A Fragment of War History.* New York: D. Van Nostrand, 1870.

Haskell, John Cheves. *The Haskell Memoirs.* Edited by Gilbert E. Govan and James W. Livingood. New York: G. P. Putnam's Sons, 1960.

Hawkins, Rush C. *An Account of the Assassination of Loyal Citizens of North Carolina.* New York: J. H. Folan, 1897.

Heitman, Francis B., comp. *Historical Register and Dictionary of the United States Army.* . . . 2 vols. Washington, D.C.: Government Printing Office, 1903.

Hesseltine, William B., and Hazel C. Wolf. *The Blue and the Gray on the Nile.* Chicago: University of Chicago Press, 1961.

Heth, Henry. *The Memoirs of Henry Heth.* Edited by James L. Morrison, Jr. Westport, Conn.: Greenwood Press, 1974.

History of the Seventeenth Virginia Infantry, C.S.A. Baltimore: Kelly, Piet & Co., 1870.

Holzman, Robert S. *Stormy Ben Butler.* New York: Macmillan Co., 1954.

Hood, J. B. *Advance and Retreat: Personal Experiences of the United States and Confederate States Armies.* New Orleans: Hood Orphan Memorial Fund, 1880.

Horn, John. *The Petersburg Campaign, June 1864-April 1865.* Conshohocken, Pa.: Combined Books, 1993.

Hotchkiss, Jedediah. *"Make Me a Map of the Valley": The Civil War Journal of Stonewall Jackson's Topographer.* Edited by Archie McDonald. Dallas: Southern Methodist University Press, 1973.

Howard, McHenry. *Recollections of a Maryland Confederate Soldier and Staff Officer under Johnston, Jackson and Lee.* Baltimore: Williams & Wilkins Co., 1914.

Howard, Oliver Otis. *Autobiography of Oliver Otis Howard, Major General United States Army.* 2 vols. New York: Baker & Taylor Co., 1907.

Hunter, Alexander. *Johnny Reb and Billy Yank.* New York: Neale Publishing Co., 1905.

Hunton, Eppa. *Autobiography of Eppa Hunton.* Richmond: William Byrd Press, 1933.

Irby, Richard. *The Captain Remembers: The Papers of Captain Richard Irby.* Edited by Virginia Fitzgerald Jordan. Blackburn, Va.: Nottoway County Historical Association, 1975.

_____. *Historical Sketch of the Nottoway Grays, Afterwards Company G, Eighteenth Virginia Regiment, Army of Northern Virginia.* Richmond: J. W. Fergusson & Son, 1878.

Jensen, Les. *32nd Virginia Infantry.* Lynchburg, Va.: H. E. Howard, Inc., 1990.

Johanson, Dorothy O., and Charles M. Gates. *Empire of the Columbia: A History of the Pacific Northwest.* New York: Harper & Row, 1967.

Johnston, David E. *The Story of a Confederate Boy in the Civil War.* Portland, Ore.: Glass & Prudhomme Co., 1914.

Johnston, Joseph E. *Narrative of Military Operations. . . .* New York: D. Appleton & Co., 1874.

Jones, J. B. *A Rebel War Clerk's Diary at the Confederate States Capital.* Edited by Howard Swiggett. 2 vols. New York: Old Hickory Bookshop, 1935.

Jordan, David M. *Winfield Scott Hancock: A Soldier's Life.* Bloomington: Indiana University Press, 1988.

Jordan, Ervin L., Jr., and Herbert A. Thomas, Jr. *19th Virginia Infantry*. Lynchburg, Va.: H. E. Howard, Inc., 1987.

Kean, Robert G. H. *Inside the Confederate Government: The Diary of Robert Garlick Hill Kean, Head of the Bureau of War*. Edited by Edward Younger. New York: Oxford University Press, 1957.

Krick, Robert K. *Lee's Colonels: A Biographical Register of the Field Officers of the Army of Northern Virginia*. Dayton: Press of Morningside Bookshop, 1979.

_____. *Parker's Virginia Battery, C.S.A.* Berryville, Va.: Virginia Book Co., 1975.

_____. *30th Virginia Infantry*. Lynchburg, Va.: H. E. Howard, Inc., 1983.

Lee, Fitzhugh. *General Lee*. New York: D. Appleton & Co., 1894.

Lee, Richard M. *General Lee's City: An Illustrated Guide to the Historic Sites of Confederate Richmond*. McLean, Va.: EPM Publications, Inc., 1987.

Lee, Robert E. *Lee's Dispatches: Unpublished Letters of General Robert E. Lee, C.S.A., to Jefferson Davis and the War Department of the Confederate States of America*. Edited by Douglas Southall Freeman and Grady C. McWhiney. New York: G. P. Putnam's Sons, 1957.

_____. *The Wartime Papers of R. E. Lee*. Edited by Clifford Dowdey and Louis H. Manarin. Boston: Little, Brown & Co., 1961.

Leighton, Caroline C. *Life at Puget Sound . . . 1865-1881*. Boston: Lee & Shepard, 1884.

Lewis, John H. *Recollections from 1860 to 1865. . . .* Edited by Jim D. Moody. Dayton: Morningside House, 1983.

Lincoln, Abraham. *The Collected Works of Abraham Lincoln*. Edited by Roy P. Basler. 9 vols. New Brunswick, N.J.: Rutgers University Press, 1953.

_____. *Poetry and Prose by A. Lincoln*. Edited by Paul M. Angle and Earl Schenck Miers. Kingsport, Tenn.: privately issued, 1956.

List of Staff Officers of the Confederate States Army, 1861-1865. Washington, D.C.: Government Printing Office, 1891.

Loehr, Charles T. *War History of the Old First Virginia Infantry Regiment, Army of Northern Virginia*. Richmond: Wm. Ellis Jones, 1884.

Long, A. L. *Memoirs of Robert E. Lee: His Military and Personal History. . . .* New York: J. M. Stoddart & Co., 1886.

Long, E. B., and Barbara Long. *The Civil War Day by Day: An Almanac, 1861-1865.* Garden City, N.Y.: Doubleday & Co., Inc., 1971.

Longstreet, James. *From Manassas to Appomattox: Memoirs of the Civil War in America.* Philadelphia: J. B. Lippincott Co., 1896.

Manarin, Louis H. *15th Virginia Infantry.* Lynchburg, Va.: H. E. Howard, Inc., 1990.

Manring, Benjamin Franklin. *Conquest of the Coeur D' Alenes, Spokanes & Palouses.* Spokane, Wash.: J. W. Graham, 1912.

Marks, J. J. *The Peninsular Campaign in Virginia. . . .* Philadelphia: J. B. Lippincott & Co., 1864.

Marshall, Charles. *An Aide-de-Camp of Lee: Being the Papers of Colonel Charles Marshall. . . .* Edited by Sir Frederick Maurice. Boston: Little, Brown & Co., 1927.

Maury, Dabney H. *Recollections of a Virginian in the Mexican, Indian, and Civil Wars.* New York: Charles Scribner's Sons, 1894.

McCabe, James D., Jr. *Life and Campaigns of General Robert E. Lee.* Atlanta: National Publishing Co., 1866.

McMurry, Richard M. *Two Great Rebel Armies: An Essay in Confederate Military History.* Chapel Hill: University of North Carolina Press, 1989.

Message from the President of the United States, to the Two Houses of Congress, at the Commencement of the First Session of the Thirtieth Congress. Washington, D.C.: Wendell & Van Benthuysen, 1847.

Messages of the President of the United States . . . on the Subject of the Mexican War. Washington, D.C.: Wendell & Van Benthuysen, 1848.

Miller, J. Michael. *The North Anna Campaign: "Even to Hell Itself," May 21-26, 1864.* Lynchburg, Va.: H. E. Howard, Inc., 1989.

Miller, Robert Ryal. *Shamrock and Sword: The Saint Patrick's Battalion in the U.S.-Mexican War.* Norman: University of Oklahoma Press, 1989.

Montgomery, James Stuart. *The Shaping of a Battle: Gettysburg.* Philadelphia: Chilton Co., 1959.

Moore, Frank, ed. *The Rebellion Record: A Diary of American Events.* 12 vols. New York: various publishers, 1861-68.

Moore, Robert H., II. *The Richmond, Fayette, Hampden, Thomas, and Blount's Lynchburg Artillery.* Lynchburg, Va.: H. E. Howard, Inc., 1991.

Morgan, William H. *Personal Reminiscences of the War of 1861-5.* Lynchburg, Va.: J. P. Bell Co., 1911.

Morrison, James L., Jr. *"The Best School in the World": West Point, the Pre-Civil War Years, 1833-1866.* Kent, Ohio: Kent State University Press, 1986.

Mosby, John Singleton. *The Memoirs of Colonel John S. Mosby.* Edited by Charles Wells Russell. Boston: Little, Brown, & Co., 1917.

Murder of Union Soldiers in North Carolina: Letter from the Secretary of War . . . May 3, 1866. House Executive Document no. 98, 39th Congress, 1st session, 1866.

Murray, Keith A. *The Pig War.* Tacoma, Wash.: Washington State Historical Society, 1968.

Official Records of the Union and Confederate Navies in the War of the Rebellion. 2 series, 30 vols. Washington, D.C.: Government Printing Office, 1894-1922.

Official Register of the Officers and Cadets of the U.S. Military Academy, West Point, N.Y. West Point, N.Y.: privately issued, 1843-46.

Parker, William L. *General James Dearing, C.S.A.* Lynchburg, Va.: H. E. Howard, Inc., 1990.

Pender, William D. *The General to His Lady: The Civil War Letters of William Dorsey Pender to Fanny Pender.* Edited by William W. Hassler. Chapel Hill: University of North Carolina Press, 1965.

Pickett, George E. *The Heart of a Soldier, as Revealed in the Intimate Letters of Genl. George E. Pickett, C.S.A.* Edited by La Salle Corbell Pickett. New York: Seth Moyle, Inc., 1913.

_____. *Soldier of the South: General Pickett's War Letters to His Wife.* Edited by Arthur Crew Inman. Boston: Houghton Mifflin Co., 1928.

Pickett, La Salle Corbell. *Pickett and His Men.* Atlanta: Foote & Davies Co., 1900.

_____. *What Happened to Me.* New York: Brentano's, 1917.

Pickett, Thomas E. *A Soldier of the Civil War, by a Member of the Virginia Historical Society.* Cleveland: Burrows Brothers Co., 1900.

Piston, William Garrett. *Lee's Tarnished Lieutenant: James Longstreet and His Place in Southern History.* Athens: University of Georgia Press, 1987.

Poague, William T. *Gunner with Stonewall: Reminiscences of William Thomas Poague. . . .* Edited by Monroe F. Cockrell. Jackson, Tenn.: McCowat-Mercer Press, 1957.

Poindexter, James E. *Address on the Life and Services of Gen. Lewis A. Armistead. . . .* Richmond: privately issued, 1909.

Report of the Chief of Engineers. Senate Executive Document no. 1, 28th Congress, 2nd session, 1844.

Report of the Chief of Engineers. Senate Executive Document no. 2, 29th Congress, 1st session, 1845.

Report of the Secretary of War. Senate Executive Document no. 2, 36th Congress, 1st session, 1859.

Richards, Kent D. *Isaac I. Stevens, Young Man in a Hurry.* Provo, Utah: Brigham Young University Press, 1979.

Richardson, David. *Pig War Islands.* East Sound, Wash.: Orcas Books, 1990.

Riggs, David F. *7th Virginia Infantry.* Lynchburg, Va.: H. E. Howard, Inc., 1982.

Robertson, James I., Jr. *18th Virginia Infantry.* Lynchburg, Va.: H. E. Howard, Inc., 1984.

_____. *General A. P. Hill: The Story of a Confederate Warrior.* New York: Random House, 1987.

Robertson, William Glenn. *Back Door to Richmond: The Bermuda Hundred Campaign, April-June 1864.* Newark: University of Delaware Press, 1987.

Rodenbough, Theophilus F., and William L. Haskin, eds. *The Army of the United States: Historical Sketches of Staff and Line. . . .* New York: Merrill & Co., 1896.

Rodick, Burleigh Cushing. *Appomattox, The Last Campaign.* New York: Philosophical Library, 1965.

Rollins, Richard, ed. *Pickett's Charge: Eyewitness Accounts.* Redondo Beach, Calif.: Rank and File Publications, 1994.

Roman, Alfred. *The Military Operations of General Beauregard in the War Between the States. . . .* 2 vols. New York: Harper & Brothers, 1884.

Ross, Fitzgerald. *Cities and Camps of the Confederate States.* Edited by Richard B. Harwell. Urbana: University of Illinois Press, 1958.

Ruffner, W. H. *A Report on [the] Washington Territory.* New York: Seattle, Lake Shore & Eastern Railway, 1889.

Sanger, Donald Bridgman, and Thomas Robson Hay. *James Longstreet.* Baton Rouge: Louisiana State University Press, 1952.

San Juan Island National Historical Park, Washington. Washington, D.C.: National Park Service, 1991.

Schiller, Herbert M. *The Bermuda Hundred Campaign: "Operations on the South Side of the James River, Virginia—May, 1864".* Dayton: Morningside, 1988.

Schlicke, Carl P. *General George Wright, Guardian of the Pacific Coast.* Norman: University of Oklahoma Press, 1988.

Scott, Winfield. *Memoirs of Lieut.-General Scott. . . .* 2 vols. New York: Sheldon & Co., 1864.

Sears, Stephen W. *To the Gates of Richmond: The Peninsula Campaign.* New York: Ticknor & Fields, 1992.

Seventh Annual Reunion of the Association of the Graduates of the United States Military Academy. . . . New York: A. S. Barnes & Co., 1876.

Shaara, Michael. *The Killer Angels.* New York: David McKay Co., Inc., 1974.

Sheridan, Philip H. *Personal Memoirs of P. H. Sheridan.* 2 vols. New York: Charles L. Webster & Co., 1888.

A Short History of Genl. G. E. Pickett. Park Place, N.Y.: Knapp, ca. 1888.

Shotwell, Randolph A. *The Papers of Randolph Abbott Shotwell.* Edited by J. G. D. Hamilton and Rebecca Cameron. 3 vols. Raleigh: North Carolina Historical Commission, 1929-31.

Simpson, Harold B. *Cry Comanche: The 2nd U.S. Cavalry in Texas, 1855-1861.* Hillsboro, Tex.: Hill Junior College Press, 1979.

Simpson, John H. *Diary, 1862, of Rev. John Hemphill Simpson.* Compiled by Mary Law McCormick. Arlington, Va.: privately issued, 1986.

Smith, Gustavus W. *The Battle of Seven Pines.* New York: C. G. Crawford, 1891.

Smith, Justin H. *The War with Mexico.* 2 vols. New York: Macmillan Co., 1919.

Sommers, Richard J. *Richmond Redeemed: The Siege at Petersburg.* Garden City, N.Y.: Doubleday & Co., Inc., 1981.

Sorrel, G. Moxley. *Recollections of a Confederate Staff Officer.* New York: Neale Publishing Co., 1905.

Stevens, Hazard. *The Life of Isaac Ingalls Stevens.* 2 vols. Boston: Houghton, Mifflin & Co., 1900.

Stewart, George R. *Pickett's Charge: A Microhistory of the Final Attack at Gettysburg, July 3, 1863.* Greenwich, Conn.: Fawcett Publications, Inc., 1963.

Stiles, Robert. *Four Years Under Marse Robert.* New York: Neale Publishing Co., 1903.

Stine, J. H. *History of the Army of the Potomac.* Philadelphia: J. B. Rodgers Printing Co., 1892.

Stribling, Robert M. *Gettysburg Campaign and Campaigns of 1864 and 1865 in Virginia.* Petersburg, Va.: Franklin Press Co., 1905.

Sublett, Charles W. *57th Virginia Infantry.* Lynchburg, Va.: H. E. Howard, Inc., 1985.

Taylor, Walter H. *Four Years with General Lee.* . . . New York: D. Appleton & Co., 1877.

Trask, Benjamin W. *9th Virginia Infantry.* Lynchburg, Va.: H. E. Howard, Inc., 1984.

Tucker, Glenn. *High Tide at Gettysburg: The Campaign in Pennsylvania.* Indianapolis: Bobbs-Merrill Co., Inc., 1958.

_____. *Lee and Longstreet at Gettysburg.* Indianapolis: Bobbs- Merrill Co., Inc., 1968.

Turnley, P. T. *Reminiscences of Parmenas Taylor Turnley.* . . . Chicago: Donohue & Henneberry, 1892.

Utley, Robert M. *Frontiersmen in Blue: The United States Army and the Indian, 1848-1865.* New York: Macmillan Co., 1967.

Walker, C. Irvine. *The Life of Lieutenant General Richard Heron Anderson of the Confederate States Army.* Charleston, S.C.: Art Publishing Co., 1917.

Wallace, Edward S. *General William Jenkins Worth, Monterey's Forgotten Hero.* Dallas: Southern Methodist University Press, 1953.

Wallace, Lee A., Jr. *1st Virginia Infantry.* Lynchburg, Va.: H. E. Howard, Inc., 1985.

_____. *A Guide to Virginia Military Organizations, 1861-1865.* Richmond: Virginia Civil War Commission, 1964.

_____. *17th Virginia Infantry.* Lynchburg, Va.: H. E. Howard, Inc., 1990.

_____. *3rd Virginia Infantry.* Lynchburg, Va.: H. E. Howard, Inc., 1986.

Warfield, Edgar. *A Confederate Soldier's Memoirs.* . . . Richmond: Masonic Home Press, 1936.

Warner, Ezra J. *Generals in Blue: Lives of the Union Commanders.* Baton Rouge: Louisiana State University Press, 1964.

_____. *Generals in Gray: Lives of the Confederate Commanders.* Baton Rouge: Louisiana State University Press, 1959.

War of the Rebellion: A Compilation of the Official Records of the Union and Confederate Armies. 4 series, 70 vols. in 128. Washington, D.C.: Government Printing Office, 1880-1901.

Washington: A Guide to the Evergreen State. Portland, Ore.: Binfords & Mort, 1941.

Waugh, John C. *The Class of 1846, from West Point to Appomattox: Stonewall Jackson, George McClellan and Their Brothers.* New York: Warner Books, 1994.

Welles, Gideon. *Diary of Gideon Welles, Secretary of the Navy Under Lincoln and Johnson.* Edited by Howard K. Beale and Alan W. Brownsword. 3 vols. New York: W. W. Norton & Co., Inc., 1960.

Wert, Jeffry D. *General James Longstreet, the Confederacy's Most Controversial Soldier: A Biography.* New York: Simon & Schuster, 1993.

Wilhelm, Thomas. *History of the Eighth U.S. Infantry, from Its Organization in 1838.* 2 vols. New York: Headquarters, Eighth Infantry, 1873.

Williams, T. Harry. *P. G. T. Beauregard, Napoleon in Gray.* Baton Rouge: Louisiana State University Press, 1954.

Winks, Robin W. *Canada and the United States: The Civil War Years.* Baltimore: Johns Hopkins Press, 1960.

Wise, Jennings Cropper. *The Long Arm of Lee, or the History of the Artillery of the Army of Northern Virginia. . . .* 2 vols. Lynchburg, Va.: J. P. Bell Co., 1915.

Wise, John S. *The End of an Era.* Boston: Houghton Mifflin Co., 1899.

Woodson, William D. *War Recollections of Lieut. Wm. D. Woodson, Company K, 28th Virginia Regiment. . . .* Lynchburg, Va.: Liggan & Holt, Printers, 1911.

Wood, William Nathaniel. *Reminiscences of Big I.* Edited by Bell Irvin Wiley. Jackson, Tenn.: McCowat-Mercer Press, Inc., 1956.

Wright, Marcus J. *General Officers of the Confederate Army. . . .* New York: Neale Publishing Co., 1911.

Yearns, W. Buck, and John G. Barrett, eds. *North Carolina Civil War Documentary.* Chapel Hill: University of North Carolina Press, 1980.

Young, William A., Jr., and Patricia C. Young. *56th Virginia Infantry.* Lynchburg, Va.: H. E. Howard, Inc., 1990.

INDEX

at Plymouth, 144
at Drewry's Bluff, 149
opposes cavalry raid, 162
at Five Forks, 164, 167
captured at Sayler's Creek, 170
Couch, Darius N., 14
Couer d'Alene Indians, 36
Croxton, Charles, 64
Crozet, Alfred, 18
Culpeper Court House, Va., 95, 111-12, 131
Culp's Hill, 115
Cumberland River, 82
Cutlar, Lyman, 43-44

D

Darbytown Road, 81-82
Davis, Fort, 34
Davis, Jefferson, 40, 72, 81, 87, 100, 109,
131, 133, 136, 138, 143, 172
Davis, Robert H., 40
Dearing, James, Jr.:
in "Game Cock Brigade," 62
in Siege of Yorktown, 66
at Williamsburg, 68
at Seven Pines, 76
commands GEP's artillery, 92-93
in Suffolk Campaign, 101, 104
on march to Gettysburg, 112
and Pickett's Charge, 117, 122, 126
in Department of North Carolina, 134,
143
De Courcy, John F., 44
Delafield, Richard, 9
Dinwiddie Court House, Va., 163-64
Dismal Swamp, 104
Deep Bottom, 159
Donelson, Fort, 82
Douglas, James, 43-48
Drewry's Bluff, 100, 149, 155, 159
Drewry's Bluff, Battle of, 149, 155
Duncan, James, 22
Dutch Gap, 159

E

Early, Jubal A., 151-52
Edenton Road, 104-05
Edgemont, Va., 112
Egypt, 177
Elizabeth City, N.C., 137
El Paso, Tex., 34
Emmitsburg Road, 118, 123, 125
England, 42-43, 47, 50
English Channel, 3
English, T. C., 52
Essex County, Va., 57, 60, 91
Ewell, Richard S., 112, 115-16, 131

F

Falling Creek, Va., 101, 107
Falmouth, Va., 95, 99
Fauquier County, Va., 3, 5, 54
Field, Charles W., 150, 155-56, 160
Five Forks, Battle of, x, 163-67
Florida, C.S.S., 53
Flowerree, Charles C., 135, 149
Forsyth, James W., 35, 44
Fort Smith, Ark., 33
France, 47
Franklin, Battle of, 161
Franklin, La., 30
Franklin, Va., 104
Frayser's Farm, Battle of, 89, 155
Fredericksburg, Battle of, 95-98, 153
Fredericksburg, Va., 56, 58, 64, 89, 95-96,
98-99, 107-08, 112
French, Samuel G., 103, 105
Friend, Thomas R., 123-24
Fry, Birkett D., 11, 119

G

Gaines's Crossroads, Va., 112
Gaines's Mill, Battle of, 83-88, 90, 92
Gallega Reef, Mexico, 20
"Game Cock Brigade," 61-62, 68-69, 71, 76,
78-81, 83, 88-91, 95, 101
Gardner, William M., 14
Garnett, Richard B.:
at Antietam, 90-91
early war service, 91
admired by GEP, 91
commands brigade under GEP, 95
at New Bern, 102-03
in siege of Washington, N.C., 103-04
on march to Gettysburg, 112, 118
awaits Pickett's Charge, 120-21
death of, 126
Garnett, Robert S., 36, 91
Gates, Collinson P., 18
Gates, Fort, 29-30, 33
Gettysburg, Battle of:
First Day, 114-15
Second Day, 115-17
Third Day, ix-x, 1-2, 117-27, 174
Gettysburg, Pa., 113-15
Gibbon, John, 10
Gibbs, Alfred, 11, 14
Goldsboro, N.C., 103
Gordon, George H., 14
Gordon, G. T., 119-20
Gordonsville, Va., 162
Goree, Thomas J., 66-67, 156
Grant, Ulysses S.:
prewar friendship with GEP, 19-20, 40
early war reputation, 82